LIBERALISM AND TRANSFORMATION

Liberalism and Transformation

The Global Politics of Violence and Intervention

Dillon Stone Tatum

UNIVERSITY OF MICHIGAN PRESS

ANN ARBOR

Copyright © 2021 by Dillon Stone Tatum
Some rights reserved
CC BY-NC-ND

This work is licensed under a Creative Commons Attribution-NonCommercial-NoDerivatives 4.0 International License. Note to users: A Creative Commons license is only valid when it is applied by the person or entity that holds rights to the licensed work. Works may contain components (e.g., photographs, illustrations, or quotations) to which the rightsholder in the work cannot apply the license. It is ultimately your responsibility to independently evaluate the copyright status of any work or component part of a work you use, in light of your intended use. To view a copy of this license, visit http://creativecommons.org/licenses/by-nc-nd/4.0/

For questions or permissions, please contact um.press.perms@umich.edu
Published in the United States of America by the
University of Michigan Press
Manufactured in the United States of America
Printed on acid-free paper
Open access e-book first published July 2021;
additional formats first published November 2021

A CIP catalog record for this book is available from the British Library.
Library of Congress Cataloging-in-Publication data has been applied for.

ISBN 978-0-472-07505-8 (hardcover: alk. paper)
ISBN 978-0-472-05505-0 (paper: alk. paper)
ISBN 978-0-472-90249-1 (OA)

https://doi.org/10.3998/mpub.11979108

S|H   **The Sustainable History Monograph Pilot**
M|P   Opening up the Past, Publishing for the Future

This book is published as part of the Sustainable History Monograph Pilot. With the generous support of the Andrew W. Mellon Foundation, the Pilot uses cutting-edge publishing technology to produce open access digital editions of high-quality, peer-reviewed monographs from leading university presses. Free digital editions can be downloaded from: Books at JSTOR, EBSCO, Internet Archive, OAPEN, Project MUSE, and many other open repositories.

While the digital edition is free to download, read, and share, the book is under copyright and covered by the following Creative Commons License: BY-NC-ND 4.0. Please consult www.creativecommons.org if you have questions about your rights to reuse the material in this book.

When you cite the book, please include the following URL for its Digital Object Identifier (DOI): https://doi.org/10.3998/mpub.11979108

> We are eager to learn more about how you discovered this title and how you are using it. We hope you will spend a few minutes answering a couple of questions at this url:
> **https://www.longleafservices.org/shmp-survey/**

More information about the Sustainable History Monograph Pilot can be found at https://www.longleafservices.org.

To my family: Milam, Kelly, and Theron.

CONTENTS

Acknowledgements xi

CHAPTER ONE
Introduction: Liberalism and Violence 1

CHAPTER TWO
The *How* of Emancipatory Liberalism 16

CHAPTER THREE
Transformation and Civilization: Liberalism, Empire, Intervention 40

CHAPTER FOUR
Transformation and Self-Determination: Internationalists at War 64

CHAPTER FIVE
Transformation and Totalitarianism:
Intervention and Cold War Liberalism 86

CHAPTER SIX
Transformation and Terror:
State Failure, Development, and Human Rights 110

CHAPTER SEVEN
Conclusion: Toward a Minimalist Liberalism 137

Notes 153

Bibliography 179

Index 199

Digital materials related to this title can be found on the Fulcrum platform via the following citable URL: https://doi.org/10.3998/mpub.11979108

ACKNOWLEDGEMENTS

This book benefited from enormous assistance by several institutions and individuals. I would like to acknowledge the help, feedback, and inspiration I have received over the years from various places, though I know I am likely forgetting many. Any faults in this book are my own.

This book started as a Ph.D. dissertation, though the book itself bears only a cursory resemblance to the final draft of that project. In terms of financial and institutional support for that work, I would like to thank the very generous funding and resources offered by both the Columbian College of Arts and Sciences and the Elliott School of International Affairs at the George Washington University. This included several semesters of teaching-free research support in the form of graduate assistantships, the Rickey Fellowship, and tuition assistantships.

Henry Farrell, Marty Finnemore, and Charlie Glaser were among the first to give formative feedback on the project. The early process itself was unusually difficult, and I am grateful for the assistance provided by several people who took the time to read the entire draft and give solid comments. These include Robert Adcock, Ingrid Creppell, Amy Hsieh, Michelle Jurkovich, Diogo Lemos, Dan Nechita, Alex Reisenbichler, and Ken Vincent.

Pieces of this project have been presented at a variety of venues, including the International Studies Association conferences (2014–2018), as well as the International Studies Association-Northeast Conference (2015) in Providence. Among those in attendance, I am particularly thankful for the feedback offered by Alena Drieschova, Jamie Frueh, Cameron Hill, Tony Lang, Rodger Payne, and Andrew Ross. For their assistance at various points throughout the writing process, including commenting on drafts and bouncing around various ideas, I would like to thank Kerry Crawford, Ryan Krog, Henry Nau, Fabiana Perera, and Allison Quatrini. For their generous time, I would also like to thank Melani McAlister and Ingrid Creppell.

A version of the concluding chapter was presented at a workshop on John Dewey that was held in October 2017 at University College Dublin. I would like to thank the participants and organizers for a brilliant discussion.

Part of chapter 5 was previously published as "A Pessimistic Liberalism: Jacob Talmon's Suspicion and the Birth of Contemporary Political Thought" in the *British Journal of Politics and International Relations*. Many thanks to the journal and SAGE Publishing for making that piece available for reprint.

A few colleagues are deserving of special mention. Alyx Mark, Brett Richards, and Scott Weiner volunteered more time than was reasonable to ask for. Alyx was a friendly ear for airing frustrations, Brett introduced me to literatures I likely would not have encountered, and Scott volunteered to read more drafts of various chapters than anyone else close to this project.

I would also like to extend thanks to my home institution, Francis Marion University, and the faculty in the Department of Political Science and Geography. Significant writing, rewriting, and research was made possible by a series of summer research grants, generous teaching schedules, engaged colleagues, and the most important things a writer needs: a computer and a printer. The university also contributed funding through professional development grants for conference travel to present early versions of the chapters and related research.

The University of Michigan Press, and particularly the fine work of Elizabeth Demers, Haley Winkle, the production staff at Longleaf and Michigan, and three anonymous reviewers made this project come to life—many thanks for their efforts. This book was made freely available in digital formats thanks to a grant from the Andrew W. Mellon Foundation.

My greatest intellectual debts are to some excellent professors at the George Washington University. Michael Barnett has been an amazing mentor, and has been incredibly generous with his time. I would not have been able to write this book without his support and mentorship. Alex Downes deserves special thanks for his kind encouragement throughout the project, and particularly for his assistance in pointing me in the right direction for data sources. Eric Grynaviski read numerous drafts of many of the chapters, and provided some of the sharpest critiques and suggestions that I have received. I can say, without hesitation, that I had the opportunity to study under three of the most innovative minds in the field, and for that I am forever grateful.

It would be a tremendous oversight not to thank the brilliant, engaged, and critical students I have had at Francis Marion University. Students in my seminars "Political Violence and Terrorism" and "Politics of War and Security" deserve special mention. Teaching those courses helped clarify issues related to concepts and theory utilized in this work. Sometimes, caught up in the minutia of our own research, we often forget the debts we owe our students—our greatest (and certainly most frequent and curious) interlocutors.

I would, lastly, like to thank my family. Kelly Gamble—an amazing scholar and writer in her own right—deserves special recognition for all of her love and support over the years. Epictetus once said: "Be careful to leave your sons well instructed rather than rich, for the hopes of the instructed are better than the wealth of the ignorant." She has always instilled the ethics of learning into me, and I am forever indebted. My brother and best friend, Theron Tatum, has never been anything but supportive, and has always been one of my greatest allies through thick and thin. Finally, my husband, Milam Chandler, has been by my side through some of this project's highest highs and lowest lows. This finished project is as much his as it is mine. This project is dedicated to these three; everything I do, I do for you.

CHAPTER ONE

Introduction

Liberalism and Violence

> Liberalism has changed all political conceptions in a peculiar and systematic fashion. Like any other significant human movement liberalism too, as a historical force, has failed to elude the political.
>
> —Carl Schmitt, *The Concept of the Political*

BY 1792, JACQUES-PIERRE BRISSOT had made a name for himself in the First French Republic as a journalist, a particularly outspoken liberal intellectual, and an Anglophobe. Early in the year, he called for an outright French imperial project on the continent, with the purpose of emancipating those republican brethren of Europe enslaved by despotic rule. For Brissot, "war was necessary against the enemies of humanity, who viewed the nation of many millions to be equivalent only to the person of a single king."[1] This would not serve as idle propaganda for the republic. Brissot became an influential political actor and legislator in the new Assembly.

In November of 1792, he was a prominent voice in convincing the National Convention that France should establish a republican empire across Europe. The Convention decreed as much on November 15 of that year. By the end of the month, France annexed Nice and Savoy in the name of freedom. A month later, the French forcibly opened the Scheldt River to free trade.[2] France inaugurated the nineteenth century—the century of liberal democracy—with violence and intervention in the name of freedom. The great liberal revolution in an age of kings, one inspired by the likes of Jean-Jacques Rousseau and Voltaire, was characterized by war and conquest.

As the beginning of the nineteenth century represented a transformative and violent moment for international liberalism, so did the end of the twentieth. At the denouement of the Cold War, Francis Fukuyama heralded, in a positively Hegelian way, the triumph of liberalism as the "absolute truth" toward which history had moved. Liberalism, for writers like Fukuyama, represented "the end point of mankind's ideological evolution."[3] Indeed, Western capitalism and market liberalism appeared to have triumphed over the Soviet Union in a protracted battle for ideological supremacy. Yet new forms of violence in the name of humanity characterized even this period of hope. In the 1990s, the world witnessed military interventions in the Middle East, Africa, the Caribbean, Eastern Europe, and Southeast Asia in configurations never before imagined, leading some to argue that these new forms of intervention were uniquely liberal ones.[4]

Liberalism has been a characteristic feature of international order since at least the nineteenth century, and its relationship to violence should prove puzzling to scholars of international politics. There are several instances in modern history where we find liberalism—as a set of political principles, institutions, cultures, and collective identities—mobilized to defend and shape state action and the use of force. These forms of violence, in the counterfactual, would not have been configured in the way that they were without international liberalism providing the context of social action for states. For example, governments often cast colonial wars in the nineteenth century as being part of a broader process of market expansion and "civilizing" progress. Andrew Jackson explicitly couched his "removal policy" of the indigenous peoples of the Americas in a language where tribes represented the antithesis to progress, civilization, and American destiny.[5] John Stuart Mill's writings on empire, as well, indicate a clear liberal logic for coercion and violence over Britain's colonial possessions.[6]

Moreover, in contemporary international politics, actors carry out and justify violence with a universalist logic of emancipation and individualism, which would not be possible without such a language of liberalism. Even in wars that are widely acknowledged to have been waged for other reasons, a discourse of liberalism justified and brought meaning to episodes of force. One prominent illustration is the 2003 coalition intervention in Iraq, led by the United States. In attempting to sell the war, President George W. Bush branded the proposed intervention as an emancipatory one:

> America believes that all people are entitled to hope and human rights, to the nonnegotiable demands of human dignity. People everywhere prefer freedom to slavery, prosperity to squalor, self-government to the rule of terror and torture. America is a friend to the people of Iraq. Our demands are directed only at the regime that enslaves them and threatens us. When these demands are met, the first and greatest benefit will come to Iraqi men, women and children. The oppression of Kurds, Assyrians, Turkomen,

Shia, Sunnis and others will be lifted, the long captivity of Iraq will end, and an era of new hope will begin. Iraq is a land rich in culture and resources and talent. Freed from the weight of oppression, Iraq's people will be able to share in the progress and prosperity of our time.[7]

I argue that one strand of liberal ideology, what I have termed *emancipatory liberalism*, has a long, and diverse, historical connection with violence and intervention in world politics. This ideological program has been of broader importance to the constitution of international relations since the mid-nineteenth century. Emancipatory liberalism is a paternalist liberalism with the primary aim of freeing individuals from the chains that bind them. It includes an understanding of the liberal project as a universal one: a project that requires the fortunate and enlightened to "save" those who are in trouble. The aim of this book is to draw out the effects of emancipatory liberalism, its interaction with institutions of war, intervention, and force, and the interplay between practices of violence on the ground and the discourses of liberty that give rise to them. The intertwined history of violence and emancipatory liberalism shows the deep connections between ideology, culture, discourse, and intervention in international society.

In another vein, this book is about discourses and their power in international politics and world history.[8] Discourses structure international politics, influence the way that states act, and allow actors to interpret their positions, practices, and beliefs about the world. Emancipatory liberalism does this in three specific ways. First, it allows for the justification of violence. It provides not just the rhetorical cover for physical fire, but constitutes the realm of justifiable action. Second, emancipatory discourses affect the way intervention is practiced, institutionalized, and operationalized. Third, emancipatory liberalism, and its historical specificity, has an impact on how the agents of violence and intervention confront resistance.

The reader of this book will encounter a variety of "authors" of this emancipatory discourse of world politics: a cast of characters as diverse as only a playwright could imagine. Scholars, intellectuals, policy makers, novelists, editorial writers—discourses of emancipatory liberalism are constituted by an array of cultural forms, a panoply of methods for thinking about global politics. As such, I approach this historical study from a discourse perspective.

Finally, this book invites readers to reflect on global ethics and transformation in world politics. It shows how ethical imaginings of the world have direct effects on actions of transformative importance. It suggests that discourses are fluid, changing, and complex. This has implications for the development and potential of alternative and dissident perspectives. Additionally, it opens the space for such an alternative perspective. In this critical history of the use of violence in international politics, a central theme is that world society need not be one structured around violence and intervention. Keep this in mind; my desire is to provide tools to emancipate ourselves from emancipation. "Minimalist" liberalism as the basis for international society—a topic further elaborated in the concluding chapter—finds a foothold in a variety of dissenting discourses that have existed, in one form or another, alongside emancipatory imaginings of violence and intervention.

This introductory chapter previews some of the major themes of the book. First, I place emancipatory liberalism in the broader context of thinking about violence and international order. How does emancipatory liberalism fit into contemporary conceptions of liberal world order? International relations theory has largely overlooked this historical narrative. Second, I propose a way of thinking about the history of global liberalism as a story of intervention and violence: a narrative that takes place within a written and spoken discourse, but also within the broader milieu of institutions, politics, and war. Throughout is a running theme about the purposes of such a critical history, alternative visions, and counterpolitics. Other conceptions of liberal world order exist—and have, perhaps, always existed—in opposition, conflict, and contradiction to emancipatory conceptions of world order.

Liberalism, Violence, and a New Narrative

International relations (IR) theory is concerned with the theory, history, and practice of liberalism, as well as the phenomenon of violence. Beate Jahn argues that liberalism, without question, still dominates international affairs.[9] Others have argued that, at least rhetorically, IR is about studying violence.[10] The history of both liberalism and violence in international politics, and the way these histories intertwine, however, is underdeveloped and undertheorized. Arguments about liberalism tend to focus on texts in isolation from the material effects of liberalism. A focus on institutions and U.S. hegemony often neglects the role of violence in maintaining that order. And, finally, liberal IR theory itself has crafted a triumphalist narrative; liberalism is ending humankind's confrontation with violence altogether. This book links and challenges these narratives. I argue that texts in the history of international liberalism are intimately related, and inseparable, from practices of violence in world politics. The liberal world order is as much about intervention, force, and war as it is about institutions, trade, and peace. A "liberal triumphalism" is itself an expression of a long-standing liberal sentiment. It is, indeed, part of—not an explanation for—the discursive history of liberal internationalism.

Defining Liberalism

Despite being a "protean prey" conceptually,[11] I define liberalism along two dimensions in this book. The first dimension is about the thematic similarities between thinkers and ideologies across time and space. Charles Mills sums up these themes succinctly, and deserves quoting at length:

> "Liberalism" [. . .] refers broadly to the anti-feudal ideology of individualism, equal rights, and moral egalitarianism that arises in Western Europe in the seventeenth-eighteenth centuries to challenge the ideas and values inherited from the old medieval order, and which is subsequently taken up and developed by others elsewhere.[12]

Liberalism, in this formulation, is based upon modern understandings of individualism—that ethics and politics should center on the welfare, liberty, and development of the individual. Furthermore, equality in terms of rights, privileges, and participation are cornerstones of liberal ideology. In world politics, this extends beyond the bounds of political communities into formulations that are often *cosmopolitan* in orientation. Liberalism, in short, is an ideology that expresses the desirability of a world that is fair and equal, with individual welfare as the primary thematic focus.

The second dimension of the concept of liberalism qualifies this ideology in relation to its contexts and histories. Liberalism does not always live up to its lofty promises, and, in fact, liberal thinkers often develop a logic of exclusion, racism, and violence within the historical, social, and political contexts it operates.[13] Thus, liberalism sometimes justifies "illiberal" action, and other times has exclusions and violence built in.[14] Duncan Bell has pointed out that perhaps the most useful way to think about liberalism is through this contextual lens: "liberalism" is work written by people who have considered themselves "liberals."[15] This conception gives us leverage for understanding the content of "liberalism" as a political and ideological program.

One potential counterargument against this conceptualization of liberalism is that it is overly general and attempts to group together national-political and theoretical traditions that are diverse as well as historically specific. This book's primary goal is to provide an inclusive definition, and to use the historical analysis in subsequent chapters to flesh out these contextual differences in each of the instances presented. My approach is to provide a broad definition of liberalism, and to demonstrate certain commonalities between "emancipatory liberalisms" and their relation to violence in world politics in specific historical instances.

Studying Liberalism in World Politics

Scholars of liberal empire have narrated well the intellectual history of early liberal internationalism. Enduring themes of this expansive research agenda focus on the way that liberal intellectuals attempted to justify empire while simultaneously developing theories of private property, liberty, and (sometimes) equality. Uday Mehta illustrates this point succinctly in suggesting that:

> In its theoretical vision, liberalism, from the seventeenth century to the present, has prided itself on its universality and politically inclusionary character. And yet, when viewed as an historical phenomenon, the period of liberal history is unmistakably marked by the systematic and sustained political exclusion of various groups and "types" of people.[16]

An overt focus on intellectual history often misses the material connection that liberalism has had on the deployment of violence. Bell makes a clear distinction between intellectual sources of liberal empire and material acts of imperialism; imperialism is not just theory or a set of texts.[17] While this broader point is certainly true, the framing of theoretical arguments, as opposed to material practices of violence and intervention, is historically problematic. Bell goes further along this line, implying that texts are fundamentally different from social practices: "[studying ideology] encompasses the interpretation of texts, the study of social practices, and the analysis of visual/material culture. [. . .]"[18] Casting the dichotomy between liberalism as a set of texts and imperialism as a set of social practices associated with violence and domination obscures the historical relationship between the discursive and the material in a liberal politics of violence and intervention.

Two additional examples show that this connection is underdeveloped. First, in Jeanne Morefield's important book *Covenant without Swords,* she traces the intellectual origins and tensions in the work of Alfred Zimmern and Gilbert Murray—two early twentieth-century "idealist liberals." She is modest, however, about her claims to the effects their thinking had on the practice of intervention in the interwar liberal order. She writes: "This is not to say [. . .] that the power of Murray's and Zimmern's arguments alone convinced the British government and Conference participants to enact their particular approach to international organization in 1919."[19] Second, even works that do connect liberal ideology to episodes and processes of violence, like John Owen's work, often focus more on the way that perceptions and interpretations of a state's liberality can create the conditions for war. These studies often avoid digging into the substance of liberalism—discursive, ideological, ideational—which creates opportunities (and often moral imperatives in the minds of liberals) to intervene and deploy violence.[20]

Furthermore, contemporary discussions of the development of liberal world order devote much of their attention to the way that liberalism's history intersects with global institutions, while largely bracketing liberalism's connection with violence. Some provocatively suggest that the existing liberal international order is in a crisis because hegemonic leadership of global institutions is declining (a "crisis of governance"[21]), while others suggest that this crisis is what liberal world order looks like: a fight between liberals who value restraint and pluralism, and those who value universalism and imposition.[22] In this vision, world order is about the promises and pitfalls of supporting an "institutionalized rule-based order."[23] These analyses all share a focus on institutions, broadly conceived, and leadership in the maintenance of liberal world order.[24] None of these approaches, however, seriously addresses violence, or questions the historical foundations of liberal world order.

One important exception in this vein is critical scholarship that examines the effects that a liberalized world politics has in constructing spaces of "disorder" in the Global South. But even this work pays less attention to theorizing the connection between this world order and direct deployment of violence. More notable in this regard is Michael Hardt's and Antonio Negri's influential argument about neoliberalism, and the way it has created a global structure that reduces enmity to conditions of lawlessness. Violence is committed in connection to new global criminals (e.g., terrorists) who threaten the institutional bases of liberal world order.[25] Others have examined the way that neoliberalism merges security and development discourses together in such a way that modern humanitarianism is contributing directly to crises in the developing world, marked by "new wars" along the borderlands of international society.[26] These approaches neglect, however, that liberalism more generally is complicit in traditional forms of violence (war, intervention, etc.): a history that is sacrificed for an argument solely about the contemporary condition.

Curiously, liberal IR itself constructs a narrative that not only ignores the connection between liberalism and violence, but also declares liberalism the "end of history" and associates it with the decline of violence.[27] This liberal triumphalism takes the form of not only liberal peace theory, but also broader accounts of liberalism's pacifying effects. Liberal peace theory suggests that liberal-democratic states do not go to war with each other. Some liberal peace scholars have taken this argument even further, to argue that liberal states are inherently more peaceful.[28] Andrew Linklater's study of cosmopolitan harm conventions makes the suggestion that "civilizing processes," led by the liberalization of world politics, are leading to a decrease in harm. He writes:

> Cosmopolitan harm conventions can be said to be immanent in the way in which all societies have been organized, in that all must protect members from superfluous pain and suffering, and all have at least the capacity to extend similar rights to all other persons. The universal human rights culture, augmented by recent developments in international criminal law, is the main contemporary expression of that shared potential.[29]

Linklater gives little attention to what Michael Doyle refers to as the "crusading" impulse of international liberalism.[30] Some see in international liberalism a teleological movement toward the global diffusion of liberal democracy, or maybe even an inevitable world state. In these arguments, the struggle for recognition of universal rights is a key mechanism in the creation of a cosmopolitan, and universal, world order—one founded on liberal democratic principles.[31] In short, triumphalism has supposedly heralded a Kantian "perpetual peace": a utopia where harm, violence, and war are outdated, or at least reduced significantly. This book challenges this narrative. As chapters 3–6 show, triumphalism like this is, ironically enough, a recurring theme in the discursive history of liberal violence.

Violence

The study of violence in IR would appear at first glance to be a vibrant research agenda, but, scholars rarely address the concept itself in a systematic and empirical way. Violence as a concept is conspicuously missing in most mainstream IR.[32] Most of the studies in IR that deal with violence are more interested in specific types of violence (e.g., war) and interrogating their causes, rather than thinking more clearly about the implications of violence in international politics. What is violence? How does violence relate to representational practices? How might violence be, in many ways, inseparable from our very visions of international order?[33] Violence is a central part of world politics, as well as the discipline of IR. The history of international violence, however, has often neglected the relationship between discourses, justificatory schemes, and the ethical bases of international violence. What is required to interrogate the idea of violence, and its grounding in discourses of liberalism, is a critical reading of international liberalism as an emancipatory project.

There are notable exceptions to this trend of ignoring violence, though these exceptions are few and far between. The study of humanitarian intervention has importantly focused on ideas; however, this attention has largely been on norms of intervention, rather than on discourse and ideology.[34] Studies focusing on the decline of violence have looked at the connection between liberalism and violence, but this relationship is one of opposition (i.e., liberalism causes the decline of violence) rather than one of co-constitution. And, studies of identity have examined discourse in relation to processes of conflict, though this literature tends to be oriented to concept development and deconstruction, rather than a more comprehensive account. There is much more to explore in relation to violence in international society, particularly in relation to discourses, institutions, and practices of intervention.

This book intertwines these narratives of a liberal international system and processes of violence and intervention. It challenges a liberal triumphalism by situating the evolution of international society within the context of justifying and employing violence. Furthermore, it contributes to a way of rethinking violence in international politics. Moving the focus away from simply the causes of war and peace to interrogating the history of an international ethics of violence—developed within, and operating through, narratives of progress, civilization and development—helps us recognize the complex interaction between the ideas, justifications, institutions, and practices of intervention.

Emancipatory Liberalism and a New Narrative

Emancipatory liberalism, the subject of this critical history, is one form of international liberalism, and refers to the trend in liberal thought of utilizing physical means for the sake of freeing individuals from obstacles to their own self-realization.[35] This form of liberalism often takes on the character of paternalism: the intervention in others' affairs for the purported sake of their own welfare.[36] Emancipatory liberalism is not a liberalism of restraint; it is a liberalism focused on empowerment and active freedom. This broad focus has domestic-institutional implications.

First, emancipatory liberalism imagines effective, and appropriate, institutions as those that are distinctly *liberal*—they are institutions created in the image of a Western emancipatory ethic.[37] Second, the idea of frugal governance, in an emancipatory worldview, is replaced with that of radical governance[38]—constructed around a discourse of the "rights of man," rather than of limited government. This is directly related to the way that emancipatory liberalism, as a culture, imagines governance: a means of ridding domestic institutions of tyranny, and institutional inefficiency, which would otherwise have illiberal affects in domestic politics. Third, emancipatory liberalism is not necessarily democratic. While democracy would become an important part of an emancipatory culture in the late part of the twentieth century, oftentimes actors saw direct hierarchy (as in the case of empire or spheres of influence) as an appropriate method of operationalizing the liberal project.

Isaiah Berlin's influential discussion of *positive* liberty is most similar to the present conception of emancipatory liberalism and its focus on active freedom.[39] In international politics, emancipatory liberalism is oriented toward positive liberty, placing a value on bestowing the power and resources necessary to fulfill one's potential. This can lead to the operation of violence through intervention, however, and confirms Berlin's own concerns with the paradoxes of positive liberty. As he writes: "If this leads to despotism, albeit by the best or wisest wishes—to Sarastro's temple in *The Magic Flute*—but still to despotism, which turns out to be identical to freedom, can it be that there is something amiss in the premises of the argument?"[40] As this book demonstrates, this contradiction is one with which intellectuals and policy makers have been preoccupied.

A focus on emancipatory liberalism, as a type of liberal internationalism, allows for a rethinking of the narrative of the rise of global liberalism and its relationship to force. Charting the multiplicities of liberal discourses about intervention and violence, and demonstrating the deep connections between such discourses and actual practices of intervention, provide the resources to engage in a sustained critique of liberalism's place in modern political considerations about war, security, and peace in international society.

Violence and Its Discourses: War and "War by Other Means"

A central theme of this study is the role that discourse plays in constituting practices of violence and intervention. By "discourse," I mean the collection of texts that makes up a cultural system—providing the symbolic order in which social and political agents act.[41] Discourse theory has seen a resurgence in IR scholarship. There is now a plethora of research in this regard, especially in the realm of genealogical analysis inspired by Michel Foucault.[42] Much of this literature is interested in the history of the development of norms, however, rather than a more open exploration of the role that discourse plays in constituting international politics.[43] In the case of emancipatory liberalism, discourse has a multiplicitous, and sometimes contentious, relationship with practices of violence and intervention. Nonetheless, any understanding of international liberalism must grapple with liberalism as a textual artifact—a set of symbols, cultural systems, and deep systems of meaning that are created by, and constitute, the writers who expound those ideas. These connections are not always clear and can sometimes be difficult to parse out historically.

There are two essential functions that discourse has in relation to practices of violence in world politics. First, discourse provides cultural resources that actors draw on in the practice of violence. Discourse works to constitute the lifeworld of actors; it forms cultural worlds that make lived experience meaningful. Sociologists Peter Berger and Thomas Luckmann said it best: "language [...] typifies experiences, allowing me to subsume them under broad categories in terms of which they have meaning not only to myself but also to my fellow men."[44] Discourse creates these broad categories by giving substance to cultural systems. This is apparent in everyday life. Take the example of fashion. At any point in time, most of society shares at least broad understandings about what kinds of clothing are culturally acceptable. What belongs in the categories of "fashionable" (e.g., dark blue jeans) and what belongs in the categories of "unfashionable" (e.g., fanny packs) is part of a shared world created by the way we represent fashion discursively—in speech, in magazines, on television. Similarly, emancipatory liberalism as a discourse helped constitute broader international cultures shared by both elites and publics. In the Cold War, for instance, an ideological fear of totalitarianism was expressed in public discourses like editorial pages, intellectual production, and policy communities. Discourse has real, structural effects through its mediation of culture.

Discourses also construct identities, or what may be referred to as "subject positions."[45] Subject positions are discursively defined relationships between distinct identities or "subjects" within a particular social system. In relation to everyday life, for example, within the sets of discourses developed and institutionalized by the American university system, as a professor I have a subject position vis-à-vis other actors within that institution. I am hierarchically above undergraduates (at least institutionally), my dean and chair are hierarchically superior to me, and I am at a level of certain equality with other junior faculty members. This gives me a set of normative prescriptions about my roles in certain social situations (e.g., giving out grades, doing university service, etc.). It also, however, constitutes the ways I identify with similar actors (other junior professors), and potential conflicts with different actors (students/administrators).

Discourses of emancipatory liberalism construct similar sorts of subject positions, and these changed enormously over time. The period of liberal empire investigated in chapter 3, for instance, was a period of dichotomy between supposedly "reasoned" and "civilized" European liberalism and the barbarism and stunted progress of the colonial periphery. This allowed Western states to justify, often unquestioningly, the prerogative of intervention in "less developed states." Subject positions create real effects on how violence is used.

Furthermore, symbols, identities, and cultural resources often act as technologies. By "technology," I do not mean in terms of a "tool kit" or a rationalist understanding of strategy, however.[46] I refer to technologies of power, as Michel Foucault defined them. For Foucault, discourses interact with other types of domination as means for a particular end, namely, the governing of the subject.[47] It is important, however, to recognize that the history of emancipatory liberalism does not suggest a clearly intentional reasoning behind all forms of war making. Liberal states oftentimes did not simply use liberal vocabularies to justify motives that were "impure," or to impose sinister forms of domination on other peoples with an emancipatory window dressing. Liberal intellectuals and publics give us little reason to suppose that they did not truly *believe* these ideas. Discourse as a constitutive feature of the self creates a duality between a technology that can be used by dominators and a mechanism that constitutes those dominators' very identities.[48]

Second, discourse and the "writing of war" are inseparable from violence in and of itself. Violence is not simply the deployment of troops or the use of tactics of intervention with physical implements. Discourses of emancipatory liberalism, as vessels of power that can constitute identities, hierarchies, cultures, norms, and justificatory schemes, are in an important way direct forms of violence. Foucault puts this eloquently (and famously) in his inversion of Clausewitz's aphorism: "power is war, the continuation of war by other means."[49] This "silent war"[50] waged through discourse raises a myriad of questions about liberalism and its relationship to violence. How do ideologies of liberty (re)produce forms of power and domination in international politics? In what way are seemingly benign—and often technical—understandings of other places and other peoples forms of violence and domination? And, as is critically examined in the concluding chapter, how do we emerge on the other side of this perpetual war inscribed in discourse?

This book, thus, does not just try to locate war *outside* of texts—viewing discourse as a simple causal relation to intervention outcomes. It is true that discourse constitutes cultures and identities that create the conditions that make violence possible, justifiable, and defensible. Discourse interacts with institutions and material factors to create a physical world that is characterized by violence and intervention. But this is only one side of the coin in narrating a history of emancipatory liberalism. This book does not solely try to locate war *within* texts, either. Jacques Derrida's phrase that "the text is all and nothing exists outside of it"[51] highlights the importance that texts-as-discourse play in the "writing of war" itself, but it does not capture the complex interrelationships that discourses of emancipatory liberalism have had with the institutions, values, and practices of war and peace in international society since the mid-nineteenth century.

Global Ethics: A Minimalist Alternative

If an emancipatory liberal world order is intimately connected to practices of violence and intervention, what are the implications of this empirical study for an understanding of international ethics? Chapter 7 outlines an alternative liberal "vision" of world politics—what I have termed a liberal *minimalism*. Chapters 3–6 demonstrate that emancipatory liberalism lives in a tension and dialogue with other liberal imaginaries. Protominimalisms, in one form or another, have been an integral critical force in international society for the last century and a half. The final chapter fleshes out the implications of these findings for a rethinking of global ethics and international political theory.

Minimalism is a form of liberalism that is pluralistic, pragmatic, and democratic. It embraces difference, and recognizes the problems with universalism and paternalism.[52] In particular, such a minimalism is one that is *radically democratic*. Following Laclau and Mouffe, it is a central contention that a liberal democracy requires an understanding of liberalism that not only celebrates difference, but requires it for the creation of a world society that can stand up to the problems associated with power.[53] If emancipatory liberalism, throughout history, is united by a relatively coherent set of principles that—though varying in operationalization—represent an important force in the evolution of military force, then dissent, deliberation, and defection are the only means available for challenging it. Though chapter 5 shows that emancipatory liberalism witnessed its own internal dissent during the Cold War, an entirely new imaginary of deliberative agonistic democracy is necessary.

Prototypes of minimalism have been present throughout the development of a liberal international society and provide historical models on which to reflect. Anti-imperialist movements in America in the late nineteenth and early twentieth centuries stressed the need for America to reject a European imperial worldview, though this was hardly a celebration of difference. Pluralism during the Cold War was dissent against a development discourse, but was closely tied to emancipatory liberal concerns with totalitarianism—so much so, that the interaction between Cold War pluralism and development liberalism had causative effects on intervention. A powerful critique of transformative intervention and state building in the post–Cold War order emerged, though such lines would become often blurred in practice. Minimalism is a utopian liberal-democratic vision, but one that should guide a pragmatic ethics of the international.

Organization of the Book

This book, in great part, is an "effective history" of emancipatory liberalism in world politics. Chapters 3–6 make up the bulk of the historical chapters that chart the trajectory of violence and liberal internationalism since the mid-nineteenth century.

Chapter 2 theorizes the effects of liberal discourses on the employment of violence in world politics. First, it examines the ways that discourse constitutes liberal orders, through a politics of identity, positionality, and hierarchy. These political processes have material effects and contribute to a broader global liberal culture. Second, the chapter connects this process of order-making to the practice of violence and military intervention. How does a global liberal culture affect the way that states carry out interventions? In what ways are these practices textual, material, or both simultaneously? Third, it raises preliminary issues about the contested nature of discourses, and the way that liberal discourses change and effect material changes in international institutions.

Chapter 3 is the first of four empirical-historical chapters that show these processes at work. Looking at the period from 1848 to the turn of the twentieth century, it examines the role of an imperially oriented liberalism in the development of modern institutions of violence and intervention. These discourses had a profound effect on the way that states carried out intervention in the nineteenth century, and particularly in the way that violence was seen as having an emancipatory purpose in the context of the imperial periphery. Interrogating the work of figures like John Stuart Mill, Alexis de Tocqueville, and Frédéric Bastiat, this chapter demonstrates how common ways of thinking about civilizational development had effects on the deployment of force. The Second and Third Anglo-Burmese Wars are used as case studies to demonstrate these effects.

Chapter 4 shows the progression of this civilizational discourse in the first half of the twentieth century. The post–World War I experience of American and European liberals reconstituted international order in new ways, reviving older discourses of empire, while developing newer ideas of self-determination that affected intervention dynamics. I simultaneously engage the work of pro-Mandate liberal thinkers, including feminist pacifists like Jane Addams, and French social scientists like Yves Guyot and Émile Durkheim, to show the similarities and divergences in Anglo-American political thought regarding the relationship between liberty and the use of force in an interwar order. British intervention in Iraq in the 1920s is used as a case study to show the effects of these ideas on Mandate-era military interventions.

Chapter 5 analyzes a period of great change in international liberal order during the Cold War. World War II, the beginnings of the Cold War, and the explosion of a new development culture simultaneously limited international intervention while transforming its aims, methods, and reach. Drawing on the works of writers like Jacob Talmon, Simone de Beauvoir, and Gore Vidal, I show how—in a variety of ways, and a variety of contexts—Cold War liberalism was obsessed with the specter of totalitarianism. I use the Dominican Crisis of 1965 as a case to illustrate how these discourses mapped on to foreign policy decision-making processes.

The final historical chapter is focused on the post–Cold War period. The globalization of liberalism has made intervention claims on the basis of human freedom more universal, while simultaneously opening up the possibilities of unrestrained violence in the name of progress, civilization, and humanity. This violence is particularly aimed at so-called failed states (a term of recent vintage), and toward the subjects of terror. I analyze contemporary texts in international political theory and public policy in order to show how expert knowledges constructed these categories out of existing emancipatory liberal tool kits. I use the intervention in Afghanistan in 2002 as a case study.

The concluding chapter explores the implications of these investigations in the context of the development of international political theory. I suggest that a turn to a pragmatic liberalism, and nonintervention, is a way forward. Uncovering the threads of liberal resistance to intervention aids in this task, and demonstrates that there are possibilities for cultural change in world politics in the context of the use of force. This chapter wraps up these discussions, and indicates promising areas of further exploration.

CHAPTER TWO

The *How* of Emancipatory Liberalism

> Imagination has brought mankind through the Dark Ages to its present state of civilization. Imagination led Columbus to discover America. Imagination led Franklin to discover electricity. Imagination has given us the steam engine, the telephone, the talking-machine and the automobile, for these things had to be dreamed of before they became realities. So I believe that dreams—day dreams, you know, with your eyes wide open and your brain-machinery whizzing—are likely to lead to the betterment of the world. The imaginative child will become the imaginative man or woman most apt to create, to invent, and to foster civilization.
>
> —L. Frank Baum, *The Lost Princess of Oz*

WRITTEN IN 1917 amid crisis in Europe, Baum's statement about imagination in Western civilization is a telling example of an argument about the human capacity toward creativity and ingenuity—the harbingers of modernity—that will free us from the darker times of human history. Baum was not alone in this of thinking about the relationship between changing ideas of the "good life" and the development of Western civilization, the forward march of progress, and the emancipation from despotism. This system of thought was widely shared by liberal political communities and their intellectuals throughout the nineteenth and early twentieth centuries. Ways of thinking about the world as structured around the rights of individuals were the means by which world order could become progressive. International liberalism as a political project contains in it an emancipatory element—what I have termed "emancipatory liberalism"—that has not always visualized freedom and pacifism as complements. Since the mid-nineteenth century, liberals have often envisioned the project of freedom through the sights of a rifle, the windshield of a bomber, and the periscope of a submersible. Imagination has no limits.

"The mandate given to France in Syria gives her not only the right but also the duty to maintain order and security," wrote Prime Minister Alexandre Millerand to a French commander in Syria during the interventions of the 1920s.[1] This imagining of duty and purpose was not so different from that of prevailing intellectual winds in Europe at the time. Jan Smuts, an influential character in the intellectual development of the League of Nations, would make a similar point: "The mandatory state should look upon its position as a great trust and honour, not as an office of profit or a position of private advantage for it or its nationals."[2] This is not unlike the connection between development liberals, who argued for democracy as a means of protecting against the international spread of totalitarianism, and policy makers like Senator William Fulbright, who, during the Dominican Crisis of 1965, stated that he had "very little confidence in the capacity of the Latins" to resolve the issue themselves.[3] It is difficult to separate a discursive politics of emancipatory liberalism—the philosophical arguments for liberal interventionism—and the actual practice of violence in world politics. The history of emancipatory liberalism is a long one. It is one of imagination in action.

To theorize the processes at play in the long narrative of emancipatory liberalism's interaction with episodes of violence and intervention, this chapter elaborates a guiding framework. This framework, drawing on a broadly Foucauldian approach to the historical study of discourse, provides a structure for a complex history, allowing for a critical examination of crucial moments in the history of liberalism and violence. The literatures of the discourses of international liberalism are vast,[4] as are the literatures on the history of violence and intervention.[5] The task of integrating these two narratives into a single, if not intricate, history, however, requires thinking clearly about the ways that liberalism interacts with institutions, the use of violence, and political events/change. Subsequent chapters may make sense without having read this chapter, but understanding the reasons *why* discourses matter, and *how* emancipatory liberalism influences the way states use violence can help us take an often disjointed, fragmented, and contested history, and make it intelligible.

This chapter comprises three sections. First, I develop a theory of *how* discourses, the way that we write about and speak about the world, constitute liberal world orders. I focus on the role that discourses of emancipatory liberalism play in constituting state identities and hierarchies, constructing institutions, and developing full-fledged cultural/ideological projects. Building on discourse theory, and recent attempts to understand the role that discourse plays in international politics, I argue that discourse works on multiple levels to construct not just the ideational aspects of world order, such as identity, but also institutions. Existing approaches to discourse in international relations have often looked either *inside* the discourses to expose relations of power, or looked *outside* the discourses to show how speaking, arguing, and writing about world politics has effects on norms.[6] My approach, however, returns to a Foucauldian concern with the complex historical interaction between discourses and the institutions, identities, and physical practices of power nexuses.[7]

Second, I address the question of violence. How do emancipatory liberal discourses impact processes of violence and intervention? I elucidate a few different themes. Emancipatory discourses provide a common set of "maps" for states to justify the use of force; the "the writing of" and the "waging of" war are inseparable. This argument proceeds from the premise that actors' justifications for action should be judged as sincere unless there is reason to doubt them.[8] Contrary to realist arguments about double-talk and lying,[9] justifications provide an important window into understanding why actors do what they do, how they imagine their "doings," and the effects of those actions. Speech act theory has demonstrated clearly how words can be inseparable from action.[10]

Furthermore, the way that actors practice interventions, and the way that resistance is confronted, are structured by emancipatory liberalism's interaction with real-world politics. Thinking about and practicing intervention does not happen in a vacuum. Thinkers, publics, and policy makers have had to confront the prospects, and realities, of resistance. This includes local resistances to violence and endogenous forms of resistance: different liberal visions of world order, different interpretations, and different voices.

Third, the chapter approaches the issues of contestation and change. Is emancipatory liberalism a monolith? How do these discourses—and practices of violence—change over time? This study avoids a Hegelian teleology of international liberalism. In fact, this is precisely what it critiques. Rather than positing a single engine of change as a "driving force" of a linear history, I show how four periods—characterized as much by rupture as by continuity—complicate a universal narrative, and demonstrate the folly in considering even the possibility of an "end of history."[11]

How Discourses Constitute Liberal World Orders

Discourse is a central concept in understanding emancipatory liberalism's complex relationship to violence and intervention in international politics. Emancipatory liberalism is a set of discourses that have had real effects on international practices of violence since the mid-nineteenth century. Most simply, discourses are signifying systems that create our lived experience, structure society, and give meaning to our realities.[12] They are the "meat" of the social world, the bases of a symbolic order,[13] and the prerequisites for action. There are a wide range of theoretical debates about the role that discourse plays in politics and society. This section draws, in a synthetic way, on work in IR and social theory/philosophy about discourse and its relation to two specific aspects of order: identity and institutions. Identity is a part of liberal world order in that it gives substance to the actors embedded within that order. In the history of emancipatory liberalism, this has included not just liberal states, but also individuals and broader societies that states represented. Institutions, as well, are a central feature of world order. They provide a set of regulatory schemas that set limits, and develop possibilities, for action.

A brief reconstruction of insights about discourse from critical IR theory and contemporary social/political philosophy gives us three broad structuring themes we can develop about the "shape" or "contours" of discourse most generally. I describe these connections generatively, moving from social actors to structures of order and then to social processes. The remainder of this section explains how discourses construct identities—focusing on the role that discourses play in constituting subject positions, and in creating hierarchies, oppositions, and relations of Otherness—as well as institutional contexts and broader cultural constructions—what might be termed the "common sense" of world order. In developing these general themes about the way that discourse constructs liberal world orders, some caution is necessary. General theoretical propositions are important in guiding any empirically grounded study of world politics; however, discourse, by its very nature, is contingent, contested, and fluid. As Jennifer Milliken succinctly notes, "good studies of discourse not only focus on their order-creating effects, but also on contingency."[14] If this early caution is not entirely satisfying, the historical chapters will demonstrate, at the least, that it is a truism.

Specifically, this book develops a discourse theory about emancipatory liberalism's relationship to violence by building on a broadly Foucauldian framework of historical discursive analysis. Foucault himself found the possibility of separating discourse analysis from history to be logically and practically impossible. His work exemplified, in his mind, an analysis of "history as a discourse."[15] In the same vein, this narrative of emancipatory liberalism focuses on the way such discourses-as-history have changed over time, how they have contributed to the construction of broader normative orders, and how they have influenced the ways that actors *act* in world politics. Such a historical-discursive approach allows us to examine the ideology of emancipatory liberalism from a multiplex of relationships to identity, institutions, and common sense. Furthermore, it gives us a clearer understanding of method, and of how discourses like emancipatory liberalism are inseparable from state action.

Some general methodological insights can be gained from such a framework. First, identities are inseparable from discourses. As Foucault makes clear throughout his corpus of later work, the subject is embedded in complex networks of power-knowledge that ascribe meaning and mechanisms of control upon the individual. Emancipatory liberalism as a discourse constitutes the actors that act, and the subjects who are acted upon. Second, Foucault's understanding of institutions demonstrates that institutions have a dual relationship with discourse. Discourse constructs institutions, and institutions put boundaries on the ways we can "speak" about the world. His most significant works in this regard, *Discipline and Punish* and *History and Sexuality* examine this two-way relationship between discourse and institutions.[16] Third, a Foucauldian genealogical approach helps us to understand how discourses are implicated in the taken-for-granted linguistic practices of elites and political communities. Sexuality, for instance, and the norms associated with the way we talk about and write about sex, not only affect the institutions and elite knowledges of sex; they also inform the everyday understandings we have about how subjects relate to objects of desire.[17]

Identities

Discourse is constitutive of the actors within a social system. Discourse has identity implications; it constructs subjects. More than that, discourse reproduces the cultural contexts that give actors meaningful relationships, and allow them to engage in activities to fulfill roles that discursive systems elucidate. This means that discourse functions as both a stabilizer of identity, and proof of identity's fluidity and instability through repeated iterations, changes, and rewriting of discourse. This "logic of iterability" rejects a conception of history focusing on simple repetition, and instead looks to contexts, changes, and different situations of articulation.[18] Discourse may recur, reemerge, or reproduce throughout the *longue durée*, but it is always context specific, always adapting, always somewhat differently expressed. Discourses of emancipatory liberalism, for instance, endow actors with identities as "liberal" agents. These identities, however, differ, change, and are interpreted in numerous ways throughout history. Actors are "speaking subjects"[19] who not only employ discourses, but also are fundamentally shaped by the speech acts that they (or Others) employ.

Three elements of identity construction are central within a liberal world order: the constitution of the "liberal state," the creation of an "Other," and both vertical (hierarchical) and horizontal (relational) orderings.

First, discourses of emancipatory liberalism construct states as "liberal" states. This aspect of identity formation is a continual historical process with both internal and external dynamics. Internally, domestic political culture and institutions constitute liberal states, and give them a unique identity. Much of IR talks about order this way: a liberal world order is an order based on the collective interests and identities of states that are internally liberal. Michael Doyle, for instance, suggests that "what we tend to call liberal resembles a family portrait of principles and institutions, recognizable by certain characteristics—for example, individual freedom, political participation, private property, and equality of opportunity—that most liberal states share...."[20] These internal aspects of state identity play a key role in constituting liberal world order, but are not exhaustive. External dynamics are significant. For example, during the Cold War, liberalism was not simply defined by the internal constitution of states, but also by the allegiances *between* liberal states in battling the threat of totalitarianism. It is not surprising that many public intellectuals, including people like Gore Vidal and Noam Chomsky, saw the potentiality of American totalitarianism even within the context of liberal-democratic institutions. Liberalism is not solely a type of domestic government, but a global idea placed against a set of oppositions.

Second, emancipatory liberalism works to construct "Others"—those who exist outside, beyond, or at the margins of liberal world order. The creation of an Other is a necessary part of the construction of self-identity. In fact, as Derrida famously (and rather playfully) noted, Otherness is one of the most fundamental aspects of identity: "every other is every other other, is altogether other."[21] Furthermore, theorists like William Connolly have pointed out how identity itself is the construction of Otherness through the processes of a "politics of evil"—where the Other is defined in negative relation to the Self. Not only is Otherness fundamental to the creation of identities; Otherness often relies on the construction of evil, enmity, and radical alterity.[22]

Othering has two significant attributes. Othering creates dichotomies, and these dichotomies are foundational for global order.[23] In the interwar period, for instance, this dichotomy often took the form of "child races" and generated a quite literal liberal paternalism.[24] Othering, also, is not just a deliberate strategy of a written text. It is deeply integrated in public culture, becomes a taken-for-granted, unreflective way of representing the world,[25] and is often difficult to disentangle from the formality of language itself, i.e., one cannot talk about life without also acknowledging its Other, death.[26] In the post–Cold War era, for example, these deeply ingrained forms of Othering made it nearly impossible to separate underdevelopment from terror, and resulted in new solutions—war, intervention, etc.—to solve the "root causes." Discourses of emancipatory liberalism have always contained within them a contrast—a point of Otherness, a point of disorder that could be ordered.

Specifically, a liberal world order has enemies. Enemies are those Others who are a threat and affect security of the order. Enmity is not just a phenomenon that brings a group together through "negative association."[27] Enemy-making is a public act, involving a complex array of intellectual and popular, normative, and discursive imaginings.[28] In a liberal world order, these enemies are not always concretized entities. Enemies do not have to be the Spartans, the French, or the Holy Roman Empire. Enemies are often abstract, ideational, and conceptual. During the Cold War, for instance, the enemy of liberal world order was totalitarianism. A wide variety of intellectual and public texts grappled not only with the problem of totalitarian governance, but also contributed to justificatory schema for intervening in areas where this purported enemy threatened liberty and the interests of liberal states. Similarly, in the post–Cold War order, the concept of "state failure" created a new enemy, a new kind of threat: that of disorder and its associated horrors. While the concept of the Other itself is not one of hostility,[29] and does not imply a sense of violence, enemy-making as a form of Othering can create the discursive conditions for it.

Third, liberal world order is composed of both hierarchies and sets of relational identities. In terms of hierarchies, emancipatory liberalism constructs subjects and places those subjects within a world order in relations of rule. Cultural aspects of world politics—like norms, and by extension, discourses—not only constitute realms of what is "appropriate," but also rank states and other actors in relations of hierarchy.[30] Work focusing on pre-twentieth-century international relations has already pointed out the role of hierarchies in perpetuating difference; of particular note are histories of the "standard of civilization" that created a clear distinction between Western civilization and the rest of the world.[31] Emancipatory liberalism functions to create its own hierarchies well into the twentieth and twenty-first centuries, however. In the Cold War, an emancipatory developmentalism functioned in this way, creating a hierarchical distinction between modernized states and "less-developed countries." This began as an academic exploration—modernization theory being one of its earliest instantiations. But these ideas intertwined and cross-pollinated with a host of other modes of discourse: policy, popular, intellectual. Besides just constituting difference, emancipatory liberalism places difference within ordered, vertical relationships.

In terms of relational orderings, emancipatory liberalism defines not only *who* actors are, but also implies certain sets of acts that are legitimate, necessary, or even morally imperative for an actor with that identity. Liberal states have liberal roles and aims. This phenomenon is called "positioning," where the narrative within the discourse gives actors limited potential actions within a speaking context. Rom Harré gives an example of this from everyday life by focusing on the sentiment "I'm sorry you're not feeling too well. Can I get you anything?" Within this narrative context, "A positions him or herself as the active and helpful member of the duo and positions B as passive and helpless."[32] This relational positioning, and the role/actions it makes possible, are inscribed in emancipatory discourses as well. In the liberal empire period, for instance, the concept of "civilization" created roles and obligations within the context of broader historical narratives about progress. During the period stretching from 1900 to the 1930s, a narrative about self-determination and "sacred trusts" gave liberal states a repertoire of roles, positions, and relationships that made intervention a central part of their identities.

Identity formation is something important that discourses do. Furthermore, emancipatory liberalism as a set of discursive formations has been a long historical process of identity formation that has not only endowed liberal states with self-identity, Others, enemies, hierarchies, and relationships, but—through these processes—has also helped *construct* a robust liberal world order.

Institutions

Discourses also shape institutional contexts: the specific social/political forms that actors are embedded/act within. Discourse theory has illustrated the complex ways that discourse (what is "articulable") interacts with the "visible": those extra-discursive elements of the social world.[33] Some analysts have even suggested that the primary aim of discourse analysis is the focus on what is outside the discourse, what is material, what is lived[34]—that is, the institutional. An entire literature on discursive institutionalism has shown how institutions are constructed, reproduced, and given meaning by background identities and discursive systems within which agents are embedded.[35] Institutions are as much physical, material aspects of international reality (i.e., I can physically touch the walls of the World Bank building in Washington, D.C. I can attend forums and conferences at the United Nations, etc.) as they are constituted by, and implicated in the employment and reproduction of, discursive formations.

Social institutions—including the vast array of institutions that regulate aspects of international politics—are, fundamentally, products of discourse.[36] In the most general sense, representations, expectations, and webs of significance through which cultural systems are organized characterize institutions.[37] Emancipatory liberalism, as a discourse, has been historically integral to the development of international institutional environments, in diverse ways. And, despite common periodization that liberalism was closely connected to post–World War II institutional developments,[38] this interaction between international liberalism and the institutional contexts in which states interact goes back much further. There is one element of the cultural construction of international institutions that concerns us here: the embedding and formalizing of a liberal ethic in institutional arrangements.

Emancipatory liberalism affects the development of institutions in the sense that cultural values become embedded in institutional design. As Keohane and Goldstein note, "Once ideas have influenced institutional design, their influence will be reflected in the incentives of those in the organization and those whose interests have been served by it."[39] This can be both a conscious or unconscious phenomenon. For example, following World War I, the creation of mandates acted as a conscious effort for liberal European powers to confront the moral dilemmas of empire, while simultaneously operating under the ethical imperatives of civilizational development.[40] Political realists in the interwar era recognized this in their critique of liberal internationalism, by arguing that such institutions simply reflected the ideals of the powerful.[41] Institutions, in one way or another, are part and parcel of the cultural/discursive environments within which they exist.

Institutions affect the social context that actors find themselves in, including the opportunities and constraints that are placed upon actors regarding the employment of violence. By *opportunities,* I mean institutions can provide states with rules and values by which they can justify and frame violence. This is evident in many cases of intervention, including the 1983 intervention in Grenada, where cooperation with the Organisation of Eastern Caribbean States (OECS) was, in part, a response to the lack of legitimacy the United Nations (UN) accorded to the intervention. In addition to opportunities, *constraints* are also an effect of institutions. States are limited by the institutional contexts in which they exist, making certain practices unthinkable within that context. States cannot use violence, legitimately, for every reason, and therefore states have to make a compelling case for war, intervention, and the use of force within the context of the institutional environment in which they operate. Using the previous

Grenada example, involving the UN or OECS at all provided the United States with important cover for an operation that would impact the geopolitical situation of several important international players—most notably the United Kingdom. It is important to note that the effects of institutions on transformative intervention are historically variable in terms of quantity and quality.

Additionally, institutions act as forums for public debate, whereby states can draw on existing discourses to sway other actors that the use of violence is appropriate. Sometimes this can take the form of persuasion (or attempted persuasion), where actors draw on dominant—and easily recognizable—symbols, metaphors, concepts, and ideas to persuade others within an institutional context that the use of violence is justified.[42] Sometimes this works, and sometimes it does not, but the successes can be as interesting as the failures. The United Nations Security Council functioned—albeit unsuccessfully—as one such forum during the United States' attempt to justify intervention in Iraq in 2003. In other cases, actors can be "trapped" into an action through strategies of rhetorical coercion—where the use of a discourse within an institutional context has real, physical, power.[43] The British intervention in Iraq in the 1920s was as much a function of British ideas as it was a function of coercion by a League of Nations discourse about duty and responsibility of the sacred trusts of mandates. This intervention was doomed to failure largely because of these discourses.[44] Institutions are social environments developed around sets of discourses, ideas, and ideologies; they are also the battlegrounds for those ideas.

Institutions are not just shaped by discourse; there is also a feedback process: institutions contribute to changes in discourse as well. Public debate within institutions, as well as conflict over existing norms, forms of knowledge, and authority can play a role in the way that a discourse is written, articulated, and contoured. Furthermore, as Foucault pointed out, the interaction between institutions and discourse is mutually constitutive. Institutions like the asylum, the clinic, and the prison are shaped by discursive systems, but those forms of knowledge would not be intelligible without those institutions themselves. Madness as a concept (discourse), for example, does not prefigure the asylum (institution); they created each other.[45] Two examples relevant to liberalism and violence are appropriate. During the Cold War, developmentalism as a discourse evolved substantially, and not just from endogenous aspects of emancipatory discourse. The institutional facts of early development politics fundamentally altered this discourse: the veritable "boom" in a development industry tied up with Cold War competition. In the contemporary period, as well, multilateral institutions not only created new norms for the use of force,[46] they also fundamentally transformed the content and method of elaborating a discourse. Justifications had to appeal to a wide variety of audiences, a broader background political culture, and universal themes like terror and state failure.

Common Sense, Publics, and Cultural Politics

Discourse affects actions and interactions in world politics through the ways that it regulates culture and practice. Discourses, quite directly, construct what might be termed "knowledgeable practices": the everyday processes through which discourse catalogs—and makes legible, reasonable, and proper—certain types of action, techniques, habits, and behaviors.[47] In the first place, discourse often *is* action. Speech act theory has shown that the distinction between word and deed is often illusive.[48] In the second place, discourse provides shared resources for actors to use in contexts of action. Shared knowledge is required for any action, and this knowledge is interpreted, understood, and given social meaning by discourse.[49] The "doing" of international politics, and of social and political life more generally, is a function of the types of relationships, solutions, legitimacies, and logics that a discourse makes intelligible—legible in a literal sense—to the participants in a social and political system. Discourses create a cultural common sense politics.

By *common sense*, I follow Hannah Arendt's understanding of the term as referring to a shared "sense of the world."[50] The broadly Foucauldian approach employed here can help us understand how discourses of emancipatory liberalism help to construct regimes of common sense that impact the cultural imaginings of world politics. Following Foucault's lead in works like *Archaeology of Knowledge* and *Discipline and Punish*, Edward Said employs Foucault's understanding of power in popular culture to help explain practices of imperial Othering: "... European culture gained in strength and identity by setting itself off against the Orient as a sort of surrogate and even underground self."[51] In a similar way, emancipatory liberalism provided the discourse to construct a background culture that translated these concepts into the vernaculars of everyday life—in aesthetics, in opinion pieces, and in popular rhetoric.

Constructions of common sense connect emancipatory liberalism to broader cultural imaginings of world order. Whereas the identity and institutional politics of emancipatory liberalism often happen at a high level of analysis (states, prominent intellectuals, policy makers, international institutional contexts, etc.), emancipatory discourses also affect publics and the ways that citizens of nation states make sense of the acts of violence being justified to them. This cultural aspect of discourse limits resistance, provides legitimacy, and gives a wide range of latitude for governing authorities to exercise power.[52] Such common-sense understandings are constructed via popular media, such as television, film, newspaper editorials, novels, intellectual production, and political rhetoric. These media shape the social world in which people live, providing meaning through the linking of key concepts. For example, news editorials during the nineteenth century frequently used discursive tropes from the policy and intellectual communities to talk about non-European countries, including languages of civilization, barbarians, and even animal metaphors. Readers and consumers not only understood and were versed in these concepts; their heavy publication in widely purchased media indicates that these ideas were justifiable to a great portion of them.

Discourse also contributes to the (re)producing of understandings about what is considered a threat. Violence, security, and threats are not simply connected to discourse through elites, but are also related to broader common-sense understandings about violence, its legitimacy, and its sources. In fact, security itself is a broad cultural system that "organize[s] particular forms of life."[53] So-called security formations make legible and intelligible actions and justifications that states and other actors must make to their publics and constituencies.[54] In justifying the Iraq War and the Afghanistan War, for instance, the Bush administration drew on justifications about human rights, state failure, and terrorism—justifications based not just on intellectual or policy discourses, but also on broad, public, common-sense notions about security and the legitimate use of violence. The politics of liberal violence is not just an elite politics. It is a broader cultural phenomenon.

Furthermore, common sense does not just provide a connection between international discourses and broader publics; it also conditions expert knowledge—the ways that scholars, practitioners, and policy makers conceptualize world politics from the vantage point of taken-for-granted ideas. Theories of civilizational development, "child races," modernization, and state failure are not neutral scientific theories that exist in vacuums. They are products of, and (re)producers of, a complex discursive structure of liberal world order.

While this book is not a study in the domestic constitution of political liberalism, it is important to note that the question of publics and the construction of discourses is imbued deeply within a matrix of power. On the one hand, powerful elites—either in the form of policy makers or cultural elites—have a role to play in "setting the agenda" of public reception of certain discourses, and particularly discourses about politics. On the other hand, publics themselves are active interpreters of such attempts at creating "common-sense" discursive structures.

While some approaches to ideological hegemony—and particularly Gramscian approaches—focus on the ways that elites construct ideologies that benefit their own interests, and then have these ideologies taken for granted by the populous (cultural hegemony),[55] the interplay between publics and elites is much more complex. Nonetheless, as the empirical chapters demonstrate, liberal discourses are embedded deeply in structures of common-sense and public conceptions of liberalism's purpose, aims, and goals.

Table 2.1 summarizes the ways that discourse constructs a liberal world order. Understanding the discursive bases of world order, and how emancipatory liberalism is a constitutive part of that order, is a key component of making sense of the ways that emancipatory liberalism impacts the writing and waging of war, intervention, and violence.

How Discourses Affect Action: Writing and Waging War

Discourses, as I have argued, construct liberal world orders through their complex relationship to politics of identity, institutional formation, and common-sense cultural constructions about international politics. Discourses, however, also have a direct impact on the way that violence is deployed and practiced in world politics. Discourses of emancipatory liberalism constitute a world order founded on vocabularies about freedom, emancipation, and development. These structures have an impact on the way liberal actors act: the way violence is justified and deployed on the ground, and the ways resistance is confronted. A Foucauldian framework alerts us that discourses are not just constitutive of normative orders; they also affect the ways that we act. As Dianna Taylor notes, for Foucault, "subjectivity is not a state we occupy but rather an activity we perform."[56] Discourses of emancipatory liberalism do not just construct the liberal world orders that states act within. These discourses confront actors with constraints and opportunities in the way they act.

Justifying Violence

Emancipatory discourses affect the way that actors justify the use of force and the deployment of violence. By *justification*, I refer to the articulation of actions as being legitimate within the context of a specific normative universe. Legitimacy is a key component of any kind of action in world politics, and especially violence. Violence must "be circumscribed by a set of rules acknowledged by the international community," and justification appeals to these rules.[57] Justification is not just cheap talk, window dressing, or evidence of hypocrisy; justification is

TABLE 2.1. How Discourse Constructs a Liberal World Order

Identity	*Defines the "liberal state" *Creates hierarchies and enemies through the process of "Othering"
Institutions	*Embeds values in institutional design *Creates opportunities for/constraints on action *Develops forums for public debate
Common Sense	*Constructs public languages, understandings, and symbols about threat *Creates taken-for-granted expert knowledges

meaningful and intimately related to action.[58] First, justification itself is a form of action; it is a speech act. Second, justification is not solely based on "spin," but reflects preexisting discursive structures that make certain types of speech possible. This is not to say that hypocrisy is not a part of some types of justification; however, it is not synonymous with justification itself. Third, successful forms of justification allow states the ability to engage in forms of violence and intervention that are normatively "legitimate" within the context of a discourse. Justifications for British intervention in Iraq in the 1920s, for example, only made sense—and were successful—in that they helped in the "universalization of the Western model" of liberal governance.[59] Justification takes many forms and fulfills many functions. It is, in many ways, central to an actor's ability to effectively deploy violence.

Justification appeals to identity claims. Justification of violence draws upon elements of securitization, or the creation of us-versus-them dichotomies. Justification itself is "a social practice founded on an intersubjectively and normatively based ordering."[60] More than that, it turns violence and intervention into a way to preserve, maintain, and protect an identity or a way of life. Two examples are worth mentioning. Civilizational dichotomies that were common during the nineteenth century worked to bring legitimacy to progressive developmental histories: the idea that some parts of the world required a "strong man" to put them on the proper path. This did not just represent a general philosophical narrative that was popular in Europe at the time; it was also a way of constituting the identities of liberal European states as well as the "Other" in the colonial periphery. During the Cold War, a similar logic was used to justify military intervention in Latin America, with the idea that some people (notably Cubans, and other Caribbean/Central American peoples) were either naturally inclined to communism, or more likely to be persuaded by its expansion.

Identity claims are a central component of attempts at justification, and offer mechanisms of positioning that are crucial to making justification operative as a speech act.

Furthermore, practices of justification relate to institutions in two ways. First, justifications based on emancipatory liberalism connect practices of violence to preexisting institutions. This allows actors to legitimate force by appealing to institutional authority. Second, connecting the use of violence, intervention, and force to institutions is a way to further buttress institutional legitimacy by demonstrating that even supposed threats to order—violence, force, intervention—are part of a single institutional logic. Institutions do not just play the role of providing sets of norms that constrain actors; through mechanisms of authority, and through an endogenous logic of survival, institutions are deeply related to processes of justification. They are opportunities.

Finally, justificatory practices of emancipatory liberalism rely on the common-sense understandings created by discourse. Justification has multiple audiences. In the first place, actors must appeal to other political elites, who share common-sense understandings about the proper use of violence, the targets of that violence, and the vocabularies that are used to give legitimacy to those acts of violence. These forms of common sense often take the form of expert and scientific discourses, but can also be more general, philosophical, or cultural references that are taken for granted. In the second place, actors must appeal to publics. Justification, and the symbols, tropes, and rhetoric attached to it, draws upon common cultural meanings that publics attach to the deployment of violence and intervention. Often the local populations who are being affected by this violence are not audiences of justification. Sometimes these discourses preclude the existence of certain groups of people from the public sphere altogether. In the nineteenth century, this was "barbarians" or "child races,"[61] the "Third World" during the Cold War, and failed states/societies in the post–Cold War order. Most bluntly, justification must draw on discursive common sense to be successful.

The foregoing discussion of justification should not be taken to imply that material interests do not matter. In fact, it is often difficult to disentangle the complex interplay between material interests, ideas, and the justification for very real material effects. While this study focuses on the material effects and structures of justification, it is also infused with a panoply of material interests—rooted in imperialism, capitalism, local elite/worker dynamics, etc. While justificatory frameworks can help us understand a lot about how liberalism deploys violence in theory and practice, these material aspects matter as well.

On the Ground: Deploying Identities, Institutional Discourses, and Common Sense

Justification of violence and intervention is not the only role emancipatory liberal discourses play in the deployment of violence. The carrying out of interventions on the ground is also profoundly affected by the embeddedness of actors within complex webs of discourse. Practice theory in IR has shown, more generally, how discourse affects the physical "doings" of international politics.[62] Discourse does not just have an influence on the justification of violence, but also what comes after: peace building, state building, reconstruction, etc.[63] While justification is an act in and of itself, it only provides a partial picture of the ways that emancipatory liberalism has historically affected the patterns and practices of violence in international society.

Identities frame the relationships between governors and subjects post-intervention. This is apparent not just in the scope of violence on the ground after initial interventions, but also in the way that administrative realities are imagined in the aftermath. In Iraq in the 1920s, for example, self-governance was tempered by certain racist understandings about Iraqis as incompetent, or as "child races"—a common discursive trope at the time. Furthermore, institutional contexts provide rules of the game for implementing governance after the deployment of violence. What states can get away with in deploying violence, and in peace-building or state-building after conflict, is affected by institutional contexts, and the way that institutional ideals conceptualized relationships between interveners and the objects of intervention.

Common-sense understandings, especially as they relate to administrative realities in the aftermath of the use of force, play a significant role in peace building and state building, during and after intervention. Recall, common-sense understandings can relate to intersubjective understandings that discourse creates in a community about what the social world does/should look like, and also expert knowledges: common understandings about science, administration, and technocracy. The latter is especially important in this case. Emancipatory liberalism constructs entire repertoires of shared knowledges that influence the way that administration, planning, and strategy is developed during and after conflict.[64] A dramatic data point bears mentioning. During the invasion of Iraq in 2003 and its aftermath, the coalition entered with specific understandings of what a well-constituted liberal state would look like, and engaged in processes of state building/nation building meant to fit that model. That this model was imposed through processes of paternalism mattered less to the interveners than the soundness of the model—generated through taken-for-granted understandings of liberal governance.[65] Common sense, and specifically expert knowledge, are part of emancipatory discourses and are conspicuous in the practice of intervention and post-war reconstruction.

Confronting Resistance: How Actors Deal with Contradictions and Challenges

Deploying violence is not as straightforward as having a good justification, and being able to operate effectively, and competently, within a particular moral universe. There are always challengers to violence, there is always resistance, and there is always contestation. The first set of challengers are other actors within a particular community. Emancipatory liberal politics itself is the site of contestation and resistance. The Cold War, for example, saw perhaps the most dramatic battles between divergent strands of emancipatory liberalism. The developmentalists and the anti-totalitarians of the period often had very different visions of the emerging post-war order.[66] These were not just ideological battles; they affected practices, including the Dominican Crisis of 1965. The second set of challengers come from outside of emancipatory liberal discourses—from the victims of violence, the "facts on the ground." The British learned this the hard way in Iraq in the 1920s and 1930s, when their actions resulted in a series of revolts. How do emancipatory liberals approach, deal with, and counter resistance?

There are two primary ways that actors approach resistance and challenges. On the one hand, actors can draw on discursive resources to argue that challengers exist *outside* of prevailing discourses—that their arguments are wrong or otherwise deviant. Communism, for example, was outside the realm of legitimate governance in the eyes of Western liberal states during the Cold War. Communism and its discourses were presented as symptoms of totalitarianism or "tyranny." On the other hand, actors deal with challenges and resistance by incorporating such challenges into existing discourses: an attempt to diffuse challengers by incorporating alternative visions into predominant discourses of emancipatory liberalism. Self-determination arguments were added onto more traditional civilizational development arguments in the post-WWI era, incorporating anti-imperial arguments into more standard arguments for intervention. Antiwar, pro-democracy activists like the American suffragist Jane Addams were some of the strongest supporters of League of Nation mandates. These differing strategies vary in levels of success in particular instances, and, in fact, are not mutually exclusive. State failure discourses beginning in the early 1990s, for instance, attempted both of these strategies simultaneously. Alternative ways of imagining governance were deemed to be illegitimate, illiberal, and ineffective. Yet, at the same time, notions of "peace building" were imbued with arguments for local involvement in "shared governance" schemes, which were aimed—at least rhetorically—at involving local populations in post-intervention contexts. Challenges were common, and actors were often creative in the ways they dealt with them.

Rather than argue that the history of liberalism is a story of hypocrisy, or a disjuncture between theory and practice,[67] it is a central contention of this book that liberalism has historically been both a constitutive feature of world politics, and it has provided the reasons, the methods, and the context for actors in their decisions about force, intervention, and violence. Specific cases in the deployment of liberal violence illustrate this well, whether it is nineteenth-century interventions in Burma, or twenty-first-century wars against "enemies of democracy." The vocabularies have changed; however, the means of operationalizing words into deeds have been relatively consistent.

How Discourses Are Contested and How They Change

Emancipatory liberalism is not a static idea, possessing a single essence, logic, or trajectory. Actors contest discourses and discourses change. Just as the way the Western world wrote about "madness," punishment, and sexuality changed significantly over time,[68] international discourses also evolve, rupture, shift, reverse, and conflict. After all, "the world of speech and desires has known invasions, struggles, plundering, disguises, and ploys."[69] As one such data point, the change from a civilizational narrative in the nineteenth century to one focused—concomitantly and often in tension—on self-determination in the interwar period is demonstrative of a simultaneous evolution of a discourse, and radical disruptive change. Thus, while this is a story of the development, change, and practice of an idea, this should not be taken as a claim that this idea is transcendent, beyond historical time, or immutable/unchangeable. Foucault contra Hegel.

Contestation has divergent effects on a discourse as a system of thought in a particular period. In the first place, contestation is evidence of the robustness of a particular discourse, the taken-for-granted character of a set of symbols, and the common ground for debate to happen. Contestation only makes sense in the context of discourses that are strong, influential, and taken for granted. This is because contestation causes actors to understand norms, rhetoric, and ideologies in diverse and complex ways. Actors in a liberal world order may be writing, reading, and acting within the context of the same discourse, but operate

TABLE 2.2. How Discourse Affects the Deployment of Violence

Justification	*Violence is framed as a way to preserve an identity. *Violence is placed within the context of institutional legitimacy. *Violence is "sold" to publics and elites through common discursive tropes.
On the Ground	*Identities frame the relationships between governors and subjects post-intervention. *Institutional contexts provide "rules of the game" for implementing governance after the deployment of violence. *Expert knowledges constitute post-intervention administration.
Confronting Resistance	*Actors dismiss resistance by questioning the legitimacy of the alternative discourse. *Actors incorporate alternatives into their pre-existing discourses.

with different "cultural scripts."[70] Two examples deserve brief mention. During the interwar period, discourses of self-determination and the ideas of a "sacred trust" were not the only significant parts of an emancipatory liberal discourse. Since at least the 1890s, America, especially, had witnessed the development of an outspoken liberal anti-imperialism that criticized institutional mechanisms as new forms of colonialism. And, most dramatically, the Cold War saw battle lines being drawn between developmental liberals who were ready to reconstitute the "third world" in its entirety, and more cautious liberals, whose greatest fear was about what the excesses of interventionism could bring. Therefore, the recognition that emancipatory liberalism as a discourse is, and has always been, contested should not cause us to think this is all a worthless endeavor: why chart a critical history of an idea that is not and never has been coherent? Contestation shows the coherence—albeit with shaky and unstable foundations—of a discourse.

In the second place, contestation demonstrates just how contingent and slippery discourses can be. Justifications for the Iraq War in 2003, for instance, drew heavily not only on discourses about liberation and emancipation, but also on contradictory ethical and strategic tropes. This was not about a simple application of existing discourse, but a combination of tactical appeals to common symbols, and acting on shared understandings about America's role in the world.

If discourses are slippery, how do we explain discursive change? Some common themes stand out. Events, and what comparative political studies calls "critical junctures,"[71] can rather quickly change both the nature of discourse and the way that institutions police it. This book is less interested in explaining *why* emancipatory discourses changed over a lengthy period of historic time; it is more interested in how these changes affected the nature of the discourses, and—therefore—affected the way that liberal actors conceptualized and operationalized violence in world politics. British intervention in Burma in the late nineteenth century, for example, looked very different than British intervention in Iraq in the 1920s. Not only had there been gradual changes in institutions, broader ideologies, and the introduction of new vocabularies, but critical junctures—including dealing with the constitution of a post-WWII order—intertwined in significant ways to produce different effects. In short, change is an important part of this narrative. Not just evolutionary change, but also fundamental, external forces.

Beyond such critical junctures, however, institutional change (gradual or rapid) can also feed back into discourse, causing changes in the way that violence is conceptualized, justified, and practiced. The institutional environment can often take on a life of its own and change the very discourse that helped constitute it.[72] Critical moments in the shaping of international institutional environments have had a profound set of effects on *what* actors can say, *how* they say it, and *why* they say it. The significance of regional institutions during the Cold War, for instance, was profound. When it came to intervention politics, the discursive battles were often played out within these smaller institutions. The interactions between organizations like the OAS and the IAPS and the United Nations during the Dominican Crisis were complicated and conflictual. The effects of emancipatory liberalism, then, are not one sided; this discursive system shaped history as much as it has been shaped by major institutional changes.

Finally, discourse can change simply because the voices that articulate it change, attitudes that contribute to the idea skew, or public opinions evolve. "Change," Mark Bevir suggests, "occurs contingently as, for example, people reinterpret, modify, or transform an inherited tradition in response to novel circumstances or other dilemmas."[73] Furthermore, new actors and new global structures can change the contexts of discourse. Decolonization, for example, opened a whole host of novel issues and voices to a conversation that was once largely limited to Western voices—voices mostly sympathetic to paternalism and imperialism.[74] Radical disjunctures, including the introduction of terms like "failed state" into the public consciousness in the 1990s, did not just have a policy impact. They also changed the way that a panoply of actors (in the realms of politics, media, aesthetics, etc.) conceptualized security threats to liberal order. International politics has never been static; even the actors have changed, and certainly ideas have changed.[75]

Conclusion and Notes on Methodology

The following four chapters narrate the development of emancipatory liberalism from the mid-nineteenth century to the present, showing its intellectual and cultural origins in global discourses, and mapping out its connections with processes of violence, force, and intervention. Such a study is, most broadly, a form of genealogy: an attempt to construct "historical-philosophical accounts of how reality comes into being."[76] As such, it is a general methodological approach of this book to mediate between how philosophers and broader cultural formations—especially those pronounced in popularly consumed media—related to implements of violence and intervention. Genealogy is a historical examination of the dense, multiplicitous, and often messy interrelationships between the discursive (what is said, what is written, what is argued, what is justified) and the nondiscursive (the institutions, events, political processes, and uses of force and violence).[77] This book is not an intellectual history. It, however, historicizes the development of emancipatory liberalism as a form of discourse, justification, and knowledge of the international, and shows how this discourse is inseparable from the way states use violence. After all, "knowledge is not made for understanding; it is made for cutting."[78] This book is interested, first and foremost, with this "cutting." It is therefore a "critical history."[79]

The questions of what kinds of discourses, what kinds of institutions, and what kinds of violence are important ones. In relation to the discourses themselves, I have focused on two types of texts in charting the historical development of emancipatory liberalism. The first set of texts are philosophical texts: important writings by central thinkers who attempted to systematically develop an emancipatory liberal theory of world politics, and a "progressive" understanding of violence and intervention. These texts allow for a deeper interrogation of the effective history of international liberalism. These texts were chosen because they "represent [. . .] not the average, but rather the whole statistical curve"[80] of the common, contradictory, and multiplicitous ways of imagining emancipatory liberalism. Some of these texts are by major philosophers who have already been extensively studied in relation to the development of liberal empire and internationalism—including J. S. Mill and Alexis de Tocqueville—and others are more obscure, or at least underanalyzed—such as Jacob Talmon, Jane Addams, and Yves Guyot. Attention is given to the "diagrams,"[81] the maps, the imaginings of world order that these authors reasoned toward. The politics of intervention and violence are woven into this narrative. An examination of the way that these diagrams, these maps, these imaginaries interact with processes of violence are part and parcel of this examination of texts and intellectual production.

IR work on discourse has engaged in text selection strategies from a variety of angles. Some have focused on selecting texts that are important works in the genealogy of the politics being examined.[82] Others have focused on idiosyncratic texts that help to draw out the specific interpretive claims the authors are making.[83] This book takes both of these approaches seriously in engaging canonical works by important authors, less-well-analyzed works by well-known theorists (including Mill's *Principles of Political Economy*), and more obscure thinkers whose works are otherwise illuminating of the political, discursive, and cultural processes under investigation. Thus, the method for choice of texts is generalizable in two senses: (1) the texts chosen should represent texts that could be reasonably considered important texts of the periods under study by other scholars; and (2) the texts chosen assist in the narration of an alternative history of emancipatory liberalism's encounters with violence and intervention.

The second type of texts are what we might consider *cultural* texts. These are texts meant to show the general milieu of thinking about the international during the period examined. Newspaper editorials are one such set of texts that provide a window into understanding broader modes of thought. Editorials elucidate the way that elites think about political phenomena: they give us the opportunity to map out patterns of discourse and witness recurrence of common themes and common languages. News editorials and other types of popular cultural production, however, also give us insight into popular sentiment through a simple economy of discursive production. The languages and ideas in editorials must make sense and resonate with a broader portion of the population, otherwise newspaper companies will not sell newspapers.[84] Works like editorials, popular fiction, and other general elements of culture are analyzed throughout the book to give range and depth to systems of thinking about international liberalism during the periods of study.

I do not engage in statistically driven content analysis of texts, though such methods are gaining more traction in the study of discourse in IR.[85] Rather, the analysis of cultural texts—and specifically pieces of news, essays, and fiction—is developed through a close reading and genealogical analysis of the text itself. Thus, I distinguish between *textual* analysis, which involves a theoretically informed reading of cultural texts, and *content analysis,* which aims at the statistical analysis of a large range of texts. I rely on the former as a tool of analysis in order to provide a rich and in-depth understanding of the genealogy of emancipatory liberalism.

In choosing texts to focus on, I developed archives of both types of texts, and used a principle of selection based on how representative a text was in terms of the discursive universes it inhabited. While my choice of theorists, texts, and cultural artifacts in some sections may seem idiosyncratic, the methodological wager made in this book is that if a researcher were to write a similar history, with a similar archive of texts, they would come to similar *descriptions* and *interpretations* of other representative texts. Thus, following cautions against selection bias, this study uses a contextualized and interpretive approach based on selecting texts that are representative—or at the mean of the distribution of such texts.[86]

The book also analyzes the way these discourses about liberalism and emancipation affected cases of violence and intervention "on the ground." In doing so, I present a series of case studies connecting the intellectual milieu of emancipatory liberalism to the politics of intervention. Each of these cases is an example of what Clyde Mitchell calls a "telling case" or one that "makes previously obscure theoretical relationships sufficiently apparent."[87] Chapter 3 uses the single case of British intervention in Burma during the Second and Third Anglo-Burmese Wars to illustrate the connections between civilizational intellectual discourse and the deployment of force in the British Empire. Chapter 4 examines the dual cases of the French in Syria and the British in Iraq in the 1920s to highlight the similarities in British and French deployments of force in the context of emancipatory liberalism. Chapter 5 analyzes the U.S. intervention in the Dominican Republic to demonstrate how Cold War emancipatory liberalism's intellectual concern with totalitarianism translated into violence. And, finally, chapter 6 uses the case of coalition intervention in Afghanistan—as well as the language used to justify the Russian invasion of Crimea—to show how post–Cold War imaginings of liberal world order were universalized, even by countries (like Russia) that appropriated this language for self-interested motives.

Examining cases of British, American, and French interventions presents its own opportunities and problems. In the first case, it allows a sustained examination of how transnational discourses of emancipatory liberalism function despite differing domestic contexts. Emancipatory liberalism as a set of discourses has comparable effects regardless of the regime in question. The reader, for instance, will notice similarities between French intervention in Syria and British intervention in Iraq during the interwar period, despite different histories. Differences do exist, however—particularly in the cases of imperialism, where all three countries had notably different experiences (Britain often relying on proxy rule, the French on direct control, and the United States oscillating from anti-imperialism to Cold War spheres of influence). The benefit of examining cases across these great powers is to understand the ways that emancipatory liberalism operates as a discourse that transcends political boundaries, while also being sensitive to the historical contexts of intervention.

There are two significant counterarguments to this methodology. The first is that attributing causal power to discourses is a difficult proposition to sustain. I make no strictly *causal* claims in this book. I do, however, make constitutive claims about the relationship between discourses and force.[88] Emancipatory liberalism provides a vocabulary, a justificatory framework, and the ammunition (both literal and figurative) necessary for the realization of intervention projects. As this book will demonstrate, these emancipatory liberal languages were not just extant in the realm of philosophy or editorial/public culture, but mapped onto concrete practices of intervention. The reader should recognize patterns in the way states have used force that are deeply connected to patterns of thinking about, and arguing for, violence in international society. The second counterargument may be that it is difficult to talk about a broader discourse when such a wide panoply of voices is speaking. Is emancipatory liberalism coherent? Does it constitute a broader structure for thinking about world politics? Demonstrating this is the task of the empirical chapters that follow; however, the discontinuity and conflicts within and outside of the discourse of emancipatory liberalism are often just as interesting.

CHAPTER THREE

Transformation and Civilization

Liberalism, Empire, Intervention

International history between the mid-nineteenth century and the turn of the twentieth century exemplified two broad historical trends. The first is the rise of what some referred to as a "new imperialism,"[1] which represented the most comprehensive period of European imperial expansion. By 1878, Europeans occupied or controlled almost double the amount of land in the world than they did in 1800.[2] The second of these trends is the rise of liberalism in the political life of Europe. Several revolutions occurred in the 1840s, which owed their origin to both resistance to absolutism in an age of kings, as well as a growing intellectual and theoretical concern among European thinkers about the importance of freedom, equality, and personal liberty. These trends were related; they mutually reinforced each other. This chapter examines how imperialism, internationalism, and the cultural politics of a new emancipatory liberalism in world politics interacted to impact violence and intervention.

The argument of this chapter is twofold. First, emancipatory liberalism from the mid-nineteenth century to the early twentieth century was based on a civilizational liberalism. Liberals grounded this emancipatory liberalism in philosophical and popular understandings about progress and the contrast between a rational Europe and an irrational (or "barbaric") outside. I demonstrate this through a close reading of significant texts of intellectuals and policy makers in Britain, France, and the United States during the period, drawing out common themes between those specific texts in relation to a broader discourse of emancipatory liberalism. Additionally, I examine popular writings—including newspaper editorials—to show how these ideas were parts of a larger public culture. Second, I show how these discourses, and the cultures that they constitute, map onto the politics of war and intervention. I argue that these discourses structured the ways actors justified and practiced intervention, with the conceptual frameworks of policy makers, war makers, and administration makers centering on civilizational development narratives.

Besides focusing on a period integral to emancipatory liberalism's connection to violence in international politics, this argument is a challenge to the scholarly literature on liberal empire. This chapter cuts against the grain of recent research that questions the coherence and hegemony of civilizational discourses in the mid-to late nineteenth century. Duncan Bell, for instance, argues that intellectuals in Victorian Britain began to abandon the civilizational narrative during this period. He states that "during the last thirty years of the century, enthusiasm for the civilizational mission waned."[3] Karuna Mantena makes a cognate argument to this effect. She argues that British liberal thought shifted from a linear civilizational development narrative to one that was more "culturalist," or interested in understanding other cultures through the lens of social theory in the late nineteenth century.[4] This chapter shows that this civilizational narrative was not only a strong ideological component of liberalism in Britain and France particularly, but that these narratives made up discursive frameworks that guided a politics of violence and intervention.

Furthermore, while most of the liberal empire literature on this period is about the British Empire,[5] this analysis compares the way that liberal intellectuals in a multiple countries and contexts shared distinct themes about emancipation and violence. Such an analysis of global discourses of liberalism shows just how significant and substantial arguments about civilization, progress, and intervention were in those periods. The case of the Anglo-Burmese Wars, examined here, further shows how even unilateral intervention by Britain mirrored discourses emerging from France as well. In providing a broader view of emancipatory liberalism in intellectual and policy production, I show that these discourses had much wider-ranging effects and deeper cross-border connections than is often emphasized in the intellectual history of international liberalism of the period.

This chapter proceeds in three main parts. First, I examine the way that actors conceptualized emancipatory liberalism in the latter half of the nineteenth century. I focus primarily on three big issues: the way writers conceptualized the liberal state and its goals/duties, the ways writers thought about spatial, temporal, and hierarchical relationships between liberal states and Others, and how these ideas were furthered and disseminated through popular media. The themes of civilization and progress were central to a nineteenth-century emancipatory liberalism. Second, the chapter examines the role these broad emancipatory discourses played in the practice of violence by liberal states. I use a detailed case study of British intervention in Burma during this period to demonstrate the power that discourse had in justifying intervention, placing intervention within institutional contexts, and governing "on-the-ground" in post-conflict environments. Finally, the chapter concludes with reflections on this period's broader significance to the long history of emancipatory liberalism.

Writing World Order: Civilization, Progress, and Liberal Imaginaries

This history begins in 1848, a pivotal time in the transition from an era of authority to the modern era of liberal sensibility and governance,[6] as well as a moment of crisis for actors in reimagining the role that violence and intervention should play in international politics. Liberalism, and particularly a concern for global (though conditional) individual rights and protections, emerged before this crisis, however. For example, by the early nineteenth century, though universal rights became widely recognized as the basis of political justice, and their recognition the basis of political authority,[7] ideas such as "self-determination" were greatly limited to those actors with certain "civilized" and enlightened characteristics.[8] In international politics, these were imagined as primarily features of European great powers and their agents. This distinction related to reason and self-determination was an ordering factor that determined cultural hierarchy within the realm of international politics. Gerry Simpson argues, succinctly, "The early part of the nineteenth century introduced a formal distinction between sovereign entities that are not quite part of the society of states, and those, mostly European states at the centre of this society."[9] This intertwining of an emerging liberal ethic in international politics, and understandings of civilization, laid the groundwork for future discourses of empire and paternalism. Separation of the "rational," "civilized" Europeans from the rest of the world was a set of social processes embedded in discursive structures about individual rights and liberties.[10]

The revolutions of the late 1840s demonstrated the popular importance of emerging liberal sentiments, and sparked debates about governance and universalism that would impact later iterations of emancipatory liberalism. Who is entitled to self-governance? What is the appropriate structuring of governing authority, both domestic and international? Though conservative absolutism was exhaling its last breath on the European continent, civilizational distance brought about by a new liberal rationalism made liberty an important part of international affairs, while, simultaneously, liberal thinkers imbued duty and protection with paternalism.[11] These events, especially the events of 1848, would have a substantial impact on debates about what it means to free people who belong to other political communities. This was both an intellectual and political conversation. In fact, 1848 had such an immediate impact on liberal discourse that even English liberals—whose country had been largely unaffected by continental revolution—began to reimagine their own positions on liberty.[12] Such a crisis created new cultural battle lines, and resulted in rather paradoxical political positions. For example, philosopher and colonial administrator John Stuart Mill, in frustration with both Irish calls for bloodless revolution and English demands for better governance in Ireland, broke with former intellectual allies—most notably his old friend Thomas Carlyle— arguing that the problem with Ireland was that England had poorly governed the country for centuries.[13]

This position that poor governance, and lack of proper intervention, was part of the problem in the lack of development in "backward" places was not confined to Ireland. Writing in the same year, in his monumental *Principles of Political Economy,* Mill noted the necessity of Jesuit supervision of Paraguayan Indians in order to foster capital accumulation: "The real difficulty was the improvidence of the people; their inability to think for the future: and the necessity accordingly of the most unremitting and minute superintendence on the part of their instructors."[14] These cultural attitudes would set the stage for future understandings of civilizational relationships, and intervention for the purposes of civilizational development. The following century saw European liberals—and their governments—inscribing liberal governance onto spaces where it was possible, and desirable, to do so.

Emancipatory Identity Politics: Imagining the Liberal State and Its Other in the Nineteenth Century

One of the central sites for the writing of world politics after the mid-nineteenth century was the issue of identity. Political thinkers elaborated and debated the identities of liberal states—as counterpoised to the identities of liberalism's "Others"—within the context of broader conversations about liberal world order. Political theory of the mid-to late nineteenth century had as one of its principal tasks the defining of what the liberal state looked like, and how other parts of the world related to the liberal state. One of the most widely researched examples of this is Mill's writings on identity. Mill not only wrote extensively on British identity, but also its broader connection to global networks of interdependence. Bell notes:

> [Mill] always saw the colonies as embryonic nations, bound ultimately for independence, their sheer physical distance from Britain rendering them

indissolubly separate. This did not constitute part of a single political field—a field in which the colonies and Britain were envisioned not simply as bound together by economic flows, shared interests, and webs of communication, but as comprising a shared political community grounded in a thick common identity.[15]

The central questions of identity were threefold: What does the liberal state look like (and—what is its relationship to violence)? Who are its Others/how do its Others fit within a hierarchy of liberal world order? And, finally: Who are the enemies of such a world order? Mill was not alone in developing these questions and their answers. This was a broader theme in liberal political thought in the nineteenth century.

The defense of liberal political culture, and liberal institutions, as superior to all others was a focal point of identity arguments. The relationship between liberal states and violence emerges from these identity claims. For writers like Mill, Herbert Spencer, and others, representative institutions characterize a liberal state, and such institutions are the best kinds of institutions that well-constituted states can have. Spencer's illuminating essay "Representative Government—What is it Good For?" demonstrates just how pervasive these identity claims about liberal states, violence, and good governance were. Spencer spends much of the essay inveighing against the many "flaws, vices, and absurdities"[16] of representative institutions. However, his conclusion is that the deficiencies of representative government constitute a good state that can fulfill its proper functions of protecting its subjects from "aggression." He writes that the deficiencies of representative governance are good things: "In becoming so constituted as to discharge better its essential function, the government becomes more limited alike in the power and the habit of doing other things. Increasing ability to perform its true duty, involves decreasing ability to perform all other kinds of actions."[17] For Spencer, the liberal state is simultaneously one that we limit, but also one tied intimately to violence. The liberal state's main role is to provide security by checking aggression. Its failures in all other functions are good for liberty.

Spencer was not alone in making arguments about liberal states' identities in relation to representative governance and violence. These arguments were as long-standing as the natural-rights-based arguments of theorists like Edmund Burke from the eighteenth century, famously arguing that the British Empire had a "moral duty" to engage in colonial practices.[18] Even theorists at the margins of liberal thought, including British socialists, who had very different understandings of liberal state identity, often justified empire on a sense of moral duty. For example, J. A. Hobson advocated for a "socialist imperialism."[19] Regardless of differences in specific conceptions of what a liberal state looked like, what its institutions should resemble, and liberal conceptions of identity, the duty/role of the state was often tied directly to violence and empire. As Uma Narayan argues, "most liberal political theorists had no difficulty endorsing colonialism."[20] And these endorsements were often tied explicitly to the function and identity of a liberal state.

Processes of "Othering"—of creating opposing identities—ran through the discourses of emancipatory liberalism during the latter half of the nineteenth century, carving out both spatial and temporal differences. Spatially, the concept of "barbarism" or "savagery" was an imagery meant to separate liberal Western Europe from the rest of the world, and especially the colonial periphery. After all, as French politician and writer Alexis de Tocqueville noted, "everything in Egypt is curious."[21] This Orientalism, and racio-spatial ordering of the world, was deeply tied up with the interests of empire.[22] The Sepoy Rebellion of 1857 was a key moment of anxiety for intellectuals like Tocqueville, threatening European domination, but also—potentially—representing a reversion from civilization to barbarism on the subcontinent. "[T]here is not one civilized nation in the world," according to Tocqueville, "that ought to rejoice in seeing India escape from the hands of Europe in order to fall back into a state of anarchy and barbarism worse than before the conquest."[23] The emancipatory efforts of liberal Europe to civilize the world, to impute reason to "barbarians," were under threat; it was Tocqueville's hope that Britain would crush this trend, even if violence were necessary. Writing to his friend and interlocutor William Nassau Senior, Tocqueville's worries were tempered: "I am quite sure you will conquer."[24]

Intellectuals like Tocqueville did not just consider barbarism to exist spatially within the sphere of imperial possessions; rather, barbarism was characteristic of any lands that were not liberal republics. Discussing Russia with Senior, in the context of the Crimean War, Tocqueville highlights this sentiment clearly: "It is impossible that that semi-barbarous empire, with its scarcely sane autocrat, its corrupt administration, its disordered finances, and its heterogeneous populations, should ultimately triumph over the two most powerful nations of Europe [. . .]."[25] And, China was even more of an abomination: "the most wretched of governments."[26] Mythscapes about Russian and Chinese politics as unreasoned, unordered, and illiberal colored Western European understandings about war and peace on the continent.[27]

Temporally, emancipatory liberals were correspondingly interested in issues of unequal development, progress, and the eventual march of reason.

Mid-nineteenth-century liberal thinking about empire was so profoundly embedded in discourses about historical progress and civilization that justificatory schemes for violence and domination in the colonial periphery did not even require that the liberal writers in question be strong proponents of empire. Much of the liberal empire literature focuses heavily on identifying supporters/critics of empire, and then analyzing the connections between their political theories and their justification of imperialism. Much less attention, however, is given to the broader significance of liberal thinking in constituting a realm of possibility for justifying imperial undertakings.[28] One illustrative thinker in this regard is the French economist Frédéric Bastiat, whose writings on liberty and political economy are tinted with an anti-violence and anti-imperial perspective, while simultaneously laying the discursive groundwork for a justification of violence and intervention—one that would mirror real-world justifications of transformative foreign policy.

Bastiat's critique of empire takes two tacks. The first is a fundamental critique of *fonctionnairisme*: the enlarging of the bureaucratic state.[29] Bastiat aimed his gunsights particularly at socialist sentiments in France, where he equated the swelling of bureaucracy with developing a corrupt empire for its own sake.[30] The second tack is a critique of war and violence more generally. In his seminal 1850 work *Economic Harmonies,* Bastiat sees war as an impediment to humankind's progress; it is a waste of an individual's capacity to labor and innovate. He writes:

> If we take into account the extent to which labor has been wasted by war, if we consider the extent to which what remained of the product of labor has been concentrated in the hands of a few conquerors, we can well understand why the masses are destitute, for their destitution cannot be explained in our day on the hypothesis of liberty.[31]

Bastiat's writing, however, has an internal justification for imperial violence and intervention; much of his general philosophy of history and his understanding of the contrary identities of Europeans and Others echoes languages used by both pro-empire intellectuals and policy makers who deployed violence as a means of intervening in the colonial periphery.

In terms of philosophy of history, Bastiat's thinking is intimately related to Mill's consideration of civilizational development.[32] Bastiat's narrative of historical progress is driven, however, by providential design: humankind is destined by God toward perfectibility. As he writes, "[this] cannot be doubted when we consider the nature of man and his intellect, his distinctive characteristic, which was breathed into him along with the breath of life, and by virtue of which the revelation of Moses could declare that man was created in the image of God."[33] Civilization is connected to this providential teleology; Basquiat eloquently critiques theorists who see in civilization the corruption of humankind. On the contrary, civilization is the mechanism by which man can perfect himself. In attacking François-René de Chateaubriand's argument about the horrors of civilization, Bastiat retorts "[this argument] has been repeated since the time of Heraclitus, but it is not, for all that, any less wrong."[34] Civilization moves the individual, and, by extension, society, forward through history—from man's imperfection to the possibility of perfectibility.

This narrative of perfectibility sees progress as humankind's continual struggle against evil in the process of civilizational development, where man is the inevitable victor thanks to his God-given intellect. "What makes for Man's perfectibility is his intellect," he writes, "or the capacity that is given him to pass from error, the source of evil, to truth, the source of the good."[35] While carrying common Enlightenment themes about reason and progress into the mid-nineteenth century context of revolution and fundamental social change, Bastiat notably sees this historical trajectory as one of inevitability—as being ordained by God himself.

Bastiat also exemplified common liberal understandings about European identity in contrast to that of other peoples. Bastiat does this through both a reading of non-European societies as backward and at earlier stages of development (*pace* Mill), and as a contemporary threat to Western society more generally. Bastiat is clear throughout *Economic Harmonies* that even though man is made in God's image, not all men are equal. In discussing the historical interests that individuals have vis-à-vis certain institutional arrangements, for example, he suggests "these wants were the chief and most absorbing preoccupation of the great majority of the human race."[36] Who is this minority? This distinction is further developed in Bastiat's discussion of war—dividing the human race into nations of "plunderers" and nations of "workers" who are fundamentally opposed; in fact, the "nations of plunderers" are the only nations that benefit from war.[37]

Bastiat's own anti-empire stance contains within it a bizarre, and uniquely imperial, understanding of the Other's inferiority. In arguing against conquest, Bastiat elaborates that war creates an atmosphere of militarism in public culture. More than that, the use of violence to conquer makes the conquered more warlike than before. "When [the conquered race] overcomes its oppressors, it shows itself in its process of readjustment disposed to imitate them."[38] The strange discursive move of simultaneously critiquing empire while also arguing against colonial independence is a rhetorical strategy that would be used by colonial administrators and government officials to justify intervention and, ironically, new iterations of empire. The idea of United Nations mandates (discussed in more detail in the following chapter) was framed in an analogous way: dismantling the institutions of empire and creating a "sacred trust" to gradually allow subject peoples to gain self-determination. As Bastiat's writing shows, this was not mere hypocrisy: it is a logic built into the structure of liberal discourses beginning in the mid-nineteenth century.

Liberal theorists in Britain and France were preoccupied with the issue of identity, and the ways that features fundamental to European identity—progress, civilization, liberty—interfaced with broader political processes like empire and war. For Spencer, liberal identity is deeply tied to violence and aggression. Tocqueville predicted threats to the liberal world order from "barbarous" and "semi-barbarous" communities, and applauded efforts to bring those elements under heel. And, perhaps most contradictorily, Bastiat used a language of liberal, civilizing, domination to back up arguments that were anti-empire. These discourses were mobilized to defend the progressivism of anti-imperial causes, all the while reproducing the identity groups that justified emancipatory violence in the first place.

Institutions and a Permanent State of Exception: Mill's Other

Scholars have long interrogated John Stuart Mill's imperial legacy; however, most of the studies on Mill and empire have largely missed the connections between Mill's views on civilizational development and his broader concerns with international order.[39] Significant in this regard are Mill's economic writings, and particularly his monumental work *Principles of Political Economy*, which was first published in 1848, but revised in several subsequent editions until 1871.[40] *Principles of Political Economy* outlines central aspects of Mill's theories about international institutionalism, economics, and interaction with other civilizational groups, which makes it a prime site for analysis. Inattention to this work is particularly startling. Lynn Zastoupil, for instance, argues that "[a]lthough *Principles of Political Economy* and *Considerations on Representative Government* contain important passages about India and Indian administration, the main focus of these and other works [. . .] is events and issues far removed from the imperial experience."[41] Moreover, in recent works on Mill's civilizational development narrative, this absence of *Principles of Political Economy* is noticeable. Jahn, for example, cites the work only twice in the development of her own thesis in a 2005 journal article.[42] This absence of sustained attention limits our understanding of emancipatory liberalism's nineteenth-century picture of institutions, intervention, and civilization.

Mill's view of institutions was that of scientific discovery. One could discover the best institutions—and especially those aimed at the production and accumulation of national wealth—through causal reasoning. This holds some implications for considering the ways that liberals envisioned integrating values related to civilizational development into existing institutional orders. First, and most fundamentally, the rational design of institutions and the consideration of the moral and value-oriented aspects of social science were inseparable. As Mill notes the "remarkable differences in the state of different portions of the human race," the institutional solutions are ones of economic sciences: "in so far as the causes are moral or psychological, dependent on institutions and social relations, or on the principles of human nature, their investigation belongs [...] to moral and social science, and is the object of what is called Political Economy."[43] A science of civilization, Mill's broader project in works like *Principles of Political Economy*, would use moral and social theory to embed ideals about emancipatory liberalism in institutional design.

Second, Mill's political theory depends on an understanding of institutions that often considers the subject in contradictory ways. For instance, Mill is highly critical of slavery as an institution, but much of this objection has to do with efficiency, rather than a questioning of the inherent equality of the Other as an agent. He argues: "There are also savage tribes so averse to regular industry, that industrial life is scarcely able to introduce itself among them until they are either conquered and made slaves of, or become conquerors and make others so."[44] Inequality of the subject is clear in Mill's writing of *Principles of Political Economy*. He continues: "after allowing the full value of these considerations, it remains certain that slavery is incompatible with any high state of the arts of life, and any great efficiency of labour."[45] The institution of slavery is illegitimate to Mill primarily because it leads to an inefficiency of labor. While this rules slavery out as an institution for realizing Mill's civilizational-development philosophy of history, it opens the door for other methods; Mill leaves the problem he identifies (the inability of certain groups of people to contribute to industry) open for other institutional solutions.

Furthermore, Mill discusses at great length the aims of civilizing institutions, progressive processes, and particularly economic changes. In discussing the relationship between labor practices and civilizing methods, Mill argues, "to civilize a savage, he must be inspired with new wants and desires, even if not of a very elevated kind, provided that their gratification can be a motive to steady and regular bodily and mental exertion."[46] New understandings—and, significantly, European understandings—about interests are vital for non-Europeans to develop into so-called civilized races.

This set of arguments about civilizing institutions was closely connected to Mill's overriding concern in most of his writings: the desire to develop a science of "ethology."[47] This science of "character," for Mill, represented an attempt to understand the foundations of human nature, and its differences across space and time (e.g., levels of civilizational development). As Mill writes, the science of ethology would involve:

> [. . .] increased study of the various types of human nature that are to be found in the world; conducted by persons not only capable of analysing and recording the circumstances in which these types severally prevail, but also sufficiently acquainted with psychological laws to be able to explain and account for the characteristics of the type, by the peculiarity of the circumstances: the residuum alone, when there proves to be any, being set down to the account of congenital predispositions.[48]

Such civilizing institutions, including structural economic changes, were grounded in a science of human nature, and involved the wholesale transformation of the individual character of different races. Mill's *Principles of Political Economy* saw economic institutions as a way of reconstituting the individual ethos of the "savage," an emancipatory understanding of the relationship between positive liberty, science, and imperialism.

Mill's ideas about civilizing "barbarous races" through reform of primarily economic institutions is outlined in *Principles of Political Economy*. But there is another side to this coin. In many ways, Mill justifies violence through appeals to institutional/legal modes. Sometimes, economic (e.g., gradual) changes are not enough. Liberal Europe often has to resort to a politics of emergency and exception, to use a noncontemporaneous framing.[49] Curious in this regard are the legal/moral moves that Mill makes on the topic of intervention. On the one hand, Mill makes an appeal to European international legal institutions that prohibit intervention in the affairs of "civilized states." In fact, exceptions to the norm of nonintervention in Europe find their justification outside of law entirely, in the realm of moral prudence—i.e., particularly horrific and repugnant civil strife may be enough to violate those norms.[50]

Mill paints the institutional aspects of intervention in the colonial periphery, however, as outside the boundaries of law altogether. In some sense, the non-European world is a state of "permanent exception."[51] Particularly, Mill sees a clear limit to international law in dealing with "barbarous" populations. He writes: "A civilised government cannot help having barbarous neighbors: when it has, it cannot always content itself with a defensive position, one of mere resistance to aggression."[52] Those kinds of communities are an existential threat, in Mill's view, and the general civilizational discourse of the time, and therefore are beyond the pale of legal reasoning—it is a moral issue. It is an issue of life and death. It is an issue of preserving a civilizational identity against the barbarians at the border.[53]

Mill, further, uses this dichotomy between reasoned/civilized and unreasoned/uncivilized to structure the deliberative processes of institutional dynamics. Mill places consensus as something that occurs *within* Western, "civilized," communities, and casts the "barbarian" Other as unable to participate in institutions as a forum for deliberation about issues such as political economy. Mill writes that one such reason for this vision of the Other is that they are passive recipients of civilization, rather than active, deliberative, and communicative contributors. Regarding the Jesuits in Paraguay and their mission to civilize the natives, Mill writes: "To the absolute authority of these men they [the natives] reverentially submitted themselves, and were induced by them to learn the arts of civilized life, and to practise labours for the community, with no inducement that could have been offered would have prevailed on them to practise for themselves."[54] For Mill, the fact that "civilized" communities can develop institutional solutions is due to the fact that they have the ability to critically reason and actively shape those institutions through design, deliberation, and engagement. Mill's "barbarians" were not part of this process. They are not agents that could act, speak, engage: they are subjects that could only be acted upon.

This distinction is clear, as well, in Mill's more visible political works. For example, in what is perhaps his most famous work, *On Liberty*, Mill argues that levels of civilization apply to considerations of what *kind* of liberty is due. In talking about laws aimed at curtailing drinking in Britain, Mill makes an argument distinguishing "civilized" races from those of "barbarians." These policies are "suited only to a state of society in which the laboring classes are avowedly treated as children or savages, and placed under an education of restraint, to fit them for future admission to the privileges of freedom." [55] An "education of restraint" is necessary in dealing with those of lower civilizational development than Western Europeans. Mill fleshes this idea out even more explicitly (and deserves quoting at length):

> Despotism is a legitimate mode of government in dealing with barbarians, provided the end be their improvement, and the means justified by actually

effecting that end. Liberty, as a principle, has no application to any state of things anterior to the time when mankind have become capable of being improved by free and equal discussion. Until then, there is nothing for them but implicit obedience to an Akbar or a Charlemagne, if they are so fortunate as to find one. But as soon as mankind have attained the capacity of being guided to their own improvement by conviction or persuasion (a period long since reached in all nations with whom we need here concern ourselves), compulsion, either in the direct form or in that of pains and penalties for non-compliance, is no longer admissible as a means to their own good, and justifiable only for the security of others.[56]

Conviction, persuasion, compulsion. In Mill's view, this is for their own good. Mill developed these arguments further in writings like "A Few Words on Non-Intervention," which imagines intervention against "barbarous" peoples as being for their benefit.[57]

Mill's *Principles of Political Economy*, while much less closely analyzed in the liberal empire literature, presents an illustrative example of the ways that liberal thinkers connected broad emancipatory liberal themes—especially those related to civilizational development—to institutional issues. Mill's understanding of these issues was linked specifically to his concerns with economy and trade, and associated institutions, in the nineteenth century. Mill's vision of the way that values were embedded in institutions, his understanding of appropriate institutional design, and the deliberative purposes outlined provide depth for understanding how many mid-nineteenth century liberals imagined international organization and its relationship to liberal ideals. Mill's political geography was one of an enlightened, civilized, Europe—and its unreasoned counterpoint: one that was not only unable to participate in the formation of world order, but had to be folded into submission. The "barbarian" condition is a permanent state of exception.

Common Sense: The Cultural Politics of Emancipatory Liberalism in the Nineteenth Century

These emancipatory-liberal discourses were not only elite discourses, created by elites and intellectuals meant for other elites and intellectuals. They made their way into cultural common sense through their diffusion in popular media. Newspapers, in particular, were a way of transmitting these ideas to larger groups of people. The editorials written in these papers demonstrate that these discourses made sense to, and had an influence on, the thinking of broader segments of the population in the West. Vocabularies of progress, civilization, and mythscapes revolving around Orientalism and difference were mirrored in these texts. Some extracts from these texts are illustrative. I will focus specifically on Britain.

In *The Times* of London, one of the leading British papers of the nineteenth century, similar expressions of the identity and duty of Britain as a liberal state recur. Regarding diplomatic relations, the editors write:

> [...] we hope [to] show Europe that we have in our great popular assembly a council worthy to discuss and able to appreciate not only the conduct of our own Government, but the highest questions of international duty and the principles on which the foreign affairs of England as a leading member of the great European body must henceforth be conducted.[58]

The common liberal theme of international duty was not limited to intellectual discourse, but appeared within the context of editorial argument. Perhaps more starkly, the editors clearly lay out the defining features of a liberal state, and the illiberal alternative: "This country [Britain] finds herself of necessity dissevered from those nations in which she had laboured to establish more liberal institutions, and her own freedom has become to them a source of distrust and dread. The world is like Martin Luther's drunken peasant on horseback, who when you prop him up on one side falls over on the other [...]."[59] Britain is a liberal state; its duty is to liberalize other states; and, more than ungratefulness, this has caused "distrust" and "dread" aimed at Britain.

Besides just defining the liberal state, news media also engaged in a similar sort of civilizational Othering. This was notably aimed at non-European peoples, and those in the colonial periphery. In discussing political matters in Hong Kong, for instance, the editorials take a tough stance. "At no distant date," the editors write, "it was to become a model-farm of European civilization at the very gates of Canton, and be filled with a mixed population of English colonists and Chinese Settlers."[60] The institution of colonialism is imagined as a civilizing force. This discussion of emancipation through civilization, in fact, continued into an even darker realm of animal comparisons. In regards to maintaining police order in Hong Kong: "When they [the Chinese] found that they could splice on a tail the police ended by shaving off entirely the original appendage."[61] Much like the temporal philosophies of developmental thinkers like Mill, Tocqueville, and others, writers for popular audiences saw colonial subjects as, quite literally, less than human. Cultural common sense echoed many of the themes that elite discourses touched on, and most particularly discourses about civilizational difference and the "backwardness" of non-European peoples. These discourses presented to the public cultural frames through which intervention, violence, and even major war could be justified.

Dissent: America in the Late Nineteenth Century

While the above discussion focused on discourses about civilizational development, and the relationship between Othering processes, identity formation, and violence in the realm of intellectual production in Britain and France, the United States provides a window into dissent from this discourse. The United States in this period was a power of a different ideational tradition. These differences were largely contextual—and especially related to the fact that the United States had a very different relationship to empire and colonialism. A booming anti-imperialist movement pushed the discourse in the United States further toward nonintervention. One particular moment here is significant: US involvement in the Philippines. No other nineteenth-century event in US history would set the stage for discursive differences about emancipatory liberalism between the United States and Western Europe.

Following the Spanish-American War of 1898, the United States seized the opportunity to develop an overseas empire. These claims included, among smaller islands, Puerto Rico, Guam, Hawaii, Cuba, and the Philippines. Following the Treaty of Paris in December 1898, the United States annexed the Philippines from the Spanish for $20 million, and were faced with a rising insurgency on the islands.[62] The United States acted swiftly to attempt to quell dissent in the newly acquired territory. President William McKinley ordered, in the same month of annexation, a military government in the Philippines, and deployed the US military to force the rebel forces to accept American governing authority in the area. The military occupied the area, and was faced with a sizeable—more than 30,000 people—opposition against their intervention and occupation of Manila.[63] Policy during the intervention took the form of what McKinley called "benevolent assimilation," and involved the strategy of developing rationalized institutions, and social service infrastructure, with the aim of diffusing attempts at resistance through socialization.[64] The intervention lasted until 1902, when the Filipino peoples were granted limited self-governing rights under the "Philippine Organic Act," though guarantees of full independence were not granted until 1914.

Unlike the cases of Britain and France—where most important liberal intellectuals and policy makers supported empire—the United States' imperial ambitions in the Philippines were frustrated by, and entangled in, a domestic contestation over American position in the world. Race played an important role in this debate, especially in regard to racism and violence toward a large African-American population in the US South. Practical concerns, however, related to economics, trade, and the overabundance of continental territory, further advanced an anti-imperialist line of thinking about the Philippine intervention. Though this anti-imperial sentiment had, perhaps, a limited effect on the conflict (Roosevelt ended the conflict in 1902, shortly after taking the presidency), and organized attempts to limit US expansionism—such as the American Anti-Imperialist League—would eventually die out in the face of public opinion, the United States was faced with domestic constraints on the extent of its colonial ambitions that Britain and France, for example, did not have to confront in such a dramatic way.[65]

The costs of Manifest Destiny, along with a bloody Civil War, certainly limited US imperial ambitions during this period from a practical standpoint. And an anti-imperialist discourse in domestic politics also disrupted a consistent connection between liberalism in the United States and liberalism in Europe at the time. If Britain and France had been enmeshed in this ideological environment, rather than in a fairly consistent one of liberal empire and the goals of civilizational development, it is highly likely that violence would be greatly restrained. The simple fact that the Philippine intervention, for example, was intensely debated in the American public sphere demonstrates the potential political costs for leaders to engage in costly transformative interventions abroad. This was much less the case in Britain and France, where much of the intellectual debate of the 1848–1900 period was pro-imperialism.[66]

In short, American intellectuals were a significant source of dissent toward common ways of conceptualizing civilizational development, liberal identity, institutions, and the use of violence in relation to these ideals. Much of this was traceable to the anti-imperialism movement in America during the late nineteenth century; however, even in the context of dissent, many commonalities appear, particularly about Western superiority in relation to North-South differences.

Liberal political, intellectual, and policy thought in the nineteenth century was a series of discourses about the emancipatory potential of the modern liberal state, juxtaposed with the colonial Other. This understanding of the political aims, often framed as the "moral duty" of a Western liberal state, frequently entailed arguments about violence and intervention. This is true across a variety of liberal thinkers, from Mill and Spencer in Britain, to Tocqueville and Bastiat in France. Dissent was important, but limited by the conceptual architectures in which the writers of the time were immersed. While the Philippines shows that America was faced with a different set of discursive structures, other forms of violence were carried out by the United States in the name of civilizational development—most notably, the near complete extermination of indigenous peoples in North America.

How did these discourses of civilizational development relate to actual acts of violence on the ground? The following section presents a case study of British intervention in Burma in the nineteenth century to illustrate how these arguments were drawn on in order to justify, frame, and organize practices of colonial violence.

Violence and Civilization: The British in Burma in the Nineteenth Century

British-Burmese conflict began in the early nineteenth century after expansion of the Burmese empire along the Indian frontier caused concern among officials in British India about an emerging threat along the border. These issues resulted in the First Anglo-Burmese War (1824–1826). Following this war was the imposition of the Treaty of Yandabo, which ceded recently acquired territory by the Burmese to the British, required ending border hostilities, and included an indemnity payment and commercial/diplomatic relations with the British Empire.[67] This treaty would ultimately cause the bankruptcy of the Burmese empire, palace intrigue, and a court rebellion against the monarchy in the 1840s.[68] When the Prince of Pagan ascended to the Burmese throne in 1846, relations with the British further deteriorated, especially vis-à-vis stricter customs rules in Rangoon, and conflict between the Burmese government and British traders. British officials in Calcutta were unhappy with the lack of Burmese submission following the first war, and the seeming violation of the commercial arrangements. This conflict was a major impetus for the Second Anglo-Burmese War of 1852.[69]

A robbery in March of 1851 caused more extreme anti-Burmese sentiment among British officials. This event resulted in a merchants committee demanding that the British send troops to intervene against the Burmese, who were—according to them—offering protection to pirates and thieves.[70] In 1852, Lord James Broun-Ramsay Dalhousie, the Governor-General of British India, sent Commodore George Lambert to Burma to negotiate concessions from the Burmese regarding commercial violations. The Burmese largely complied with the requests, including the removal of the Governor of Rangoon. Lambert escalated matters, however, by blockading the port in Rangoon and seizing King Pagan's ship in the harbor. This led to war, which ultimately ended in the British annexation of Lower Burma.[71]

Following crises resulting from French encroachment on British influence in Burma, as well as other legal and commercial issues, increased tension between the Burmese government and the British Empire became a constant nuisance. In November of 1885, the Burmese refused an ultimatum given by the British that the Burmese accept a new British resident, that court actions against British companies be cancelled, and that the British have greater control over the foreign relations of the country. This resulted in intervention of the British in Burma (the Third Anglo-Burmese War), and the subsequent annexation of Upper Burma—giving complete control of the former Burmese Empire to the British.[72] Following the war, the British completely restructured the government of Burma. This was rather unorthodox, considering that the British Empire demolished the existing monarchy altogether, which was not an entirely common practice in British imperial strategy. These changes included a restructuring of even local administration, in order to introduce Western liberal bureaucracy in the stead of local institutions that were perceived by the British to be ineffective.[73]

Much of the historiography on the Anglo-Burmese Wars, and especially the conquest in 1885, neglects the role of discourse and justification. These debates largely focus on the often *hidden* strategies of Britain, and particularly moneyed elites, in causing the war. A particularly influential account of the Third War, for instance, argues that networks of "gentlemanly capitalists" influenced the British decision to intervene. Anthony Webster suggests that the interaction between the British government and the bourgeoisie helped the government gather intelligence in exchange for favorable arrangements for investment of capital.[74] These accounts miss the fact that justificatory frameworks were not always expressed in this way. Justifications for the intervention—and subsequent conquest of Burma—operated within the context of emancipatory liberal frameworks that articulated identity arguments, institutional arguments, and appeals to public support.

The identity claims made about the Burmese from British officials built on a broader theme of civilization and barbarism developed throughout the nineteenth century. In his account of the Third Anglo-Burmese War, military secretary and major in the British Army, J. J. Snodgrass, clearly illustrates who the enemy was. The Burmese were "warlike and ambitious," and their "arrogant pretensions and restless character had so frequently interrupted the relations of peace subsisting between [India and Bengal]."[75] Snodgrass had a low opinion of the inhabitants of Burma. Early on in his account, in discussing the natives of the Pegu (Bago in current terminology) region, he writes that they "have been accused of some of the worst propensities of savage man,"[76] citing uncorroborated reports of cannibalism, for instance, as proof of their uncivilized nature. The fact that Snodgrass situates these accounts of the people of Burma at the very beginning of his account is significant. In doing so, he alludes to justification for the war. After all, the barbarians (a term used throughout the narrative) of Burma had the potential to affect the entire regional order, and potentially interfere with British affairs in India. In concluding remarks, Snodgrass inserts some editorial views about this interference. He writes: "There is no country to the east so well suited for an inlet to our trade; and under a better form of government, a ready market would be found for a large consumption of British merchandise [. . .]."[77] The Burmese were holding up progress, trade, and the march of civilization.

The racism and superiority found in Snodgrass's writing is perhaps not unique. But Snodgrass's own discussion of the role that intervention would play in liberalizing Burma falls into a historically specific emancipatory discourse about domestic institutional change in the context of a civilizational development project. In writing about a new British settlement in Burma, Amherst Town, he argues that the British had begun steps to liberalize, and liberate, the Burmese people:

> [. . .] the inhabitants of Pegu, and even Ava, already well-acquainted with the difference between their own arbitrary laws and our more liberal and enlightened code of jurisprudence, will fly from the oppressive measures of their own chiefs, and flock to the ceded districts to enjoy a milder sway; and where security of property, and encouragement to industry, will convert these long ill-governed provinces into one of the finest countries in the east.[78]

For Snodgrass, liberalism could at the very least free natives of oppressive rule in their communities, even if this liberalism was at the cost of conquest, war, and the loss of sovereignty. It was worth it for the gift of civilization. Snodgrass's arguments about British settlements parallel Mill's comments about the role of paternalism in encouraging industry. For example, while Mill looked approvingly at the way the Jesuits in Paraguay forced the natives into industry, Snodgrass suggests that the existence of "free" cities in Burma, under British control, would not only emancipate the locals, but make them productive protoliberal citizens. This is the civilizing project of nineteenth-century British interventionism, built on a set of identity claims about a liberal West and a savage East.

The institutional structure of liberal empire, as well, gave legitimacy to justifications regarding the intervention in Burma. The public, especially, were a key site in the "selling" of the Burmese interventions. Elites accomplished this by appealing to the same sorts of common sense tropes discussed above. One instance of this was the *way* that language was deployed in the popular press. *The Times* of London spoke of the Second Anglo-Burmese War in a triumphalist tone: "The capture of Rangoon has opened the Burmese War with a brilliant feat of arms, and we shall be happy to learn that the irresistible force of the British squadron on the coast [. . .] has at once convinced the court of Ava."[79] This demonstrates that elite justification to popular audiences built on the broader discursive themes of the use of violence in nineteenth-century liberal empire. Themes of duty, civilization, and Orientalism, highlighted above, pervaded this specific case. The use of violence "convinced" Ava through a display of British force, proving British superiority, and using force as a means of persuading a society like Burma to join the path of civilization. The publics of the time would have recognized this sentiment, and the connections made between triumphant emancipatory ethics and the displays of British force.

These discourses of emancipatory liberalism were not limited to justifications to publics, or to providing *reasons* for warring with Burma, eventually extinguishing Burmese sovereignty altogether. They also intersected with the intervention practices on the ground. Discourses of civilizational development among policy makers at the time provided a framework for conceptualizing post-intervention dynamics and liberal constitutionalism in relation to a complex identity politics. As John Furnivall, a prominent historian of Burma, writes: "[the dismantling of the Burmese monarchy] was the result of a reading of pre-annexation Burmese society which saw the political system as a sort of 'oriental despotism', a king ruling ruthlessly and absolutely over an otherwise egalitarian society."[80] Intervening in Burma served the dual purpose of stabilizing a country that often caused problems at the Indian frontier, while at the same time freeing Burmese society from an inefficient and tyrannical regime by developing Western liberal political institutions. Doing so constituted the roles of the interveners as saviors of oppressed populations.[81]

Harold Fielding Hall, a high-ranking civil servant in Burma during the late 1880s,[82] wrote extensively about the country, its religion, and its government. Writing of the pre-intervention governance structures, he states:

> It would be difficult, I think, to imagine anything worse than the government of Upper Burma in its later days. I mean by "government" the king and

his counsellors and the greater officials of the empire. The management of foreign affairs, of the army, the suppression of greater crimes, the care of the means of communication, all those duties which fall to the central government, were badly done, if done at all. It must be remembered that there was one difficulty in the way—the absence of any noble or leisured class to be entrusted with the greater offices [...] there was no one between the king and the villager—no noble, no landowner, no wealthy or educated class at all. The king had to seek for his ministers among the ordinary people, consequently the men who were called upon to fill great offices of state were as often as not men who had no experience beyond the narrow limits of a village.[83]

Hall's discussion of governance in Burma reveals three things. First, it provides a justification for post-intervention governance in Burma, much more extensive than in most British colonies: one that is based on correcting poor governing institutions. Second, it isolates a cause for these poor governing institutions—namely, the lack of an intermediate bureaucratic system between the king and the villagers. Thus, this lack of rationalized governance contributed to the decay of rulership in Burma during the nineteenth century. Third—and most crucially for evidence of emancipatory liberalism's connection to violence and intervention—it suggests a liberal paternalism by detailing the importance of more "experienced" intermediaries to connect the boundaries between central government and local administration. This is precisely what the British aimed to accomplish in the dissolution of the monarchy and the implementation of liberal governing institutions. The ordinary residents of Burma had no range of knowledge beyond their village, and therefore the installation of technocrats served the purpose of resolving the inadequacies of Burmese society. Recall Tocqueville's railing against "semi-barbarous empires" and the role that disorder and poor governance has in stifling civilizational development. These ideas were directly mirrored in the way that civil administrators thought about Burmese politics after the war.

Equally important in thinking about the role of emancipatory liberalism in post-intervention administration in Burma is the way that the British dealt with minority groups after the interventions. Oftentimes in British and French imperial endeavors, metropolitan imperialists and colonial administrators made clear distinctions *within* colonial possessions about the inhabitants there, with strikingly varied effects. As C. A. Bayly notes in his masterful study of imperial history, "[...] the British, French, and Dutch [...] often separated off those parts of conquered territories which seemed to be inhabited by 'minority peoples,' especially when they were located in hill lands, forest, or desert."[84] These distinctions were further entrenched in a liberal language about civilization, race, and development. The Karen ethnic group, for example, was particularly targeted by the British in post-intervention administration, and as a justification for British intervention in the unjust Burman regime. Snodgrass writes that they "may be considered as the slaves of the soil, living in wretched hamlets by themselves, heavily taxed and oppressed by the Burmese authorities, by whom they are treated as an altogether inferior race of beings."[85] Britain saw the protection of minorities in Burma through invasion, domination, and colonization to be a prime purpose of emancipatory liberal ethics in world politics.

Resistance to the narratives of British rule in Burma were dramatically shut down—oftentimes through direct violence. In the Third Anglo-Burmese War, for instance, the British continued to face resistance from the Burmese in the north. This resistance was crushed through a campaign of violence and devastation, including the "systematic destruction of villages" and the replacement of local leaders with those who were seen as more sympathetic, or at least reliably co-opted by the British Empire.[86] The phrase often used by British politicians and writers in reference to Burmese rebels was "deviations from the laws of humanity,"[87] connecting resistance to enmity toward humanist values. Rebels were delaying the inevitable march of humanity toward civilization through their acts of resistance.

Administration discourses wrote off rebellion and resistance altogether, seeing it as evidence of the immaturity of the Burmese population. In an administration report from the 1860s, in the aftermath of the Second Anglo-Burmese War a decade earlier, an officiating secretary, Horace Spearman, discusses a failed rebellion that was started in one of the provinces. He notes that the would-be rebel was an example of the "extraordinary impulsiveness" and "unreflecting character of the Burmese disposition."[88] He suggests, further, that the locals were more satisfied with British administration than with the capabilities of the rebel leaders. Spearman writes, in referencing another incident of attempted rebellion, that he was "unable to find grounds on which to cause dissatisfaction" among the Burmese.[89] Thus, the British administration was able to effectively couch rebellion into a sort of paternalized view of the Burmese subject as being qualitatively different than the European—unreasoned, impulsive, irrational—while at the same time arguing that attempts at resistance were not even justifiable to other Burmese. Not only was rebellion irrational, it demonstrated why British paternalism was necessary for the Burmese people.

British ideological hegemony *within* the empire was relatively thorough. In fact, prominent British voices speaking out against British occupation of Burma were not effectively heard until well into the twentieth century, the most famous of which was George Orwell's in his essay "Shooting an Elephant": a devastating critique of British destruction of Burmese society.[90] As a clear example of this, we might look at the case of Prime Minister William Gladstone. While the liberal Gladstone's opposition to endeavors like the First Opium War were clear (he argued eloquently that "a war more unjust in origin, a war more calculated to cover this country with permanent disgrace, I do not know and I have not read of"[91]), he did not hazard such a critique of the occupation of Burma, which continued well into his prime ministry.

Conclusions: Emancipatory Liberalism before the Twentieth Century

A few general themes are worth reflecting on in conclusion of this chapter. Emancipatory liberals engaged in similar thinking about civilizational development. This chapter, drawing on an eclectic group of thinkers, and situating their work into historical context, shows that this trend is not just the idiosyncratic approach of one or two theorists. Rather, civilizational development discourses are recurrent during this period. They structured the way that liberal thinkers, policy makers, and publics imagined the means, methods, and objects of violence, and particularly imperial interventions, during the nineteenth century. A liberalism of civilizational development provided a common cultural vocabulary to conceptualize identity, norms, and Otherness in world politics.

Furthermore, these discourses mattered in the way intervention/violence was structured. As the case study of Burma demonstrates, these intellectual and popular discourses interacted with material practices like intervention in blatant ways. Colonial administrators used this language in post-intervention settings in Burma, and justificatory frameworks built off of these languages of civilizational development as well. While the historiography of the Burmese Wars often focuses its attention on the material (economic/strategic) interests of Britain in bringing Burma under its control, the ideational aspects are significant. This is evidenced by the *way* that the British conceived of the use of violence in Burma—through war and intervention—as part of a broader scheme to bring civilization to Southeast Asia. Lord Dalhousie and others were clear in their justifications for war; this was a conflict over the freedom of the Burmese people from the irrationalism of traditional ways of life.

In relation to thinking about dissent, the brief American case shows some evidence of alternative imaginaries. As the debates surrounding the Philippines show, however, while American intellectuals were more prone to dissent from the liberal discursive order they were enmeshed in, many of these ideas of civilizational superiority still existed. After all, the way that Americans engaged with (slaughtered) their own indigenous populations is deeply related to an Othering of the latter—a relegating of an entire group of people to the realm of "savages."

The following chapter analyzes the role of emancipatory liberalism in the deployment of violence between the turn of the century, especially the aftermath of World War I. This period is one characterized by similar themes of developmentalism, progress, and civilization, but with notable changes in both discourses and institutional contexts—most significantly, a shift to anti-imperial conflict *within* the discourse of emancipatory liberalism, as well as the introduction of the idea of "self-determination" to that system.

CHAPTER FOUR

Transformation and Self-Determination

Internationalists at War

CIVILIZATIONAL DISCOURSES IN emancipatory liberalism did not end with the turn of the twentieth century. Though the languages of empire changed, the underlying themes of putting less-developed people on the proper path of civilizational development were still prominent and recurring motifs in liberal international thought. The major differences involved layering new institutional understandings related to the use of force—namely, mandatory duties, self-determination, and the emergence of "democracy talk."[1] Liberals of the early twentieth century did not shy away from thinking about the uses of violence with liberal aims. This is surprising for at least two reasons. The first is that World War I created a guarded optimism about the end of great power conflict—learning the lessons of a brutal and destructive war. The second is that the discipline of IR, established as a means to manage conflict, spent many of its formative years trying to "order the world" rather than wage war against it.[2] Nonetheless, liberal discourses provided the framework for justifying and deploying force in world politics.

Two specific themes stand out in these discourses. Contextually, emancipatory liberals were optimistic and hopeful that institutional solutions to war and conflict would succeed in bringing peace and liberal values to the rest of the world. The League of Nations mandate system was a key component of these discourses, and many writers and politicians—from US President Woodrow Wilson to South African politician Jan Smuts to antiwar activist Jane Addams—would devote enormous effort defending these programs. The irony of such justifications is that mandatory rule over former colonies would allow states to justify the deployment of force and intervention in these areas. This is precisely what the French did in Syria in the 1920s, but it was not limited to that series of interventions. Similar events can be seen with the British in Iraq in the 1920s. Mandates and the institutional context of emancipatory liberalism in the interwar period provided the rhetorical ammo for a politics of violence and intervention.

Furthermore, even authors who did not write explicitly about mandates—including liberal intellectuals like economist Francois Guyot, sociologist Emile Durkheim, and others—worked to reproduce some of the same civilizational narratives as the liberal empire period, while integrating self-determination and democratizing discourses into the fray of emancipatory thought. While the civilizing mission was alive and well, emancipatory discourses added the element of self-rule and democracy; not only were countries like Britain and France creating modern, rational citizens, they were doing so for the purpose of expanding a conception of eventual democratic governance.

This chapter tells the story of these discourses in the early twentieth century, with a special emphasis on the interwar period. While other studies have developed narratives about interwar liberal optimism[3]—the development of IR, interwar empire talk, etc.—this story focuses on how these discourses constructed the space for interventions during this period. As such, the first sections of the chapter outline the broad contours of these discourses, drawing out illustrative examples of general themes and specific tropes. The final part of the chapter shows how these discourses were mirrored in the French interventions in Syria (its mandate during the interwar years) in the 1920s, while also briefly illustrating the similarities between French interventions in Syria and British interventions in mandate-era Iraq.

War, Mandates, and a New Civilizational Discourse

While nineteenth-century liberalism was characterized by emerging understandings of universal freedom and the political project of imperialism, the twentieth century, at least in terms of official rhetoric, seemed to usher in a period marked by self-determination and democracy. Woodrow Wilson and his "Fourteen Points," expressing a liberal idealism, suggested a new path toward global peace. But liberals of this period continued the civilizational thinking that epitomized the late nineteenth century. World War I marked a critical juncture in the history of international liberalism, but it also introduced new packaging for a long-standing theme about the role of liberal states in civilizing the rest of the world. Mandates became an important structural component of this discourse, whereas the language of "child races" and similar dichotomies helped to construct a hierarchically ordered international society. Cultural crises, or "faults," were important precipitators of these changes.

Two major faults characterized the transition between the nineteenth century and the interwar period. The first was World War I. Interstate war, on a scale previously unimaginable, caused a global reevaluation of the role of violence in international society, the means of resolving disputes, and the utility of international institutions in creating the conditions for world peace.[4] Many Western liberals imagined a new global politics based on free trade,[5] institutional cooperation/law,[6] and other means of world order. World War I was an external factor that illustrated the problems with the existing organization of world politics, and a new liberalism was the solution for the problem of great power war. The second major fault was a cultural turn toward thinking more concretely about the "nation" as the locus of political community. While the nation was an important ontological structure in the nineteenth century, it became much more of a towering figure following the first great "international war."[7] More than before, liberal internationalists spoke of the nation in a way that was almost sacred.[8] These two differences would have significant effects on changes and continuities in emancipatory liberalism during the first half of the twentieth century.

This focus on nationhood, and sovereignty, would shine a light on two ideas that were of paramount import during this period. The first was a greater emphasis on the idea of "self-determination."[9] This concept, emphasized by an emerging Wilsonian idealism, paved the way for anti-colonial resistance[10] and represented the "translation" of domestic political movements aimed at disassembling the liberal paternalism of the former era.[11] This new emphasis on self-determination existed, in dialogue, with another discourse, however: that of a world order conditioned on a hierarchical relationship between liberal, European, international society, and the rest of the world. As in the period of nineteenth-century liberal empire, this hierarchy was based on historically specific understandings of civilization and of civilizational development.[12] This was not just a function of reconciling liberalism with imperial ambitions. Instead, this represented a new concern with the maintenance of collective security and world order following great power conflict. Liberals of the interwar period were first and foremost concerned with "reconciling liberal universalism with the global status quo."[13]

Even Wilson himself subscribed to this European understanding of civilizational hierarchy, suggesting in the fifth "point" of his infamous address to Congress "A free, open-minded, and absolutely impartial adjustment of all colonial claims, based upon a strict observance of the principle that in determining all such questions of sovereignty the interests of the populations concerned must have equal weight with the equitable claims of the government whose title is to be determined."[14] Though self-determination was an important idea, it existed in an uneasy hierarchy with concerns about global order—namely, the imperial status quo. More than ever, liberals were occupied with issues of global order, and civilizational hierarchy, and a new imperial paternalism were the methods with which to deal with it.

Self-determination may have been a central discursive theme among liberals in this period, but this self-determination was conditional on a society's level of civilizational development. An example of this sort of civilizational thinking, in practice, was the League of Nations' mandate system. This system was meant to manage territories controlled by Germany and the Ottoman Empire following their defeat in World War I, by assigning trusteeship to League of Nations members (namely, great powers), who would administer the territories, though with conditions based upon native rights and legal protections.[15] While this system was seemingly progressive in comparison to other forms of imperial rule, its very structure was premised on paternalism, and a hierarchical understanding of civilization. For early League of Nations liberals, mandates were not empire redux. They were the duty of more developed civilizations to the peoples under mandatory control. Jan Smuts, a principle League of Nations architect, and later Prime Minister of the Union of South Africa, very explicitly outlined these themes in his suggestions for the League's incorporation, writing of mandate charters:

> This policy must necessarily vary from case to case, according to the development, administrative or police capacity, and homogeneous character of the people concerned. The mandatory state should look upon its position as a great trust and honour, not as an office of profit or a position of private advantage for it or its nationals.[16]

This civilizational thinking represented an even more robust development of liberal rationalist thinking in international affairs, by drawing upon biological and psychological metaphors in order to conceptualize the relationship between a liberal society of states and the rest of the world. One of these metaphors was the use of a language of "child races" to dichotomize a reasoned, civilized Europe, and a slightly "mad" imperial periphery,[17] with little legal agency. British classicist Alfred Zimmern talked about "non-adult races," infusing a metaphor of infancy with one of racial and civilizational limitation.[18] It might be argued that this rationalism and its interaction with liberal empire helped lay the foundations of modern IR theory, vis-à-vis the idealism of interwar international political thinkers.[19] Western liberalism was rational; it was ordering; it was emancipatory. Child races had not reached the age of maturity, and required a patriarch to grow them to adulthood. That patriarch was a liberal European international society.

This period, like the period of liberal empire in the nineteenth century, was characterized by a continued discursive thread of civilizational development. This thread divided the world between Western European liberals, and the colonial periphery. It was Europe's duty to help the undercivilized achieve their teleological end of full civilizational development. This way of thinking was undoubtedly paternalistic. Languages of "child races" illustrate this in the most literal way possible. Further, it was rationalistic. Civilization implies a dichotomy between those who can make reasoned decisions and those who need decisions made for them. Colonial control, and later mandates, were the institutional exemplifications of this discursive dichotomy. Democracy and self-determination were conditional upon a society's rational potential. This was just as prevalent in French liberalism as it was in British liberalism. For instance, Albert Sarraut, twice Prime Minister of France under the Third Republic, wrote extensively about the duty that France had to develop infrastructure and instill proper values in colonized societies. Sarraut uses the term *l'obligation* to describe such a duty.[20] Self-determination would emerge as a way to reframe a long-standing colonial understanding of liberalism's civilizing role.

Emancipation and Anglo-American Thought: Addams's and Hobhouse's Perspectives on Race and Antiwar Activism

Examples of this emancipatory ethic in Anglo-American thought are plentiful. One site is the way that this ethic interacted with two other potent political movements of the time period: the suffragist and peace movements in America and Britain. Major suffragist leaders, like Jane Addams and Emily Hobhouse, exemplified these themes of self-determination within the context of a civilizational liberal world order. Both, furthermore, were leading—if not marginalized—intellectuals, and they were engaged in political discussions about postwar peace, and particularly about the designs of collective security arrangements, like the League of Nations. Thus, these two writers and activists show the connection between emancipatory ideas in both theory and practice.

Addams's connection to antiwar movements was a long-standing one, and one that is well documented. She wrote extensively about pacifism, and was a notable activist in the antiwar cause during and after World War I.[21] She was the founder of the Women's Peace Party in the United States, which, during the war, would evolve into the Women's International League for Peace and Freedom (WILPF), of which she was the first president.[22] Elizabeth Agnew notes that Addams "succumbed neither to pro-war justification nor to political resignation."²³ Hobhouse, another activist involved in the peace movement, and an attendee at the Women's Peace Conference in 1915, was a particularly outspoken opponent of British actions in South Africa following the Boer Wars. Both activists were strong supporters of the ideas behind the League of Nations and the mandate system charged with a civilizing mission in the context of self-determination.

Addams is a prime example of a thinker and activist who simultaneously criticized empire, but justified and defended the implementation of the League of Nations' mandate program as part of a project aimed at civilization, progress, and self-determination. Addams's critique of empire was connected directly to her disdain for modern nationalism, which she believed had, by the 1880s, moved from being a force of inclusion to one of great destructive power. She identified nationalism as having a connection to empire as well, citing the ways that British nationalism resulted in an "imperialistic nationalism" that "had become the normal expression and is no longer challenged as a policy."²⁴ For Addams, nationalism was a primary reason for the Great War, and had a connection to certain forms of imperialism that were inimical to a pacifist ethic. From the period of the 1890s to the 1920s, Addams's name was often associated directly with attempts to tie anti-imperialism to other causes of self-determination, including women's rights and social reform.²⁵

For Addams, League of Nations mandates provided an opportunity to account for a permanent peace and provide a liberal basis for world order following World War I. The most explicit of these arguments is laid out by Addams in a 1922 article, where she uses a language of "child races" to argue for mandates. She begins the discussion in outlining arguments for economic guardianship, and suggests that the closest analogy to guardianship in the mandate system is guardianship over children. Addams goes on to compare such guardianship to her own experiences at Hull House, where she had fostered several children: "If there is one thing that is pathetic about these little bereft creatures it is that they are reaching out most eagerly to find someone to take their mother's place."²⁶ The metaphor here directly attaches a corollary between an orphan who is unable to take care of him/herself, and a former colony that is unable to do the same.

While Addams makes a forceful argument for guardianship of mandates by great powers, she noticeably injects such arguments with elements of self-determination. For example, while Addams recognizes that mandatory powers should have guardianship and control over "a so-called backward nation,"²⁷ she further argues that self-determination and a fair, transparent accounting should be made. She finds that transparency would reduce the problems of corruption, and ensure that international institutions and global bodies could keep track of potential abuses to a mandate's autonomy. She uses an analogy with guardianship of a child, again, in suggesting, "After all, any guardian who should come into court and say 'I was interested, of course, in taking care of the child, but I was also interested in lining my own pockets,' would, I think, be thrown out of court [. . .]."[28] Thus, while self-determination was a central message of the early feminist and peace movements as exemplified by Addams, there were limits. These limits were illustrated through paternalist analogies connecting former colonies to the "backwardness" of children, and were imbued with racial and spatial orderings of the world—where advanced, Western countries could be justified in using mandates to limit a country's self-determination, provided they could defend such policies to other great powers in the League of Nations.

Like Addams, Hobhouse was a virulent antiwar campaigner and early feminist activist. She came into the international spotlight during the Boer Wars, where her writing and activism helped to expose the British imprisonment of Boers in concentration camps. She developed a long-standing relationship with Jan Smuts, and was a vocal figure in the establishment of the League of Nations.[29] Despite being a radical reformer, Hobhouse's work functioned to reproduce many of the discursive divisions and fault lines present in pro-imperial British discourse of the period. In relation to race politics, for example, while Hobhouse was critical of the British government's actions in South Africa, she also drew clear lines regarding civilization and race, in particular criticizing the way that the British military cruelly allowed for British women to be humiliated and violated by black Africans, whom Hobhouse referred to by the common slur of the time: "Kaffir."[30] Hobhouse connected the horrors of British concentration camps to the barbarism and civilization that mirrored the race politics of the age.

Hobhouse further elaborated her ideas about peace in her writings and correspondence throughout World War I. In 1916, in a journal entry about her visit to Germany (which caused much controversy in Britain at the time), she writes about the connections between war and civilization: "I believe it is useless to soften or civilize war, that there is no such thing as a 'Civilized War'; there is war between civilized people, certainly, but as we now see that becomes more barbarous than war between barbarians."[31] Like Bastiat, of the nineteenth century, Hobhouse continues a popular liberal imaginary of war and violence as the province of the barbarians, it being entirely inimical to the civilization of the European continent. This is how Hobhouse could cast the evil of British concentration camps in South Africa as outrageous. They were barbaric in both a metaphorical and literal sense: They allowed the violence of nonwhite Africans to be operationalized upon the bodies of European women.

Addams, Hobhouse, and other interwar peace activists present an interesting cross section of emancipatory liberal discourses in the post–WWI era. In the first place, these actors were advocates for nonviolent resolutions of conflict, particularly in the aftermath of the deadliest war humankind had yet seen. In the second place, however, the ideas developed by these activists and writers provided legitimacy to the League of Nations mandate system. These discourses aimed at forwarding a pacifist ethic would buttress institutional frameworks that allowed actors like the French in Syria, or the British in Iraq, to justify the deployment of force in areas under their mandated control. Emancipatory liberalism during the early part of the twentieth century was caught between these dual demands on liberal societies: support peace through mandates, and wage war to crush dissent.

Furthermore, both Addams and Hobhouse illustrate that the concept of race, and racial orderings of the world by liberal activists and intellectuals, significantly interfaced with efforts of peace both during and after the war. For Addams, this was most pronounced in the ways that she conceived of League of Nations mandates as operating like that of a parent to child races. For Hobhouse, this was in the clear racial lines drawn between Europeans and the rest, and the locating of violence beyond the shores of civilization, within the realm of barbarity. League of Nations mandates would build on these languages, and states would use similar discourses to justify war and intervention in mandates.

Emancipatory Liberalism and French Social Science: Guyot and Durkheim

Anglo-American political thinkers were not outliers in their conceptualization of world politics through a civilizational narrative, mediated by an emerging concern with self-determination. French thinkers developed these ideas as well. Mandatory and neocolonial forms of control were the institutional exemplifications of this discourse. Democracy and self-determination were conditional upon a society's rational potential. Even in purportedly "scientific" disciplines, like economics and sociology, prominent and influential voices were writing about civilization, democracy, and self-determination in ways similar to political actors and thinkers.

One leading intellectual voice in this regard was Yves Guyot, a French economist and politician. Though his career as a politician was relatively undistinguished—his most prominent post was as a short-lived minister of public works in Pierre Tirard's government—he was a widely published, and widely read, free-trade economist, whose work spanned nearly sixty-five years. Of particular note for Guyot's thinking on world politics is his 1916 book *Les causes et les conséquences de la guerre*, which was a meditation on the causes of World War I, and the conditions for peace following the termination of hostilities. The book itself continues many themes of emancipatory liberal discourse related to civilizational development and racial politics. One of the principle novelties of the treatise, in fact, is its utilization of categories like "militaristic civilization" and "productive civilization" to highlight the fundamental clashes between Germany and the rest of Europe. He admittedly borrows these categories from other social theorists, namely Herbert Spencer and Gustave de Molinari, but nonetheless applies them to the case of Germany. He explains that Germany is an example of a "militaristic civilization," even citing the etymology of the word *guerre* as being Teutonic in origin.[32]

Guyot's writing on civilization is not just a retort to Germany. It has larger implications for his thinking about the relationship between civilization, empire, and development in the early twentieth century. For Guyot, proper civilizational development is directly tied to liberalism. He writes, "a productive civilization is based on freedom of contract, a militarist civilization on the limitation of liberty."[33] Britain is the paradigmatic example of the former, and Germany of the latter. Guyot's views of civilization, however, are notably different from the liberal supporters of empire from the previous century. Guyot sees economic exchange as a key component of peace and productivity—of proper civilization. Imperialism is contrary to free exchange: "imperialism implies acquisition by force, without exchange [. . .]."[34] For Guyot, then, imperialism is not the means of realizing civilizational development. Such realization involved cultivating productive civilization, and the recognition of the inherent conflict between civilizations inimical to liberty and exchange.

Despite Guyot's apparent anti-imperialism, throughout *Les causes et les conséquences de la guerre* he takes a position on race politics that is inconsistent, and often rather similar to earlier colonial discourses about racial inferiority and domination. For example, while providing an eloquent analysis of scholarship on the problems with considering race a natural category, Guyot describes what he calls "subject races," and blames many of the problems leading to World War I on the inability of Austria and Hungary to "assimilate" these groups into their respective societies.[35] This is an important point, as this argument about failure of racial assimilation would prove to be a common trope in mandate-era interventions, including French intervention in Syria only a few years later.

French sociologist Emile Durkheim offers another window into the way that discourses about race, civilization, and self-determination made their way into French social science. Durkheim's sociological theory attempted to grapple with the idea of "civilization," but in a notably different way than Guyot and their nineteenth-century predecessors. For Durkheim, a civilization was a midpoint between national society and international society. Durkheim argued for a comparative sociological study of civilizations (emphasis on the pluralization), rather than starting from the point of view that civilization is an inherently Western concept—descriptive of modern, Western, liberal societies.[36] Opening the door to a comparative study of civilizations, however, also opened the door to racial comparisons, and ultimately parroted a discourse about "subject races" or "child races" that is apparent in the writings of many liberal intellectuals of the period. While an argument could be made for the ways that race morphs into "ethnicity" or "civilization" in Durkheim's oeuvre, these concepts do similar work to the interwar ideas about race.[37]

Scholars of Durkheim have often argued that Durkheim's work represented the fateful deconstruction of scientific racism at the early part of the twentieth century.[38] In Durkheim's work on what he considered the emergence of an "international society,"[39] however, his views on race were quite different. In this comparative study of civilizations, for example, Durkheim has a clear hierarchical ranking of *types* of societies, following his own veneration of societies based on modern forms of social organization. As one interpreter points out, "Durkheim tends to conflate primitive, tribal, societies, as simple, lower, societies that are inferior in relation to modern ones."[40] Durkheim's vision of modern society, therefore, orders the world in terms of a spatial and racial imaginary, where Europe represents modernity, and more "primitive" societies are inferior.

This is not to say that Durkheim did not venerate so-called primitive societies in some ways. Durkheim's doctoral thesis was written on Rousseau and Montesquieu's historical sociologies of the movement of humankind from "primitive" life into the corruptions of modern society—themes that certainly come through in Durkheim's own studies of the dangers of anomie in modern industrial societies. Nonetheless, these reflections on civilizational orderings hold implications for thinking about concepts that were near to Durkheim's heart, and were prominent in his writings, including self-determination. For Durkheim, self-determination was something that was limited to adults: those who had limited access to cultural mores and reasoning. For a moral education, children must display obedience and passivity.[41] While Durkheim did not write explicitly about international politics from this perspective, the combination of Durkheim's moral theory and his sociological studies of "primitive" and advanced societies reconstructs a logic of paternalism that was characteristic of the time: there are some societies in the world that are inferior to Western societies; there are some people who can have self-determination, and others who must be obedient. These same sorts of ideas found their way into intellectual and policy discourses at the time, in combinations that ended in intervention.

This is not to blame theorists like Durkheim for imperialism, or for war. It does, however, demonstrate that a constellation of ideas developed in the early part of the twentieth century by prominent social theorists—experts—were utilized in ways that contributed to means of domination in the imperial periphery. Durkheim illustrates the way theories of race, civilization, and self-determination during the interwar period had logical connections to broader discourses of civilizational development as expressed by internationalists at the time. While Durkheim himself never developed a theory of imperialism, and died before the implementation of proposals for the League of Nations, theories like his were able to connect the dots between diverse strands of thinking about how civilizations (particularly the West vs. former colonies) should relate to one another.

Interwar social science, including economics and sociology, was not neutral to the causes and effects of war. Theorists like Guyot, Durkheim, and others thought deeply about matters of war and peace, civilization and self-determination. More than that, the theories developed in France at this time reproduced ideas about civilizational difference, while providing the intellectual ammo to rethink discourses of self-determination. Though Guyot and Durkheim were not actively involved in supporting the League of Nations mandate system (unlike Addams and Hobhouse), these theorists engaged in similar discursive moves, backed by the legitimacy of the emerging twentieth-century social and economic sciences.

Public Culture and Emancipatory Liberalism during the Interwar Period

During the interwar period, emancipatory liberal conceptions of race, hierarchy, empire and self-determination existed as part of the discourse produced by activists like Addams and Hobhouse, or social scientists like Guyot and Durkheim. They, also, had permeated popular culture, print media, and public discourse.

Repetitions of discourses about race, hierarchy, and identity difference were an integral part of liberal discourses during and after WWI. Popular conceptions about race were largely unchanged in the widest sense; for many, the Western individual was superior to others. There was, however, a subtle shift in thinking about the *ways* that this difference mattered. Most specifically, this was expressed in framing identity difference in terms of a "humanitarian" mission. Graham Wallas, the left-leaning cofounder of the London School of Economics, illustrates this sentiment well. In writing about the complexity of the "Eastern Question," Wallas lays out the issue as one in which a humanitarian may:

> see the map as the breeding places of various human varieties, and world politics as the problem of the encouragement of or prevention of the pure or mixed breeding of particular races in particular areas—the Chinese in Manchuria or California, the Japanese in the Pacific Islands or North Australia, the Jews, Hindoos, Germans, or Arabs in Mesopotamia.[42]

Wallas calls these humanitarian attitudes "necessary," indicating that such views about world politics constitute one of the principle issues facing the globe in the twentieth century. Writing for an educated and liberal public, Wallas is speaking a language of difference—and the incompatibility of different races. This highlights the ways that liberal intellectuals communicated issues in world politics to a broader public in languages that would have made sense. These ideas were often tied directly to the League of Nations and the mandate system.

Mandates were not just a popular idea in the minds of statesmen. As Frederick Lughard wrote in a contemporaneous setting, they were the "latest expression of the conscience of Europe."[43] This statement applies to liberal opinion beyond Europe, however, and extends into popular advocacies for the mandate system in Britain, France, and America. One such prominent example is a series of articles written in the liberal magazine *The New Republic* in the late 1910s and early 1920s, which illustrates common liberal opinion about mandates at the time. Left-wing British journalist Henry Noel Brailsford wrote one such article, which tears apart contemporary arguments from the margins about how the League of Nations mandate system is simply another vestige of capitalist imperialism. Brailsford takes these arguments seriously, but rebuts them by arguing that as long as the mandates have a defined mission, a time frame, and are truly designed for the benefit of the mandates under trusteeship, they are good for the world. For Brailsford, the backslide into colonialism is a problem to be defended against. At the same time, however, there was good in moderated colonial endeavors. He writes of the British civil servant, for example,

> it would be folly to deny that a sense of duty towards the native race does, when the conquest is completed, distinguish the British civil servant in Africa or India, and something rises in him to the heights of devotion and

courage. It is precisely this curious dualism of acquisitiveness and duty which makes it desirable that the conception of the mandatory power should be examined, with candor but not with despairing cynicism.[44]

The sense of "duty" characterizing the mandate system compelled liberals of the period to go beyond their concerns with imperialism and the return of colonialism in the postwar era, to the concern with rescuing "backward" populations from the plights that infected them. For arguments like Brailsford's, it was not the *concept* of mandates that was problematic; trusteeship was the only viable way to develop countries beyond the pale of civilization, the only way to bring those uncivilized countries into the march of civilization, and on the track to self-determination. The challenge, however, was the *method* by which mandates were implemented. The horrific parts of the colonial endeavor must be removed for the sake of preserving that positive, and emancipatory, part of the dualism to which Brailsford alludes.

French Intervention in Syria/British Intervention in Iraq

During World War I, Britain, France, and Russia signed the 1916 Sykes-Picot Agreement, which guaranteed formerly Ottoman-held lands to the three empires. While Britain gained direct control of lower Iraq, and indirect influence from the Egyptian border into present-day Iran, the French gained control of Syria and Lebanon. This control guaranteed the following: France would directly rule most of north and west Syria, as well as a sphere of influence in the countryside, including Aleppo, Damascus, and Mosul.[45] French rule over Syria occurred concomitantly with the rise of Syrian nationalism,[46] resulting in resistance toward French rule, beginning most significantly when France was granted mandatory power over Syria in 1920, following the San Remo Conference.[47] Yet, public opinion in Syria was against French rule. This dissatisfaction with French mandatory claims resulted in a series of revolts throughout the first half of the 1920s. The French intervened militarily in 1920 and 1925 to restructure governing authority and to put down revolts initiated by minority populations, including, most notably, the Druze.[48] These two interventions were premised on the development of more liberalized institutions.

Earlier tensions between the Syrian government and Georges Clemenceau's French government had been, apparently, resolved by January 1920, following a written agreement authorizing French direct control over the area. But threats from extremists in the camp of the installed leader, King Faisal I, along with some Kemalist resistance, caused anxiety for the French government. Faisal recognized these difficulties, and used them to attempt to negotiate better terms with the French. These hopes were dashed by April of that year, when France gained mandatory power of Syria. While plans floated of ousting Faisal, the French looked favorably on his calls for eventual independence by arguing that once Syria was able to stand on its feet, it would terminate the mandate. Prime Minister Alexandre Millerand, writing to the French commander in the Levant, Henri Gouraud, stated that the French should not leave until order and stability is instituted in Syrian governing institutions. He writes: "The mandate given to France in Syria gives her not only the right but also the duty to maintain order and security."[49] The French were in Syria to stay; it was her right and duty, and this might necessitate the removal of Faisal.[50]

By July of 1920, in the midst of diplomatic and military resistance from Faisal's government, the French gave an ultimatum that Faisal accept the mandate, or face forcible removal. At first, the Syrian Congress refused to budge; however, Faisal's government had no choice but to comply with the ultimatum.[51] Gouraud, not hearing of this acquiescence in time, intervened in Syria, defeating ill-prepared troops in Maysalun, al-Azma, and eventually entering Damascus by July 23.[52] Faisal was forced out of Damascus by July 28, and his government was replaced by one that was more favorable to the French. Following the first intervention in 1920, the French instituted a series of governmental and administrative reforms in Syria; these were a major catalyst for further revolt. These reforms radically weakened local elites by instituting French liberal administration in most aspects of governance, including in the local areas.

The French justified intervention in the uprisings through an appeal to liberal languages that were aimed particularly at the injustice of local governing institutions. Captain Gabriel Carbillet, a French officer who took the lead in modernization reforms for the Druze population of Syria, illustrated this clearly. Especially between the revolts, the idea that local ruling apparatuses were despotic, or antithetical to the ideas of liberty and emancipation (that the French were, ostensibly, trying to spread across their imperial possession), justified intervention. Carbillet expressed this in responding to challenges to his position: "Should I leave these chiefs to continue their oppression of a people who dream of liberty? Should I renounce the traditions of France?"[53] Carbillet, like other French officials, imagined the interventions in Syria in the 1920s as an act of benevolence—more than that, it was part and parcel of French identity claims.

Even challenges to Carbillet's assertions were remarkably one sided, in favor of liberal claims toward intervention. As historians of the period demonstrate, while

Carbillet used coercion and force to achieve modernizing aims, these were viewed by the French authorities as acceptable; however, when locals used violence as a form of resistance to the French intervention, this was just more evidence to confirm French stereotypes about the "barbarity" and "uncivilized" nature of the Syrian people.[54] A discourse of "banditry" was used to describe the Syrian people—putting their actions in line with those who are fundamentally aligned toward the *denial* of liberty, particularly the freedom to acquire and hold property.[55] Between despots, barbarians, and bandits, the French viewed, justified, and rationalized intervention as a way to bring ideas of liberty and emancipation to a people who were aggressive toward such ideas.

This discourse of barbarism and self-determination was a central feature of justifications and rationalizations of the Syrian intervention in the 1920s. The intervention represents a key illustration in such a mobilization of interwar liberal discourses. The class "A" mandates of the Middle East were viewed as at least capable of eventual self-determination. One of the reasons for this had to do with a hierarchical discourse about civilization and capability, whereas class "B" and "C" mandates were seen as being "at such a low level of civilization that they could be ruled practically as parts of the mandatory power itself."[56] Also playing into this identity imaginary was the imagination of the emancipatory project as one deeply rooted in historic French claims to be protecting the Maronite Christians in the area, removing some ideational distance between the French and the people they were attempting to "save."

The institution of League of Nations mandates in the Middle East related to French deployment of force in Syria in two ways. In the first place, putting Syria under mandatory control in 1923 was largely premised on liberal justifications. By opening the possibility of France having institutional cover for the intervention, it broadened the horizon of what was possible for French politicians and administrators to achieve. In the mandate document itself, the League of Nations acknowledges the importance of the French mandate in "facilitate[ing] progressive development of Syria and Lebanon [...]."[57] What is most significant, however, is the way that the mandate gives France a remarkable amount of leeway in how it is legitimately allowed to engage in war-making. For example, the mandate gives the French authority to position troops in the territory for "its own defence,"[58] though this definition is left rather broad in the document. Certainly the French exercised such leeway in putting down revolts in both 1920 and 1925. In many senses, the mandate served to justify the initial intervention three years previously, while providing cover for the future use of force in France's mandates.

In the second place, the mandate system made the deployment of force, and nation building, in Syria easier to justify to domestic and international audiences. Writing in *Foreign Affairs* in 1925, Louis Aubert argued that the French mandate in Syria did not just represent idealism, but the League of Nations mandate system itself benefited the justness of French policies in the region. "In entrusting to the League the oversight of four matters [including mandates] of chief concern to her," Aubert writes, "France not only has given from the start the greatest proof of attachment to the League that she can give, but has at the same time shown her preference for fair and objective policies."[59] Such arguments were common at the time, and they functioned to do two things. First, these arguments assert that French actions in Syria, including interventions for order-making and putting down revolts, demonstrated that France was living up to its multilateral commitments vis-à-vis the League of Nations. In the second place, it showed that unlike other types of colonialism—like the imperialism of the nineteenth century—League of Nations mandates were more transparent, and provided more "objectivity" in matters of rule, rather than the arbitrariness of colonial tyranny. The League of Nations made intervention justifiable.

The French established their goals, and their identities in relation to the Syrians, in terms of an analogy drawn between a liberal Europe represented by France, and a rampant militant nationalism reminiscent of Germany during World War I. These discursive tropes were "sold" to publics in the way that popular outlets like the press wrote about, and conceived of, the relationship between the French and its Other. The French newspaper *Le Temps* demonstrated this explicitly in arguing: "The Allies did not conquer Prussian militarism to allow the development in its place of a Hedjaz militarism, which will set aflame the Arab world."[60] This equation of the Syrians with the enemies of WWI, the war in which a Wilsonian liberalism triumphed, rhetorically solidifies France's understanding of itself as an emancipatory figure for Syria's people and institutions. Furthermore, building upon historical analogies, and framing France as a liberal leader aimed at stopping the rise of another militaristic power, was an effective use of political rhetoric.

In addition to using this rhetoric to convince a broader population at home about the justness of intervention, French officials used emancipatory liberal rhetoric to appeal to their armed forces abroad. Commanders in the field mobilized and motivated French armed forces by connecting the mission to common discursive tropes about racial difference, French identity, and the politics of civilization. Soldiers are not political philosophers, nor are they politicians, but these discourses made sense. One example, cited by a prominent history of nation building by the French in Syria, is in 1926, when General Maurice Gamelin, commander of the Troupes Speciales de Levant, used this rhetoric to motivate and congratulate his soldiers: "You fight here not to defend your homes or to support a conquest, but in the name of the civilization which you represent. The more selfless your ideals, the more noble will be your sacrifice."[61]

For officials like Gamelin, war and intervention were selfless causes. This mirrored discourses about civilization and self-determination of the period; such statements implied a certain civilizational difference—i.e., French soldiers were fighting barbarian Others who lacked the same attributes and accorded dignity that comes with being a representative of a French civilization. At the same time, however, these statements also touched on the same tropes that characterized the formation of League of Nations mandates in the first place: that these interventions were selfless, humanitarian, and aimed at ushering in an era where the Syrian people could eventually realize self-determination and freedom, with paternalist guiding by the French.

More than justification, and connection of the initial interventions to identities, institutions, and common discursive tropes, emancipatory liberalism also served to structure the nation-building and administrative efforts on the ground in Syria. Two examples, in particular, highlight this. In the first case, a politics of identity played a role in the way that administrators and French officials conceptualized the restructuring of the country's political system. The ideology of constitutionalism, the liberal state, and the ways these were operationalized in post-intervention governance were built upon interwar discourses about liberty, civilization, and self-determination. Particularly, the way in which the French conceptualized tribal groups as being antithetical to modern understandings of what a "state" should be worked to operationalize these discourses. Much of this categorization of groups—as, on the one hand, nomadic or "Bedouin," and on the other, sedentary—was part of an effort by the French to exert administrative control over the population during the mandate and after the interventions.[62] It also, however, demonstrates how it was nearly impossible to avoid such binary distinctions in the language of liberalism through which the mandate operated. By ordering parts of the population as antithetical to what a liberal state should look like, the French government was able to construct certain groups (namely, rebellious groups of Druze and semi-nomadic peoples) as being the enemy in post-intervention administration and nation building.[63]

In the second case, the French used languages of paternalism, inferiority, and civilization to delegitimize potential enemies in Syria throughout the occupation. A prime example of such tactics was the French attempt to block the rise of Anthony II Peter Arida to the Maronite Patriarchy in 1932. The French used a variety of rhetorical tools to try to influence that appointment, including the French High Commissioner, Comte de Martel, using terms like "stubborn," "pretty Oriental," "weak," and "impotent" to describe Arida.[64] This rhetoric would not keep Arida from election, but it demonstrates the use of terminology to highlight the difference between a mature France and a language of "child races" ("weak," "impotent," etc., draw a contrast between grown men and their Other—a racial and gendered paternalism) that was a common feature of interwar liberalism.

The Syrians were not passive in this attempt to impose Western liberal ideologies on the deployment of force and nation building in Syria. Civil society organizations in Syria were central in pointing out to the League of Nations the atrocities that the French government had perpetrated in Syria throughout the 1920s.[65] These denunciations, however, often occurred on the terrain of liberal languages. Syrian organizations were well aware of the importance of being able to "talk the talk" when it came to resistance. Such groups referred to French actions as "barbarian outrages," parroting a language about civilization that was at the forefront of liberal thinking since the mid-nineteenth century, though applying it to the means and methods of colonization in the form of mandates. In 1926, a delegation of Syrian citizens approached the Permanent Mandates Commission at the League of Nations, arguing that the French had ignored all of their claims for self-determination.[66]

The French reaction to claims of Syrian nationalism and self-determination were often harsh. Rather than attempting to defend their liberal credentials, or to incorporate these alternative discourses into existing practices, the French cracked down, and hard. In 1925, when village sheikhs began petitioning the government with grievances, Maurice Sarrail, the French High Commissioner of the Levant, requested the presence of five Druze chiefs in Damascus to discuss their grievances. Instead, the mandatory government arrested them.[67] There was no room for dissent in the French mandate.

The case of the Syrian interventions, and their aftermaths, demonstrate three things. First, it shows that emancipatory liberalism affected the way that the French justified and rationalized the intervention. As Gouraud's writings and Millerand's statements show, they saw the French as legitimately entitled to intervene, and transform domestic institutions, because of the inability of the Syrians to govern effectively, liberally, and democratically. Second, emancipatory liberalism affected French goals and identities in relation to the intervention. The dichotomies created between "traditional" Syrians and "liberal democratic"

Frenchmen, along with the analogies drawn between Syria and Germany during WWI, created a relationship wherein French goals in its mandate were legitimated through a discourse of institutional change. Third, the mandate system had a large effect on the way the French talked about intervention, if not having a significant impact on the way that the intervention was physically carried out.

The French were not the only Western power that intervened in ways that mirrored emancipatory discourses. The British's involvement in the Middle East, as well, was exemplary of a mandate-era liberal interventionism in the interwar period. Rebellions in Iraq and Palestine prompted a series of interventions by the British in the region from 1920 until the start of World War II in 1939.

The first in this series of interventions was to stop a revolt in Iraq and construct domestic institutions that would allow for self-governance. Britain was awarded the mandate in April of 1920,[68] and originally staffed most important government positions with British officials. Resentment toward this was one of the primary causes of the revolt, which began in May of that year.[69] British intervention crushed the revolt in October, and left British policy makers debating the methods by which to create a self-governing Iraq. Ultimately, the British developed institutions that included a symbolic monarchy, a standing army, Western bureaucratic institutions, and a liberal domestic constitution.[70] If Britain learned anything from the initial intervention, it was that "the Iraqi state was to be run by and for Iraqis," wherein the British would utilize the "sacred trust" of the mandate system to allow the Iraqis sovereignty and self-determination.[71] This point of view was not just a function of British economic and strategic considerations. It represented a way of thinking in British policy circles about liberal rationalism and civilizational development. This was a function of pressure from the US and the League of Nations on Britain to use the mandate as a way of providing the tools necessary for Iraqis to develop effective, liberal institutions.

Emancipatory liberalism affected the way that Britain rationalized and justified intervention in the Iraqi revolt. The British rationalized intervention as a means of benevolent paternalism. As Percy Cox, the High Commissioner of Iraq at the time, stated:

> By the end of the war, the people of Mesopotamia had come to accept the fact of our occupation, and were resigned to the prospect of a permanent British administration; some [. . .] even looked forward with satisfaction to a future in which they would be able to pursue their commerce and agriculture with a strong central authority to preserve peace and order.[72]

Not only would the intervention create peace and order, but it was suggested that it was even welcomed by many of the residents. Intervention was justified by the benefits that a mandatory government could bring to the Iraqis.

This was no mere justification, either. Cox's writings (written after his tenure in Iraq) show that the intervention was rationalized by British administrators from the point of view of a paternalist emancipatory liberalism. As he further argues about the Iraq intervention: "I can imagine no case in which H.M's Government have implemented their promises and obligations and pursued the settled policy with more complete good faith and resolution. . . ."[73] The use of the term *obligation* here is significant, particularly in the new institutional context of the League of Nations mandate system. Self-determination for the Iraqi people was an obligation of the British government, and this would be done through the restructuring of domestic institutions.

Changing liberal discourses of the interwar era also colored the way that policy makers conceptualized their identities and goals in post-revolt Iraq—often in ways that proved difficult for British administrators. Two examples illustrate this. First is the example of A. T. Wilson, who was the acting Civil Commissioner in Iraq until June of 1920. Wilson was an outspoken critic of existing thinking in policy circles about creating institutions for Iraqi self-governance and constitutional monarchism. He believed that the British had to exercise a much stronger role in the country, and that the Arabs were, as of the moment, unsuited for self-government. Wilson conceptualized British goals and identity largely from within the frame of reference used by political elites in much earlier intervention contexts, such as the Anglo-Burmese Wars. Following the beginning stirs of uprising, and after making enemies with several British officials, Wilson became the fall guy implicated in the unrest, which resulted in a further strengthening of British official opinion on the virtues of Arab self-government vis-à-vis liberal institutions constructed by the British government.[74] Wilson's own understanding of the British role in Iraq could not keep pace with evolving discourses of international liberalism, and this ultimately lead to his downfall.

Second, other political elites encountered similar issues related to the impact that emancipatory discourses had on reshaping British identities and goals. As Gertrude Bell, an important figure in the development of the Iraqi state, notes in a letter to her parents:

> The underlying truth of all criticism is however—and it is what makes the critics so difficult to answer—that we had promised self-governing institutions, and not only made no step towards them but were busily setting up

something entirely different. One of the papers says, quite rightly, that we had promised an Arab Government with British Advisers, and had set up a British Government with Arab Advisers. That's a perfectly fair statement.[75]

Even though the British went to great pains to talk *as if* they were preparing the Iraqi state for self-government, their previous understandings about the inability of Iraqis to self-govern ultimately increased their own presence in Iraq.

These contradictions between changes in emancipatory liberalism and the inability of many British administrators to keep pace with new identity formations and goals were a function of British interwar discourses about liberal rationalism and civilizational development. Rather than demonstrating that emancipatory liberalism was inconsequential to such identities/goals, the Iraq case shows just how significant these connections can be. They, ultimately, doomed state-building efforts to failure. As Toby Dodge notes, "At the heart of British thinking was a dichotomy between the explanatory weight to assign to individuals as independent agents and that to assign to social structure and 'traditional' institutions and practices. Rational individualism was dominant, but a romantic collectivism also played an important role."[76] This is not unusual for the time, as this tension was characteristic of British liberal thought during the interwar period in general.[77] While liberal Britain in the period of nineteenth-century empire intervened with notions of civilization firmly implanted into their minds, new intellectual trends in the interwar period witnessed a new, Wilsonian individualism built around self-determination and democracy, which brought these multiplicitous conceptions into conflict, but also patterned intervention and state-building in significant ways.

As the Iraq case demonstrates, mandatory powers could exercise considerable administrative and governing power under the guise of eventual self-governance. While mandates may have constrained actors in the sense that they limited legitimate intervention to specific spheres of influence, it was—in many respects—an institutionalization of older imperial relationships.[78] While interwar liberalism stressed the importance of self-determination vis-à-vis the mandate system's "sacred trust," colonial administrators often struggled in reconciling these changes with older notions of civilizational development. This issue may explain why the Iraqi intervention was, to use Dodge's phrase, "doomed" in the 1920s.

Conclusion

Interwar politics was a politics of civilization. New discourses about mandates and institutional solutions to international conflict, however, became a discourse of justification for the deployment of force in some places of the world, particularly former colonial possessions. Part of this can be explained by focusing on a power politics account—states will draw on rhetoric that is most successful in helping them achieve their security goals. This is an incomplete account of interventions during the mandate period, however. In the first place, the intellectual defenders of mandates were oftentimes peace activists, who would have found war in general to be anathema to a civilized world. Nonetheless, these vocabularies were used to justify putting down rebellions in the Middle East in the 1920s and 1930s.

In the second place, there are many *different* ways that states could have justified such interventions. It is telling that the languages that were used in the deployment of force drew upon such discourses altogether. These discourses—and especially the move toward a concern with self-determination—held legitimacy in the interwar period. They affected the *way* actors thought about war, the reasons force was deployed, and the way that wars were administered on the ground. Emancipatory liberalism of the interwar period had deluded itself; it created a discursive universe that was based on the supposition that we could end war altogether, but these discourses functioned to justify new kinds of wars, with new kinds of vocabularies, and a new range of justifications.

The following chapter analyzes the role of emancipatory liberalism and its relationship toward violence during the Cold War. This period is one characterized by discursive conflict, which, more than the liberal empire and interwar period, created ideational tensions that gave rise to the changing nature of interventions and the use of force.

CHAPTER FIVE

Transformation and Totalitarianism
Intervention and Cold War Liberalism

The point, as Marx saw it, is that dreams never come true.

—Hannah Arendt, *On Violence*

THE COLD WAR REPRESENTS a turning point in international history—and one cannot overstate its effects on the development of international liberalism. Philosopher Leo Strauss would write that "the experience of Communism has provided the Western movement with a twofold lesson: a political lesson, a lesson regarding what to do in the foreseeable future, and a lesson regarding the principles of politics."[1] This is certainly true. During this period of nearly fifty years, liberals had to confront some of their most closely held beliefs and position themselves within the context of new enemies, new projects, and new dilemmas. Cold War liberalism was a "liberalism of fear,"[2] and this fear—an almost existential anxiety—was the framing conflict within liberal thought during this time.

Furthermore, the period was one in which a liberal international society, in a postwar world, occupied itself with conceptualizing and deploying new forms of violence and new solutions. Institutionalization of liberal principles became a key development in the West, and the deployment of violence and intervention took on new meanings, both as methods—often short of major power war—to resolve conflict, and a means to refashion the world for the purposes of freedom, democracy, and economic development. If liberalism in the post-WWII era could be described succinctly, it was in stark contrast to totalitarianism, in direct opposition to the "total terror"[3] imaginary that constituted the threat of communism. Violence and intervention played an important role in realizing this opposition in practice.

This chapter makes a threefold argument. First, the threat of totalitarianism, represented by the rise of communism, divided emancipatory liberalism into two camps. One of these was a camp skeptical of liberalism's past universalism, and rationalism, suggesting that these were the constituent elements of Marxism—something liberalism should avoid. Another was a development culture, which imagined economic and political transformation as key components in the fight against Eastern communism. Both of these traditions had the same ends: stopping the encroachment of communism through an emancipatory ethic. The means to this end often differed, however. Second, these differences represented, simultaneously, a form of conflict and consensus within international liberalism—one that was not fully resolved until the end of the Cold War era, and the supposed triumph of liberal democracy.[4] Third, this had an impact on the practice of liberal violence. Intervention practices reflected these ideational divisions and cohesions.

The existing scholarly literature on Cold War liberalism is a trove of context for narrating the development of international liberalism during that period, but it also has some important gaps. The most notable issue is that the study of this period of liberal thought and practice paints a bleak picture of liberal internationalism—one that, in the context of great power rivalry, would have to become deeply realist in orientation. Amanda Anderson points out the problems with this historiography by noting, "Cold War liberalism is often assumed to simply confirm the bid for power, and the exercise of force, that is perceived to underlie liberalism's disavowal of the fact that power structures all relations and institutions."[5] She further notes that, "these [bleak] perspectives are typically counterbalanced by forms of aspiration, hope, and commitment, whether to broad social-democratic visions, procedural norms, or regulative ideal."[6] Liberals during the Cold War oscillated, both *between* theorists and *across* temporal spaces, between a liberal pessimism and a liberal triumphalism about the project of development, democracy, and transformative change.

This chapter contributes both an extension and a revision of these narratives through a genealogy of liberal reaction to the idea of "totalitarianism," and how these discursive formations interfaced with the interpretation, justification, and deployment of violence. Actors like US President Lyndon Johnson's administration, for instance, did not intervene in the Dominican Republic in 1965 in an ideological vacuum. The debates about intervention, war, and force took place within a broader context of emancipatory liberal discourses that constituted identity claims, common sense ideas, and an ethics of intervention to counter the worst fears of the totalitarian threat. Furthermore, liberals often, ironically, found totalitarianism to be an exciting opportunity to expand their vision, integrate it into a global context, and to spread a liberal messianism beyond the boundaries of Western developed nations.

This chapter proceeds in three parts. First, it contextualizes the history of emancipatory liberalism's response to totalitarianism by detailing the historical and intellectual antecedents of changes in the discourse of international liberalism. I suggest that these were not just related to the threat of totalitarianism from the Soviet Union, but were visions of totalitarian possibilities in other places as well. Second, in examining the work of American, British/Anglophilic, and French thinkers, policy makers, and intellectuals, I show that these discourses often took two tracks: one of a liberal pessimism, and one of a developmental triumphalism. The interface and conflict between these two strands of thought would characterize debates about the way that violence could be practiced in an emancipatory liberal order. Third, and finally, I look at a case study—US intervention in the Dominican Crisis of 1965—to show how both of these discourses structured political action by the United States and its allies.

Totalitarianism, Emancipatory Liberalism, and the Cold War

Midcentury liberal pessimism, and the fear of totalitarianism, are sandwiched between two sets of emancipatory liberal discourses that were quite the opposite: resoundingly triumphant. This pessimism presents two puzzles in understanding the development of international liberal discourse from the mid-nineteenth century to the present. First, what explains the intellectual turn to a liberal pessimism in the midcentury? Isaiah Berlin, Jacob Talmon, Raymond Aron, and Karl Popper represent a fundamental break from previous theorizing about liberal world order, a new way of painting a bleak picture onto the canvas of a liberalizing world. Second, the alternate question, of how to explain the subsequent decline of liberal pessimism moving into the twenty-first century, is no less interesting.

The period of empire and the interwar period's continuation of similar themes of developmentalism and progress represented the first iterations of a liberal triumphalism and optimism in world politics. In the period of "new empire," which began in the 1870s (but began its ideological development much earlier), liberal thinkers focused their sights on a developmental theory of history that would bring the rest of the world into the civilization of Western Europe. Civilizing the "barbarians" of the world, in the terminology used by thinkers like John Stuart Mill and others, was not only a duty of Western liberal states, but was also evidence of the triumph of an emancipatory liberal ethic (see chapter 3). And, in the post–Cold War era, a liberal triumphalism again emerged from the ruins of the USSR, and the success of the West in winning a protected ideological and material battle. Francis Fukuyama's "End of History" thesis—drawing on Hegelian imagery about "absolute truth"—suggested, "The triumph of the West, of the Western *idea*, is evident first of all in the total exhaustion of viable systematic alternatives to Western liberalism."[7] Fukuyama was not alone. Much intellectual effort in international theory took this triumphalist history as gospel. This was first expressed in an effort to develop liberal IR theory into a systematic alternative to political realism,[8] which peaked into a reimagining of international history altogether as the triumphant decline of violence, harm, and barbarism in the face of the rise of new global values associated with cosmopolitanism and liberalism.[9]

Cold War liberalism was often decidedly less triumphant, but no less emancipatory. The shift in international liberalism from the universalist, and ambitious, civilizational development culture of the pre–World War II period occurred at the end of the war. Some have associated this shift with a new "liberalism without illusions,"[10] or a more sensible, fearful, and cautious liberalism that was terrified by the prospect of grand visions, global designs, and the rise of totalitarianism.[11] Though liberals were not the first to express this fear of Soviet totalitarianism—in fact, it was Catholic intellectuals both before and during World War II who were the originators of coherent theories of totalitarianism[12]—liberals would take up this mantle following the defeat of fascism during the war. As Abbott Gleason notes, "Totalitarianism was the great mobilizing and unifying concept of the Cold War."[13]

This discursive change was perhaps best exemplified by two distinct intellectual movements, which shared the common fear of Soviet communism. The first of these came from left liberals, influenced by socialism, who were becoming increasingly cautious of the extremities of the socialist project in the context of totalitarianism. George Orwell exemplifies this strand, as much of his political and critical literary writings during and after the Second World War indicate an intellectual concern with the evolution of ideology in British liberal circles. In a review of Arthur Koestler's[14] corpus of work, Orwell is emphatic about his disillusionment with the sort of liberal project of the imperial and interwar periods, equating it in overt ways with the totalitarianism of Soviet communism. He writes in 1944: "Perhaps some degree of suffering is ineradicable from human life, perhaps the choice before man is always a choice of evils, perhaps even the aim of Socialism is not to make the world perfect but to make it better. All revolutions are failures, but they are not all the same failure."[15] Orwell positions his cautious left liberalism against that of George Bernard Shaw and political theorist Harold Laski, citing the ways in which their utopianism often led them into wrongheaded understandings of the socialist project.[16]

The second strand came from the emergence of a value-pluralist liberalism, which was suspicious of the sort of self-actualization liberalism of the previous era, equating it with the evolution of totalitarianism. Isaiah Berlin represented its most memorable proponent, and perhaps the most exemplary figure in terms of how liberals were wrestling with the moral bases of their project in the postwar age.[17] In his famous 1958 essay, "Two Concepts of Liberty," he writes, "One belief, more than any other, is responsible for the slaughter of individuals on the altar of the great historical ideals—justice, or progress, or happiness of future generations, or the sacred mission or emancipation of a nation or race or class, or even liberty itself, which demands the sacrifice of individuals for the freedom of society."[18] It is the rationalist, romantic, positive form of liberty that should be cautioned against. It represents an imperial liberalism, and a totalitarian one.[19]

Though Orwell and Berlin represent two distinct political positions—a left liberal, and a pluralistic, anti-essentialist one—they both exemplify the caution, and totalitarian fear, of liberal intellectuals after World War II. For Orwell, this was a caution related to the moderation of political and social aims. Such immodesty was an attribute of the excesses of Soviet Marxism.[20] And for Berlin, positive liberty, the emancipatory ethic of modern totalitarianism, caused one to desire a turn toward value pluralism, and the limitations of moral universalism. Both strands rejected the civilizational development understanding of history,[21] and began to equate it with the threat of communism: which, for Orwell, was a threat to left liberal socialism, and for Berlin, was a threat to pluralistic societies. Whereas the liberalism of civilization, which characterized the imperial and interwar periods, constituted a cultural system that justified intervention for the sake of a grand narrative of progress and development, Orwell and Berlin epitomize its antithesis in the twentieth century. In a provocative reinterpretation of Niccolò Machiavelli, written in 1972, Berlin goes as far as to suggest that of all the evils attributed to Machiavelli, at least he contributed a warning that there can be no "final solution of the question of how men should live."[22] This intellectual concern with communism in the postwar period was nearly universal, such that, as Domenico Losurdo argues, "The best way for the Western world to face this war [i.e., the Cold War] was to establish itself as the champion in the struggle against the new totalitarianism [...]."[23]

The fear of the communist threat was a recurring theme in policy discourse as well.[24] Liberal policy makers, unlike their predecessors in previous times, were worried about the practical affects that a universalism, and a heavy-handed paternalism, would have on US strategic interests. On top of this, there was a clear understanding that liberalism, as a pluralistic enterprise, should value the ability of individuals in other countries to make decisions for themselves. Secretary of State Dean Rusk, who headed the US State Department from 1961 to 1969, describes this attitude well in an interview, stating that in regard to US policy toward South Vietnam:

> [W]e can't make and unmake governments in Vietnam. We just don't have it in our capability. It would be silly for us to take steps that would cause the South Vietnamese to turn around and start shooting at us. There are limits beyond which you can [not] go in imposing your will upon somebody. You can give advice, you can persuade, you can cajole, you can sometimes put on pressure, you can sometimes threaten. But at the end of the day, these decisions have to be made by the South Vietnamese themselves because, although we've had a substantial military presence there, we can't take over running the affairs of seventeen or eighteen million people. There are limits beyond which you simply can't go.[25]

Even notable disjunctures and shifts in US foreign policy were shifts in *strategy*, rather than in the fundamental ideas of emancipatory liberalism.

Britain was dealing with its own problems in Africa during the 1960s, and relations with its former, and existing, colonies represented an important cultural shift toward a moderation of universalism and away from the civilizational paternalism of the past as well. In response to Zimbabwean claims in the United Nations Security Council that UK policies in Rhodesia were characterized by "abominable dishonesty," British Foreign Secretary George Brown argued (in quite an ironically illiberal context) that "This is primarily a great moral issue. The only solution is one which is acceptable, and is seen to be acceptable, and is determined as being acceptable, to the people of Rhodesia as a whole."[26]

This is a very different understanding of the moral issue than that of British liberals before World War II. Whereas peoples in the colonial periphery were relegated to an "infantile" status—and therefore excluded from determining their own fates,[27] democratically or otherwise—this civilizational narrative became, for many liberals, a symptom of totalitarian governance: the worst of the evils of Soviet communism.[28] Brown was not the only British liberal to make these discursive moves in the 1960s. Prime Minister Harold Wilson associated the problem of violence precisely with the reactionism of conservative and authoritarian political movements, further demonstrating the fear of Western liberals with both the rise of Soviet communism and the excesses of a civilizational paternalism.[29] Cold War emancipatory liberalism was pessimistic, fearful, suspicious—a change from the era of empire.

Cold War Liberalism: Fear, Pessimism, Violence under the Specter of Totalitarianism

The work of historian Jacob Talmon illustrates the emergence of a pessimistic yet emancipatory liberalism in the twentieth century, and highlights its origins, fears, tensions, and ruptures during the Cold War.[30] Talmon's work has been underappreciated in the history of political thought, leaving one commentator to write that "Talmon's *Origins of Totalitarian Democracy* had a 'vast influence among historians,' but the larger impact of his work has been limited and probably has declined since the 1980s, especially compared to that of Isaiah Berlin and Hannah Arendt."[31] Like the latter thinkers, Talmon's thought is fueled by a skepticism of grand narratives and the danger such narratives could ravage on the world. Berlin and Arendt were similarly influenced in their thinking by the Holocaust—perhaps the twentieth century's most horrific reminder of the terrors of ideology. "Talmon was well aware of the fact that his heroes," argues Arie Dubnov, "instead of being protectors of human dignity and individual liberty, can provide sophisticated justifications and cruel rationalizations for oppression and autocracy."[32] While Talmon was not the only theorist belonging to this tradition of a "liberalism of fear"[33] or a pessimistic liberalism, his work provides a look into a notable attempt at *tracing* the history of a crusading, optimistic liberalism—and critiquing its failures, horrors, and legacies.

Talmon's work, indeed, is nearly paradigmatic of this new trend in international liberal thought, leading some scholars to suggest that he was, in fact, a "leading representative of Cold War liberals."[34] This was partly due to Talmon's immersion in a British intellectual culture that produced a significant number of Cold War liberals.[35] Talmon, however, was an exemplary figure in his own right in the culture of suspicion and pessimism that emerged from within this tradition, particularly in the way that Talmon's own genealogical studies of liberal democracy highlighted how easily optimism and messianism could spiral out of control. This was particularly acute when, *pace* poet Johann Herder, "the whole was more real, and came before the parts" of a society—true democratic totalism.[36] Talmon's historical investigations of the aftermath of the French Revolution, as well, were not purely academic inquiries. His most significant work, *The Origins of Totalitarian Democracy*, was "written under the strong influence of Cold War realities."[37] Talmon-as-historian demonstrated just how much this suspicion penetrated all aspects of intellectual production.

Talmon's writings about totalitarianism paralleled what philosopher Paul Ricoeur termed a "hermeneutics of suspicion."[38] Ricoeur charted this critical reading—a suspicious, pessimistic reading—of texts, by focusing on three theorists in particular: Marx, Nietzsche, and Freud. All of these thinkers, for Ricoeur, shared an empirical concern with religion, and a desire to strip away the vestiges that religion put up with the idea of showing something more sinister underneath.[39] For Marx, this was demonstrating that religion was the "opiate of the masses"; for Nietzsche, this was showing how religion was involved in the creation of a "slave morality" that valued weakness over strength; and, finally, for Freud, it was humankind's psychological need for a father figure. These three thinkers took historical and textual interpretation as a project of suspicion, of genealogy in an important sense—a "historical narrative that explains an aspect of human life by showing how it came into being."[40] Such genealogies meant to expose, uncover, to show the *pessimus* (the worst) of a textual program. Ricoeur's classification of a hermeneutics of suspicion in Western thought did not necessarily entail a *nihilistic* pessimism. In other words, being suspicious—uncovering the "worst" of something—was not necessarily a spiral into the bleakest, most hopeless doom. In fact, suspicion opens us up to thinking about emancipation, about the future, about faith. Ricoeur writes, "All three clear the horizon for a more authentic word, for a new reign of Truth, not only by means of a 'destructive' critique, but by the invention of an art of interpreting."[41] On the one hand, being suspicious challenges some of our deepest assumptions about culture, politics, philosophy, and aesthetics. On the other hand, it does not necessarily entail a rejection of those projects—it is aimed at rewriting them through a specific way of interpretation.

This was Talmon's method, and his project was a genealogical one. As scholars of Talmon note, this uncovering came through Talmon's critical reading of the history of "political messianism," especially that of the French Revolution. "Rousseau, and in [Isaiah] Berlin's writings also Kant and T. H. Green," writes Dubnov, "were all preparing the grounds for totalitarianism because they began the process that eventually allowed the sacrifice of an actual 'empirical self' to an abstract 'true' or higher self."[42] Paralleling Ricoeur, Talmon's pessimism about totalitarianism was not a nihilism, however; it was pervaded by a search for truth. It was the lack of reality, and the focus on a blind idealism, that lead to the terrors of the modern age. Talmon writes, "Under the impact of the French Revolution, however, the dialogue was pursued upon a plane of absolutes. For the French Revolution had given birth to modern ideologies, indeed ideologies *tout court;* and ideologies fight shy of simple self-interest."[43] The problem with the revolution, in some ways, was that revolutionaries did not apply a hermeneutic of suspicion to their own ideas. This is how totalitarianism rises.

Two examples of Talmon's suspicion about totalitarianism during the Cold War bear dwelling on. First, Talmon's view of history caused him concern about the potentiality of a political messianism rearing its ugly head in the context of the Cold War. Talmon had already connected messianism (and namely, its radically democratic versions) to the causes of the French Revolution;[44] however, he connected this ideology to both the rise of fascism in the 1930s and 1940s in Europe, as well as to what he called "left totalitarianism" in the Soviet Union. This connection is clearly expressed near the beginning of *The Origins of Totalitarian Democracy* when he writes, of "modern totalitarianism," that it "is the outcome [. . .] of the synthesis between the eighteenth-century idea of natural order and the Rousseauist idea of popular fulfillment and self-expression."[45] For Talmon, the Soviet Union represented the worst of things to emerge from the milieu of the French Revolution, and Talmon himself was skeptical of political projects that drew on heavy mass support and promised political salvation. This was a pessimism about the ability of the masses to contain totalitarianism, and a suspicion about messianic movements.

Second, Talmon saw this less as an indictment of liberalism as a political ideal, and more of an example of how a democratic politics can lead away from a strong liberal society. He develops a dichotomy in *Origins* between "totalitarian democracy" and "liberal democracy" to clearly separate democracy and liberalism, by arguing that democracy is necessary for a liberal polity, but liberalism is neither necessary nor sufficient for a conception of democracy—collectivism is freedom for totalitarians.[46] Totalitarian democracy, unlike liberal democracy, believes there is a "sole and exclusive truth" about politics.[47] Talmon's fear, his pessimism, and his suspicions of Cold War politics were the suspicions one has of a snake oil salesman: beware the pitch. Totalitarianism is a wolf in sheep's clothing.

Talmon was not alone in such suspicion of totalitarianism in the postwar era. Another prominent illustration is French theorist Simone de Beauvoir's writings on totalitarianism—which displayed a fear and pessimism similar to the accounts of theorists like Talmon. Beauvoir is known for her pioneering writings on existentialism and mid-twentieth-century feminism; however, a uniting theme in her work is the concern with totalitarianism in its many forms. As Lori Marso notes, Beauvoir, and fellow theorist Hannah Arendt, exemplify the argument that "totalitarian and other police state regimes provide numerous and various kinds of opportunities for people to betray their responsibilities toward others."[48] Beauvoir's point of view highlights the political problems associated with the confrontation with totalitarianism.

For Beauvoir, the most troubling figure here is that of the "sub-man," that individual who is overwhelmed (with fear, apathy, turmoil) by the circumstances that float around him. The sub-man is the vulnerable one; one that can be recruited into political projects that are anti-freedom. As Beauvoir writes, "Weighted down by present events, he is bewildered before the darkness of the future which is haunted by frightful specters, war, sickness, revolution, fascism, bolshevism. The more indistinct these dangers are, the more fearful they become."[49] The sub-man, through his fear, can turn toward becoming the "serious man"—one who gives up his freedom altogether. His life becomes dedicated to an idea, or a cause—one which needs foot soldiers. This is, for Beauvoir, a means whereby totalitarianism can emerge, and where freedom can be extinguished altogether.[50]

In many ways, then, Beauvoir, like Arendt, was skeptical of grand historical narratives and ideologies by highlighting how these "ideas" could lead individuals away from freedom and into the throes of dangerous ideological projects. In this sense, Beauvoir, like other mid-twentieth-century intellectuals, including Talmon, differed from emancipatory liberals of the periods of empire. This language of ideological fear, however, was one not so different from the languages used by policy makers to justify intervention in conflicts during the Cold War. After all, in a liberal world order, one person's ideology is another person's common sense.

Even following détente, the Vietnam War, and the slowly fading memory of World War II, Western liberals continued to frame overly ambitious foreign policies as being analogous to the totalitarianism of the first half of the century. In the minds of many, however, the Soviet Union was not the primary threat anymore. The Cold War had brought out the worst in US foreign policy, and many worried that totalitarianism—if it was to rear its ugly head again—could be a consequence of US ideological crusades. The totalitarian fear had turned inward.

This change in the usage of totalitarian imagery from the pre-détente era was related to many different factors. The first was the opening of relations between the USSR, China, and the United States, which occurred under US President Richard Nixon.[51] This, coupled with increasingly unpopular US involvement in Vietnam, created an atmosphere of optimism about cooperation with the USSR and introspection with regard to the threat of global communism. The second factor was the development—beginning most notably in France—of anti-totalitarian radical philosophy, which set its sights on critiquing liberalism.[52] Third, US domestic politics, itself, was facing similar discursive shifts, as the fear of totalitarianism was, by the Cold War, causing the decline of progressivism in favor of liberalisms that were more focused on the limitation of governmental interference.[53]

Exemplary of this trend was one of the United States' most outspoken public intellectuals, author Gore Vidal, who expressed worry about the United States' descent into totalitarianism throughout the 1970s and 1980s, in voluminous essays and books about the "American Empire." Remarking on Teddy Roosevelt, in a 1981 *New York Review of Books* essay titled "An American Sissy," Vidal connects attention to Roosevelt's legacy among the New Right to fascism—simultaneously attributing Roosevelt's foreign policy to insecurities in his manhood, comparing Roosevelt himself with the likes of Mussolini, and (by implication) the New Right interventionists with both history's great "sissies" and its génocidaires.[54] This was a bigger threat to the world than Soviet communism. Perhaps the greatest fear of pre-détente liberals was realized: the West had become more like the Soviets than it could ever imagine. When asked in a *Playboy* interview about whether the Soviet Union is a threat because it, unlike America, tries to dictate to other countries how to live, Vidal replies:

> You don't think we're trying to tell the people of Nicaragua and El Salvador how to live? Were we trying to tell the people of Vietnam how to live? For decades, we have determined the governments of Germany and Japan. Things now crumble. Slowly. Of course, the Soviets' system is repressive. It's inherent in their culture. But you can be certain that if our clients were to get seriously out of line, we'd tighten the screws. Yet according to Ron and the system he works for, it's the Reds who are perpetually on the march.[55]

Totalitarianism, in sum, was a mobilizing concept for Cold War liberals. It was as much a product of pessimism (like Talmon's) about the possibility of a world order organized around big ideas as it was an ironic faith that emancipatory liberalism could provide the necessary foundations for defeating the vestiges of totalitarianism that continued to confront the West—namely, in Latin American and Asia. But this was not the only variety of emancipatory liberalism during the Cold War. A robust development culture—focusing on the totalitarian threat through the spread of modern, democratic, and progressive institutions abroad—was emerging at the same time.

Emancipatory Liberalism and the Development Boom

The Cold War signaled the birth of another cultural phenomenon within the context of international liberalism: an emerging theoretical and political focus on international development. Harry Truman declared this period a "development age," and this new movement was inseparable from the incipient battle against the spread of communism. Development functioned as a way of expanding Western influence in areas that were vulnerable to the threat of the USSR.[56] This was by no means a purely political change, however. This new era of development coincided with—and was perhaps in part caused by—a burgeoning development economics, which came about in the 1940s and saw its apex in the 1950s.[57] Though this field had its origins in the revitalization of a war-torn Europe (while at the same time opening up possibilities about social and political change—namely, growth and stability—in the Global South), it was also deeply connected to the development of colonial knowledge, calculability, and rationalism that characterized an earlier imperial period.[58] This new development politics was as much a politics of humanitarian reason[59] as it was a concern for international security. The end of World War II represented an era of development that not only reflected the new purpose of human rights, or the new means of modern economic sciences, but also the fear of totalitarianism.

By the 1950s, the threat of totalitarianism was often intimately intertwined with the political project of international development. Development schemes, and their impact on domestic social and economic policy, were directly counterposed to what was viewed, both in official circles and in the public sphere, as the Soviet alternative. "The United States stands committed, by the President," a 1957 *Washington Post* article reports, "to a new concept of foreign aid that is supposed to extend to countries in Asia and Africa the kind of long-term economic development assistance that might induce them to reject totalitarian schemes for their betterment."[60] Totalitarianism was a threat because it represented an easy way out for countries that were desperate in the face of stagnation.

The real fear that countries, especially in the Global South, "may be tempted to adopt the quicker ways of totalitarianism"[61] connected a concern with security and influence to the successes of ambitious international development projects. Though congressional funding was often an obstacle in this mission, the rhetoric of a concerted cultural struggle between liberalism and its totalitarian foe put this issue in the spotlight of prominent debates in policy circles about the virtues of development policy.[62] In the 1960s, the Kennedy administration would take Truman's "Development Era" and attempt to turn it into the "Decade of Development."[63] Besides trying to take on, in President Kennedy's words, "a much greater effort on a much broader scale," the heightening of superpower rivalry—especially following proxy wars in Korea, and the brewing of US involvement in Indochina—demanded development as a means of blocking the continued spread of communism, and ensuring international security and stability. Kennedy makes this point crystal clear in a 1961 message to the US Congress, stating:

> [. . .] widespread poverty and chaos lead to a collapse of existing political and social structures which would inevitably invite the advance of totalitarianism into every weak and unstable area. Thus our own security would be endangered and our prosperity imperiled. A program of assistance to the underdeveloped nations must continue because the nation's interest and the cause of political freedom require it.[64]

While the confrontation with the USSR vis-à-vis development policy appears, at first glance, to be a purely strategic issue of influence, its roots are much deeper. Expertise—and, particularly, intellectual defenses of philosophies of histories that highlight the benefits of development policy—had an enormous influence on the way that political officials conceptualized both the problem of underdevelopment and its solutions through social transformation and development aid. Economist Walt Rostow, for example, in developing a theory of history that staged development in relationship to a society's economic performance,[65] played a role in the way that the Kennedy and Johnson administrations framed their development policies. His modernization theory set the stage for US experiments in development during the 1960s, especially in Latin America.[66] Intellectual as much as political sources of a new development discourse connected the problems of underdevelopment with the solution of the West's increased involvement in managing the intractable problems of countries in the Global South.

A key case in this regard was US President John F. Kennedy's Alliance for Progress initiative for Latin America.[67] An ambitious decade-long plan, the Alliance for Progress represented an attempt at spreading the good word of liberal governance and development into Latin America. In a speech outlining this proposal, Kennedy states most clearly: "Let us once again transform the American Continent into a vast crucible of revolutionary ideas and efforts, a tribute to the power of the creative energies of free men and women, an example to all the world that liberty and progress walk hand in hand."[68] Kennedy's plan was idealist, ambitious, and directly aimed at the totalitarian threat looming over the Western Hemisphere: communism.

The Alliance for Progress as a robust, idealistic, and optimistic tool of development policy failed in its more ambitious goals. But even amid efforts at reorganization under the Lyndon Johnson administration, the Alliance carried with it many of its emancipatory aims, focusing more squarely on economic development as the source of transformation of Latin American countries into liberal democracies. Many former Kennedy allies and staffers were critical of the Johnson administration's attempts to change the focus of the alliance; however, as one historian notes, "the new president promised that under his leadership the ambitious aid program would flourish [. . .]."[69] Therefore, while Johnson confidantes like Thomas Mann would reshape the program for the provision of aid in the region, the liberal aims of developmentalism, progress, and struggle against the threat of Soviet totalitarianism remained. "Enlightened self-interest" had an emancipatory end goal.[70]

In terms of common sense and public culture, Latin America was, perhaps, the most important test case for the emerging development culture of the 1960s. Development aid to Chile, for example, was cast in the media of the time as a means of maintaining a secure Western Hemisphere, while at the same time producing more rapid and lasting change in the region. As the *New York Times* pointed out in 1962, in regard to debates about development in Chile: "The inter-American system [. . .] moved on two levels to implement fundamental programs for the region's economic and social development and to provide it with a means of security."[71] The worry posed by a right-wing regime in Chile was not just the fear of a new brand of totalitarianism in Latin America,[72] but also the fear of the effect of such a regime on US security interests more broadly.

Adlai Stevenson, the ambassador to the United Nations under President Kennedy, put this issue at the forefront of American foreign policy, arguing that Western liberal societies had created "the very resources of capital and technical and scientific accomplishment on which the new and emerging nations must draw," and that "accepting a common frame of international order offers the best safeguard for safety of our shores and the security of our people."[73] For US policy makers, development was both a gift of the West to the Global South and an integral part of US security interests. It was part of an ideological project that was aimed at countering the influence of communism.

The 1970s witnessed the beginnings of a shift in the development discourse from the ambitious superpower-led development strategies of the 1960s to a greater skepticism among liberals about the role of government-directed aid programs. There were two major factors in this shift. The first is that some states were experiencing domestic political problems associated with foreign aid, particularly in the United States. In regard to aid, as a *Washington Post* editorial put it most succinctly, "outside of the United States, the program as a whole is nowhere regarded as in serious difficulty."[74] The second is the rise of neoliberalism,[75] and a sea change in development discourse regarding the role of official aid in promoting successful international development in the Global South. Some commentators at the time went as far as saying that the effects of official aid were "marginal," and that external trade is the most "effective stimulant" for sustained economic growth.[76] Cold War development—a state-led project of aid and economic assistance—had, by the 1970s, given way to a new politics of the market. Trade and private investment were the central components of an effective, and international, policy of development.[77]

Political arguments for market solutions to development aside, technical discourses on economic growth further demonstrated this change from a pre-détente Cold War liberalism. A World Bank World Development Report from 1978 concludes that private investment and trade are the only viable solutions to development in the Global South:

> Those with trade-oriented economies have been able to exploit the favorable opportunities for expanding exports, and a growing number of Middle Income countries have gained access to international capital markets. But, in the poorer countries, which depend on Official Development Assistance for all or most of their capital requirements, the very slow rise in the supply of these funds has seriously hampered their growth.[78]

The "Decade of Development" heralded in the 1960s would take a radical turn in the context of a new international market liberalism, which turned the demand for state-based development aid on its head, instead shifting the focus to the virtues of open markets, and integration of the Global South into the capitalist world system. While the Cold War frame of the 1950s and 1960s faded behind neoliberal technocracy, this reappropriation of the totalitarian imagery—and, specifically, the connection between poverty and threats to international order—created a cultural environment in the 1970s where intervention was to come not at the end of a gun barrel, but at the end of a transaction.

While official development assistance saw a downturn in favor in the 1970s, by the 1980s the picture had become more complicated. For many liberals, development had moved beyond the market as more and more issues came under its umbrella. Conditional lending, along with increasingly more "intricate and everyday" methods of development practice meant that the state, along with international organizations and NGOs, would play an increasing role in bringing the Global South from poverty to economic success.[79] At least in international politics, the great powers were engines in driving development policy, and transformative foreign policy was becoming closely intertwined with the politics of poverty, state performance, democracy, and, of course, the control of alternative ideological programs. Democracy, in particular, became closely tied to this project, so much so that democracy, aid, and the fear of totalitarianism became discursively connected into a single rhetorical scheme.

In regard to the lack of congressional funding for aid to the Sandinistas in Nicaragua, President Ronald Reagan's press secretary, Larry Speakes, released a statement that embodies this spirit: "The President feels strongly [...] that U.S. policy must support free peoples who are opposing totalitarian rule supported by external forces." And, further: "We will stand up to totalitarian governments, and we will seek support for people, and we will support people who seek their basic freedom. Our response involves not only the future of democracy in our hemisphere, but it also embodies the basic political ideals of the American people."[80]

This section has charted the emergence of two strands of international liberalism during the Cold War. The first is a cautious one, emerging out of a fear of totalitarianism. This would evolve into a reflective post-détente liberalism that was not just conscious of the Soviet threat, but also of the inherent problems associated with American interventionism. The second strand is a developmental liberalism—an emancipatory project as well—which saw the solutions to the totalitarian threat in Western development science from the 1940s to the 1960s, in neoliberal markets in the 1970s, and in aid to democratic movements in the 1980s. These two interpretations of international liberalism would be central components of military intervention during the Cold War—wherein the practices of violence were profoundly shaped by visions of what it meant to free people from the totalitarian threat of Soviet communism, and what it meant to respect pluralism.

American Intervention in the Dominican Crisis of 1965

The Dominican crisis of 1965 was one significant moment in the story of mid-twentieth-century emancipatory liberalism. This case—one that would embroil the Johnson administration in a large-scale intervention in the Caribbean—mirrored the languages of anti-totalitarian liberalism of the postwar era.

The United States had experienced tumultuous relations with the Dominican Republic since before World War I. In 1913, the Wilson Plan attempted to maintain stability in the country and promote free elections. This ultimately failed due to civil unrest, however, resulting in US intervention that lasted from 1916 to 1924, immediately followed by the installation of Rafael Trujillo's dictatorship, which would last for over three decades.[81] While US interest in the Dominican Republic waned over the interwar period, renewed attention to Latin America was a notable feature of the Cold War: Trujillo was feared for being too dictatorial, causing the Eisenhower administration to attempt to remove him covertly.[82] Trujillo was assassinated in May 1961, leading to the eventual election of Juan Bosch, whose administration was similarly unsettling due to US concerns that he might be a communist sympathizer. By 1963, Bosch was removed via a coup while the United States "stood by."[83] The new president, Donald Reid Cabral, was threatened with a coup attempt in April 1965, instigated by pro-Bosch rebels.[84] This initiated a civil war, and caused the Cabral government to seek US assistance. Bosch's return to power was not welcomed by the Johnson administration and initiated a crisis for the United States. A choice had to be made between inaction and intervention, wherein intervention was the outcome.[85]

The first stage of the intervention involved the evacuation of Americans from the Ambassador Hotel in Santo Domingo. This was nearly completed by embassy personnel with Dominican military assistance by late April,[86] though this was not the planned endgame of US involvement in the Dominican Republic. President Johnson makes clear in a phone conversation with the State Department that "we are going to have to really set up that government down there, run it, and stabilize it in some way or another. This Bosch is no good."[87] An intervention initially framed as an emergency evacuation was only part of a broader transformative scheme. US troops were officially requested by the junta on April 28, and advisors suggested Johnson land troops to protect remaining Americans in the country. Troops landed the same day with the goal of working for "a cessation of hostilities, the restoration of law and order and the speedy return to normal processes of government."[88] By that date, there was a strong indication that Johnson was ready to commit troops to long-term action in the Dominican Republic. In the late evening of April 28, Johnson made it clear that "tomorrow will be the day. The decisions that will be made tomorrow will be much more important than the ones [. . .] made today."[89] Johnson was right in his prediction. April 29 saw the deployment of US troops, to the tune of 42,000, with the purpose of restoring order to the country.

Emancipatory liberal discourses of the period, and particularly the dual concerns about the totalitarian threat of communism and development politics, affected actor conception of identity and goals. This was marked by a lack of consensus about what the goals of the intervention were, however, due to discursive divisions within US liberalism. Despite the potential deployment of troops at the end of April, there was relatively little pushback by liberals in the US government about intervention. This is not too surprising, as Senate liberals were concerned (throughout the 1960s) about the spread of communism in the Americas, and the need for extensive democratic promotion in the region. Even Senator William Fulbright, a notorious critic of the Cold War fear of communism, was similarly outspoken about the need for liberal democracy in the Dominican Republic. As early as 1961, Fulbright argued that US involvement in the country could be "a concrete symbol of success through democratic methods in unmistakable contrast with the totalitarian example of Cuba."[90] This juxtaposition of democracy with totalitarianism placed the Dominican Republic in direct relation with Castro's Cuba. It was, thus, not too startling when Fulbright's only question in an April 28 meeting with the president and congressional leadership was about what role the Organization of American States (OAS) would play in an intervention.[91] Similarly, Senator Mike Mansfield, another prominent Senate Democrat, made only one suggestion, that the OAS be included in any statement to the public.[92] Violence was justified, provided there was institutional legitimacy.

Others, particularly in the press, were less satisfied with Johnson's intervention policy. While development liberals like Fulbright favored involvement in relation to development, the media cautioned against this sort of thinking, suggesting that the United States' active involvement in suppressing communism in the Western Hemisphere is what led to the Dominican Republic's problems in the first place. A *New York Times* article published in May of 1965 states, "It is therefore arguable that United States intervention was what brought the Communists to the forefront."[93] Additionally, Governor Nelson Rockefeller was vocal in opposition to US unilateralism in the matter.[94] The "moderating" of US aims in the Caribbean was in direct opposition to US interventionism, and the ultimate decision of the Johnson administration. While this cautious dissent failed to alter policy actions significantly, it demonstrates the tension and conflict between two liberal visions of world politics during the Cold War. It represented a fight over identity and goals that would never quite disappear in intervention policy over the remaining quarter century.

Johnson, in the end, would never recover from the legacy of the Dominican intervention. The fallout following the intervention was one of intra-liberal conflict. Fulbright openly criticized the administration by September of 1965, stating that the aims of the intervention were misrepresented and comparing it to Vietnam.[95] The Johnson administration immediately struck back, having Senator Thomas Dodd suggest, on the Senate floor, that Fulbright was emboldening "every Communist and crypto-Communist and fellow traveler and anti-American leftist who wields a pen in the Latin American press."[96] Relations between Johnson (who felt betrayed) and Fulbright were never the same. This made foreign policy difficult for Johnson, who lost a powerful ally in the Senate.[97]

The United States worked hard to place the intervention in the context of some sort of institutional legitimacy in order to bring the intervention in line with a global liberal consensus. Institutional legitimacy was important for the administration to hedge its bets when it came to the possibility of failure. Johnson himself was very much worried about the potential for the post-intervention operation to fall apart, leaving such a failure on Johnson's name. As he stated, rather bluntly, in a telephone conversation with Fortas, "I want it to be a hemispheric thing instead of an individual LBJ. I don't object to giving them my wife, my daughter, and my car, and my money. But I want them to say, 'here's what we've collected from all this hemisphere.'"[98] For Johnson, this was something that could tarnish his presidential legacy. Embedding the intervention in liberal institutional norms—such as multilateralism and group decision-making—could help deflect blame and responsibility.

This interpretation of multilateralism as the liberal institutional environment of the time, whether empirically true or not, was at least interpreted in such a way by the Johnson administration. In the same phone call with Fortas, Johnson discusses the way that pro-Bosch forces have been able to effectively sway liberal opinion against the United States by framing the intervention as a unilateral one.

> Bosch's group has damn near destroyed us in Europe and abroad with the liberals and the Manchester Guardians and the articles out of here about how this is a unilateral operation. And the [British Prime Minister Harold] Wilson government is wobbly now because he's got a three-man majority. And they take the position that this man Johnson is another Führer. And that's the liberal thing about the North Americans. They've sold that.[99]

A comment like this, about the comparison with Hitler, makes sense in the context of Cold War emancipatory liberalism. Liberals, as shown earlier in the chapter, were not just concerned with the development and spread of totalitarianism in the postwar order. They were also concerned with the actions and beliefs that might lead the West to turn toward totalitarianism itself. If nothing else, Johnson was a savvy reader of public and elite opinion, and was concerned that this framing would be applied to his actions in the Dominican Republic.

The Johnson administration had an enormous task before it when it came to messaging. Johnson himself noted, prophetically, in a phone call with Bromley Smith, Executive Secretary of the National Security Council, that "this is going to be bad in our country."¹⁰⁰ The administration was concerned about US public opinion, and particularly about *how* the administration would approach messaging. Worrying about dwindling Senate support, Johnson suggested to Fortas that the message had to be consistent with well-entrenched tropes about liberalism, stating, "I think [the message has] got to be anti-communist and pro-liberal. That's what I want."¹⁰¹ While this language makes it clear that Johnson was manipulating the "selling" of the intervention to elites, including members of Congress, it also shows that Johnson was well aware of the *kinds* of language that could legitimately bring liberals to his side regarding the conflict. These discourses about anti-communism, and the spread of liberalism to fight a totalitarian threat, were so well entrenched in common discursive tropes that their repetition became a key part of administration strategy.

Elites in Washington were not Johnson's only concern regarding the intervention. Johnson was certainly concerned with the war in Vietnam, and its increasing unpopularity. He did not "want to be an intervenor."¹⁰² Records indicate that Johnson was paranoid about public opinion in the United States, and perhaps even had a skewed view of the ways the public interpreted the intervention. In a conversation with former president Dwight Eisenhower, Johnson gives an unsourced statistic about US public opinion vis-à-vis the conflict—stating that 85 percent of the American public supports the operations.¹⁰³ After all, the United States, in Johnson's mind, "tried to save that country."¹⁰⁴ The rhetoric of "saving" is significant in two ways. Johnson's interpretation of public opinion—that public support was based on a reading of the intervention as a means of "saving" a country in crisis—parallels not just Cold War liberal concerns about the encroachment of totalitarianism, but also the development discourse about how transformative foreign policy could "save" countries from underdevelopment. This parallels how theorists like Rostow thought about the aims of modernization not only as a means of developing a country's capabilities, but also as a means of fighting the communist menace (recall the subtitle of Rostow's "manifesto"). The public, for Johnson, was on his side, because, like any good liberal leader, he was leading the charge against communism: emancipating the Dominicans from their fate.

Change in the messaging is evidence of the importance of liberal vocabularies, especially those related to development and totalitarianism, in persuading publics and elites to back the intervention. In the initial public announcement of the intervention, the only motive that Johnson highlights is that of rescuing embassy personnel. No other justification for war is given in that speech.¹⁰⁵ This rhetoric would soon change dramatically, however. In a speech given only a few days later, Johnson underscores another, more significant motive for intervention. No longer was this about evacuating American citizens; it was now about the "lives of thousands, the liberty of a nation, and the principles and values of all the American republics."[106] Johnson, toward the end of the speech, even goes on to suggest that the intervention itself was an effort in freeing the Dominican people from the "tyranny of communism." He states clearly: "I think it is our mutual responsibility to help the people of the Dominican Republic toward the day when they can freely choose the path of liberty and justice and progress."[107] This was not just an intervention to solve an immediate emergency. It was one with an emancipatory purpose, meant to help the country develop, and meant to stifle the emergence of communism, totalitarianism, and "tyranny" in the Western Hemisphere.

Besides decision-making dynamics, messaging, and the discourses surrounding public opinion, the operations on the ground were framed by the identity implications of Cold War emancipatory liberalism. Within one week, the mission had shifted from one aimed at protecting US citizens to one that had policing and "stability" functions—a job that involved the destruction of a potential communist state on the ground. The general in command of Operation Power Pack (the intervention's official name), Gen. Bruce Palmer, received the following message from his superior (Gen. Earle Wheeler) early on: "Your announced mission is to save US lives. Your unannounced mission is to prevent the Dominican Republic from going Communist. [. . .] [Y]ou are to take all necessary measures to accomplish this mission."[108] The administration and US generals gave the command on the ground carte blanche to accomplish the mission of disrupting the installation of a communist government in the Dominican Republic. This brought the military out of the business of evacuating the civilians, and into the business of development, nation-building, and anti-totalitarian policing. The identity of the United States as a Western liberal country engaged in a global war against a communist totalitarian threat was a central facet of US policy in the post-intervention setting.

This on-the-ground project was not limited to military actions. The US government developed plans to enlist humanitarian and development organizations like the Peace Corps in the intervention context. In October, Bundy suggested to President Johnson that the United States utilize over two hundred Peace Corps volunteers with the purpose of developing rural schools and organizing and strengthening public health, community development, and various functions related to town development.[109] These efforts were in line with contemporary intellectual currents in development, and especially modernization theory, which argued, *pace* Rostow, that for economic takeoff to happen, there had to be a fundamental restructuring of more "traditional societies."[110]

Whether responding directly to Rostow's model or just building on well-accepted discourses about modernization and development during the Cold War, US officials certainly bought into the logic based on the intersection of ideology and expertise, with a National Intelligence Estimate of 1966 concluding that "[r]eform measures of the type required for sustained economic development will be extremely difficult without a prolonged period of political stability."[111] The justification for long-term US involvement in the Dominican Republic, even after the initial intervention, was given in the language of a development culture that would only be possible through the articulation and reproduction of distinctively *liberal* emancipatory discourses. Expertise, like the deployment of Rostow's modernization theory model, and the implementation of solutions embedded in international and domestic development institutions, were directly influenced by liberal discourses, ideas, and vocabularies.

Resistance to intervention in the Dominican Crisis was significant. Internally, citizens of the Dominican Republic fought back against the US-led intervention. The intervention, itself, was a response to, and heated up, a civil war in the country. Both sides of the conflict were less than satisfied with a US-led occupation of the country. Externally, there was protest and resentment from the public in the United States, leading to some forms of resistance breaking entirely from the liberal consensus. One example was the integration of this issue into the emerging student movements of the time. Cornell University students founded an organization known as the Committee on US-Latin American Relations (CUSLAR) in response to the intervention. University chaplain Bill Rogers, one of CUSLAR's founders, called for a "new internationalism, trusting that we may find other hands that will work for us in the struggle for justice in the hemisphere."[112] For organizations like CUSLAR, the ideological bases of the current liberal world order were not enough to guarantee justice for countries subject to anti-communist interventionism.

On the ground, resistance from local actors was easily dismissed by the US administration both in Washington and the Dominican Republic. These groups were variously termed as "communists" or communist sympathizers. Even in the case of noncommunist rebellion and resistance, the administration was convinced that these forms of resistance would be pacified through the imposition of constitutional and liberal reforms in the country.[113] As in previous periods in history, emancipatory liberals utilized discourses about reform and constitutionalism to attempt to silence resistance, by demonstrating that there were no legitimate alternatives. After all, what the United States was attempting to do was to show the noncommunist resisters that their only available options were a tyrannical communist totalitarianism, or free and fair elections with liberal institutions. In the minds of Washington and US bureaucrats on the ground, that was an easy choice, and resistance was therefore actively dismissed, or viewed as holdouts to an eventual liberal triumph.

Conclusion

This chapter has argued that liberal international culture during the Cold War was characterized by a discursive concern with totalitarianism. A "liberalism of fear" between the end of World War II and détente externalized this threat toward the Soviet Union—both in terms of an emerging value pluralism, and developmentalism. After détente, liberal intellectuals began to worry more about the totalizing aspects of intervention, and feared the "mirror image" of the Cold War—the idea that the West could, in some ways, become precisely what it feared only a few years earlier. Democratization, too, became an important force following détente, becoming intimately tied to a politics of political and economic development. While the civilizing discourse of the empire period gave way to the threat of alternative political imaginaries, the interventions of this period still carried a paternalistic objective. Keeping new "Castros" out of Latin America was an American duty—from Kennedy to Reagan.

Furthermore, liberalism during the Cold War—and its focus on totalitarianism—transformed the way that actors made sense of violence and intervention. Intervention was a method for stifling totalitarian ideologies, while at the same time providing the conditions for the development of a global liberal culture constituted by liberal democratic states, whose stability would guarantee the dominance of a Western liberal world order. Pluralism would moderate these ambitions, and especially in the public sphere, as the Dominican Crisis demonstrates. Intervention's purpose, however, was one of battling a threat—the threat of an alternative political philosophy.

The epigraph of this chapter is indicative of this discursive trend. Whereas Arendt was wrestling with the implications of Marxism, the West took that maxim for granted, and with no sense of irony. For Western liberals, Marxism was the nightmare, and the dream was a utopian one—a consolidated liberal world order. The post-détente period caused liberals to step back and reevaluate the ways that intervention may be anti-liberal and antidemocratic, but this had a smaller impact than new thinking about democratization and development on intervention practices. If the liberal empire period was about civilizing the unreasoned colonial subject, the Cold War was about transforming the nature of background political culture in third-world countries by reordering regimes.

Institutionally, interventions became more affected by the international context than in previous periods. This effect was mixed, however. On the one hand, liberal states were most concerned with containing the communist threat, often at a high material and reputational cost. The Johnson administration's efforts to include the OAS in policy statements, for example, were often more marginal aspects of the decision-making process, as the case study shows. Yet, regional organizations were important allies in situations of intervention, suggesting a certain sense of necessity for regional actors to be involved in significant ways. The Cold War conflicts within liberalism would, in short, result in new institutional configurations and change the ways that publics and international actors restrained and legitimized interventions.

The aftermath of East-West conflict that was brought about by the fall of the USSR and the end of superpower rivalry would again change the dynamics of liberal world order and the deployment of violence.

CHAPTER SIX

Transformation and Terror

State Failure, Development, and Human Rights

If the cold war period represented a "liberalism of fear," the post–Cold War period represented dramatic shifts in the ways that liberals expressed those fears. The concern with totalitarianism that so pervaded liberal discourses during the previous era gave way to new concerns: the fear of state failure and "terror." This shift would be the most sudden and dramatic in relation to military intervention. After nearly four decades of concern over totalitarianism, liberals became more concerned with its inverse: the absence of robust governance. Warnings that states in the Global South are "teetering on the brink of implosion or have already collapsed,"[1] are dire ones, and represent novel ways of conceptualizing emancipatory liberalism in an era of US hegemony. Novel is not an exaggeration. Only in the early 1990s does the term "failed state" become embedded in Western policy discourses.[2] As this chapter demonstrates, the correlation between the new rise of state-failure discourses and the end of the Cold War is no coincidence. It represents a new way of thinking about international politics within the context of an evolving liberal order. As this chapter demonstrates, this discourse—and especially its intermingling with the discourses of terrorism, rights, and development—had a profound impact on the way that states deploy violence for emancipatory and transformative ends.

This chapter makes two interrelated arguments. First, the post–Cold War period represents an important shift in liberal thinking about war, development, and a liberal world order. This discursive shift moved the focus from totalitarianism to its opposite: state failure. This securitization of state institutional form integrated two seemingly separate discourses—failed states and "terror"—into a coherent security narrative.[3] Second, this set of discourses had an impact on the way that states practiced violence and intervention. It structures state rationalization and justification of interventions, connects them to institutional contexts, and integrates them into understandings of identity. The contemporary period demonstrates that emancipatory liberalism is a continually evolving project.

Two specific moves are central to these changes. In the first place, the emergence of a state-failure discourse is directly implicated, and inseparable, from a discourse about human rights. Beginning with the introduction of this terminology in the 1990s, human rights played a central role in how intellectuals and policy makers thought about the relationship between human freedom, capacity, and happiness in the context of crumbling state institutions. In the second place, discourses about state capacity and human rights were implicated in the way that "terror" is conceptualized. Terror and terrorism became associated with the decline of state authority, and its threats to human rights, stability, and a liberal world order became major items on the global agenda. These seemingly separate discourses are intimately connected, and contributed to the way that states actualized intervention policies in locations such as Iraq, Afghanistan, and elsewhere in the Global South.

This chapter proceeds in four main parts. First, I discuss the context of changing liberal vocabularies about state failure/fragility and human rights beginning in the early 1990s. The major impetus for these changes had to do with the global political climate following the fall of the Soviet Union and the end of the Cold War, as well as new imaginaries (spatial and temporal) of the coming global order. Second, I dig deeper into these discourses by examining an intellectual shift in social science literature toward the phenomenon of state failure. Political scientists and sociologists were important actors in these changes, and in the construction of new discourses about governing capacities. Third, I analyze emerging discourses about terrorism, liberalism, and race, with an emphasis on the ways that a "liberal orientalism" pervaded both the domains of expertise and popular/public culture. The final section presents a case study of the coalition intervention in Afghanistan in 2001 to show the ways that emancipatory liberal discourses mirrored practices of violence and intervention.

Emancipatory Liberalism after the Cold War: Context and Change

Following the Cold War, emancipatory liberalism focused its sights away from the issue of totalitarianism, and instead became preoccupied with the issue of human rights.[4] This can be seen as a product of three political developments which would substantially affect the nature of liberal discourses after the fall of the Soviet Union. First, the end of great power conflict opened up a space for human rights discourses to become more salient. With superpower conflict largely gone, US and Western European rhetoric about human rights could be actualized in a Western liberal order.[5]

Second, the end of the Cold War represented a turning point in a nearly fifty-year history of transnational human rights groups in getting human rights on the international agenda.[6] The apex of this historical trajectory was the Vienna Declaration in 1993, which was "a high water mark for the postwar human rights ideal."[7] Finally, and related to these developments, was a global rethinking of liberal aims in relation to democratization and the universalization of rights practices. The UN, for example, moved beyond an incrementalist strategy for human rights protections to a discourse that centered on "all human rights for all."[8] The end of the Cold War was a pivotal moment in the emergence of a new human rights discourse within emancipatory liberalism.

This emerging post–Cold War human rights discourse is one that is tied to a concern with intrastate conflict and state capacity. If the collapse of the Soviet Union created a space for the development of a universalist human rights discourse, it also created the space for increased ethnic conflict—a process that often threatened the realization of such goals in the context of changes in governing authority.[9] US President Bill Clinton highlighted this challenge, remarking that "... we reaffirm our belief that security cannot be divorced from respect from human rights and the democratic process."[10] This concern with state capacity, and the ability of Eastern Europe to comply with Western standards of human rights in the context of increasing conflict over governance, reflected the mirror image of a previous concern with totalitarianism: lack of state capacity as a threat to human rights and democracy.

Paddy Ashdown, the leader of the Liberal Democrats in the UK from 1988 to 1999, put this problem in starker terms, arguing that not only was state capacity a threat for Eastern Europe, but represented a threat to human rights, democracy, and the entire Western liberal order. He states, "The truth is, the danger to Western Europe in the 1990s that comes from the disintegration of Eastern and Central Europe is quite as great, in its different way, as the danger posed to the western democracies by the rise of fascism in the 1930s."[11] The drawing of this analogy is even more significant in that it equates the fear of state capacity and ethnic conflict to the fears of the Cold War. While the latter was the concern of emancipatory liberals after World War II, the biggest threat to democracy and human rights in a post–Cold War world is that of nation-state instability.

This issue was not one relegated only to the political elite. The connection between ethnic conflict, state capacity, and human rights played out discursively in the public sphere as well. As a *New York Times* commentator notes, the Western world should go as far as backing up human rights protections by "international guarantees, enforceable by, say, NATO, the UN Security Council, or even some ad hoc coalition of military powers."[12] In a twist of irony, totalitarianism—the biggest threat to Western liberalism—is invoked as preferable to the chaos of intrastate strife: "Perversely, it was Communist totalitarianism that checked overt ethnic violence in the archipelago during recent decades."[13] Though communism might have contributed to the development of ethnic tensions, at least stability was provided through a totalitarian governance scheme.

This discursive relationship between human rights, intrastate conflict, and state capacity was not solely a reaction to political developments. It also represented important changes in intellectual discourse following the Cold War. Following the "defeat" of Soviet communism, liberal intellectuals became increasingly bold in their denunciation of alternative governing arrangements to that of the Western liberal state—arguing that intrastate conflict was the biggest threat to a global liberal order. Francis Fukuyama is illustrative of this trend. His arguments about the "end of history" cast suspicion on allegiances to other identity categories than the nation-state, suggesting that only the liberal state represented the means by which human rights could be realized through a "struggle for recognition."[14] He writes, "[small] communities are frequently based on religion, ethnicity, or other forms of recognition that fall short of the universal recognition on which the liberal state is based."[15]

Samuel Huntington shares this concern with the threat of substate identities confronting a Western liberal world order, arguing that "the end of ideologically defined states in Eastern Europe and the former Soviet Union permits traditional ethnic identities and animosities to come to fore."[16] For intellectuals like Fukuyama and Huntington, though the Cold War opened more opportunities for the spread of Western ideas like human rights, the very process of the shrinking of political identity puts this project in threat—the biggest obstacles in a post–Cold War order are threats to the stability of the nation-state.

These discursive developments in international liberalism after the Cold War would experience important changes following a transformative moment for the Western liberal order: the terrorist attacks on the World Trade Center in New York City on September 11, 2001. Though the language of human rights and its connection to ethnic conflict remained, it took a turn into the realm of a new set of questions about the role of human rights in the context of "traditional" communities, evoking a set of paternalist understandings about the West's role in instigating cultural and political change in developing states, in new areas of concern. The Middle East and Africa would be analogous to Eastern Europe in the post-9/11 order, with its own set of intellectual and political issues.

The attacks on the United States on September 11 changed, in significant ways, the politics and liberal discourses about human rights and their relationship to state capacity and state failure. While in the 1990s this issue was largely concerned with fractured national communities in the context of post-Soviet Eastern Europe, the new human rights discourses intersected with a growing concern about state failure in the Middle East and Africa, which many have argued contributed to the attacks of 9/11. For Western liberals, not only did state failure in the Global South represent poor governance, it was characterized as a "sickness" that feeds undesirable symptoms—including abuses to fundamental human rights. As one scholar writes, "We cannot assume that states are responsible for human rights abuses—we must make them so by enabling them to police their citizens and control their agents."[17] Weak and failed states are the world's threat to human rights, according to this argument: one that has intervention built into its very vocabularies.[18]

This discourse was as much a function of political changes as emerging ideational changes. Three such changes are exemplary. First, the development of a "failed-state" discourse that began in the early 1990s had reached its zenith following the 9/11 attacks. Branwen Jones notes that the post-9/11 era represented the maturity of a long historical process whereby narratives of state fragility became used as justifications for the use of force.[19] Second, a development discourse that had been, in one way or another, a feature of liberal thought since at least the mid-nineteenth century connected such failed state imaginaries to the ability of the West to confront "backwardness" in the Global South. These discourses create visions of a "barren and backward land waiting to be claimed and tamed,"[20] where Western states must intervene with the purpose of protecting rights and security. Finally, it represented an attempt for policy makers, the media, and intellectuals to make sense of a rapidly changing global security architecture that seemed to be emerging from countries on the borderlands. As an ICISS report notes, "states that can only maintain internal order by means of gross human rights violations can constitute a risk to people everywhere."[21] Though these discourses were new, and changing, they were not ahistorical. Rather, they were the result of the evolution of a development discourse that has dominated emancipatory liberal thought since the nineteenth century.[22]

This rhetoric permeated official discourse in the United States as well as Western Europe. Most critical in this regard is the relating of human rights in the Middle East and North Africa with the instability of institutional forms in the region. US President George W. Bush connected human rights to neoliberal economic development, with his administration arguing that failing nations hindered the economic freedoms that promote human rights.[23] As the 2006 National Security Strategy Report states, "Nations that lack the rule of law are prone to corruption, lack of transparency, and poor governance. These nations frustrate the economic aspirations of their people by failing to promote entrepreneurship, protect intellectual property, or allow their citizens access to vital investment capital."[24] The threat of poor governance was a direct threat to the economic rights of citizens in the Global South, but it became framed as an integral part of US security strategy. This failed-state discourse would become prominent not just in US discourse, but also United Nations development assistance. As a *UN Chronicle* article points out, "state fragility" affects access to food and economic flourishing in the developing world—and the Western would must show "long-term engagement" in overcoming these issues.[25] Government officials, especially in linking state failure to human rights via the mechanism of economic freedom, demonstrated a rhetorical commitment to human rights by surmounting state failure.

The counterargument that these rhetorical tropes are merely political justifications are discredited when one notices the recurrence of these emancipatory discourses in the public sphere. Prominent arguments in the editorial pages of influential media outlets reflect these same connections between human rights, state failure, and international intervention that were prevalent following September 11. For example, the *New York Times* pointed to Western responsibility in upholding human rights following the creation of South Sudan, arguing "[US diplomats] have a lot of work to do—and not a lot of time—to help the leaders there improve their ability to govern and promote the rule of law. Otherwise, the desperately impoverished region runs the risk of becoming a failed state the day it is born."[26] A *Vanity Fair* interview with political advisor Richard Perle expressed similar sentiments, quoting Perle as saying, "The levels of brutality that we've seen are truly horrifying, and I have to say, I underestimated the depravity [. . .]. And then, you'll get all the mayhem that the world is capable of creating."[27] Public arguments connected Western intervention to preventing such "mayhem" for the sake of human rights and the rule of law.

Finally, the failed-states–human-rights nexus received support from its employment in intellectual circles. While some have pointed out how this discourse is itself a product of stakeholder definitions of what "good governance" is,[28] many such definitions center around some understanding of the state's ability to protect individual and communal rights. The Fund for Peace's Fragile States Index, for example, not only includes "Human Rights and Rule of Law" as a quantitative indicator affecting its rating of state fragility, but also states that "when human rights are violated or unevenly protected, the state is failing in its ultimate responsibility."[29]

Though human rights is one measure of state weakness in the Fragile States Index, framing state fragility *directly* in terms of human rights—the state's "ultimate responsibility"—reflects a cultural understanding of the state that became possible 1) after the decline of Soviet communism; and 2) in the context of post-9/11 fears about the effects state failure in the Middle East and Africa would have on global human rights. Therefore, it should be of little surprise that according to the 2014 rankings, of the sixteen states deemed to be "high alert" and "very high alert," fifteen of them were in Southwest Asia and Africa.[30]

State Failure and Human Rights: Origins

The term "failed states" was popularized by US Secretary of State Madeleine Albright,[31] but the term itself has a more complex lineage. The image of the failed state conjures up remnants of an old liberal vocabulary from two vantage points. From the first, the Hobbesian/early social contract understanding of the state is invoked—i.e., that the state is an organism that prevents the descent into normative confusion and dangerous anarchy. The state, *pace* Locke and Rousseau, respectively, is a success if it provides the context for adjudicating disputes and popular sovereignty of a political community.[32] From the second vantage point, the state has a monopoly on the legitimate use of force within its borders. This Weberian understanding of the state is a common trope in much of the early literature on state failure in international relations and comparative politics.[33] What failed states are missing are the elements of order and rule of law that allow us to live in civilization, as opposed to a Hobbesian state of nature, characterized by misperception, fear, and constant danger.

The origin of the term "failed states" is difficult to trace. Its most famous early statement is from a *Foreign Policy* article authored by two US State Department employees, Gerald Helman and Stephen Ratner. The genealogy of this term, however, is slightly earlier. In an article published in 1990 in the academic journal *International Security*, political scientist Jeffrey Herbst uses the term "failed" as a way to describe contemporary African states. He paraphrases sociologist Charles Tilly as saying "the 'enormous majority' of states in Europe failed."[34] This is framed by Herbst as a continuation of an earlier discussion of "failed states" in the political sociology literature; Herbst, however, significantly misrepresents Tilly. In the text referenced by Herbst, Tilly writes, "Most of the European efforts to build states failed."[35] The word "efforts" is missed by Herbst, and radically changes the meaning. Tilly's meaning is that it was not so much the state institutional structure of existing, and internationally recognized, states that failed; it was the *effort* to carve out such states in the first place. What occurs instead is a rhetorical move by Herbst that uses a (misrepresented) language about state-making in Europe to argue that African states are "failed." Something Tilly did not argue, and in fact *could not* argue, because, after all, Western European states cannot fail.

Robert Jackson's influential discussion of "quasi-states" from his 1990 book *Quasi-States: Sovereignty, International Relations, and the Third World*, also develops an early consideration of differences in sovereignty and state capacity. Instead of using the phrase "state failure," Jackson instead focuses on how international actors have bolstered weak states' sovereignty through institutions of "negative sovereignty." Jackson, like Herbst, draws a line directly separating the European experience from the experience of the developing world. In doing so, Jackson reproduces the discursive move that European states could not be negatively sovereign. That is not part of their historical development.[36]

Helman and Ratner's prominent 1992 article continues and extends many of these early themes about state failure. The authors, like Herbst, define failed states in a way that excludes the possibility of Western states failing; Western liberal democracies cannot fail. The countries named in the piece as illustrative cases are largely former colonies. In the one case where Helman and Ratner do acknowledge that European states may collapse, their examples are drawn from Eastern European states, including Yugoslavia and Bosnia. When they write, "Third World countries are not the only ones that could fail,"[37] their meaning is to include countries that still exist on the margins of Europe. Unlike Herbst, there is no comparison in Helman and Ratner's piece between these states and Western European states at other times in history. By definition, failed states cannot be Western liberal states.

While Helman and Ratner are not the first to write about the idea of state failure, their work shows the early equation of state failure with violations of human rights, merging these two seemingly distinct ideas together. It is telling that the connection is immediately drawn in the first paragraph of the article, where the authors state, "The massive abuses of human rights—including that most basic of rights, the right to life—are distressing enough, but the need to help those states is made more critical by the evidence that their problems tend to spread."[38] In one of the earliest texts illustrating the problems of state failure, this connection is drawn; this demonstrates a co-constitution of these discourses. One cannot understand human rights abuses without also understanding the phenomenon of state failure; one cannot appreciate the problems of state failure without also highlighting how decreased state capacity impacts human rights.

Helman and Ratner do not end their analysis by simply emphasizing the problem. The authors spend much of the piece detailing possible international solutions to state failure. Many of these solutions are ones that border on direct control of failed states through international conservatorship, and hold similarities to earlier discourses about mandates and "sacred trusts." The authors even make such a claim by appealing directly to a metaphor of illness and paternalism in describing international institutional obligation; they write provocatively:

> In domestic systems when the polity confronts persons who are utterly incapable of functioning on their own, the law often provides some regime whereby the community itself manages the affairs of the victim. Forms of guardianship or trusteeship are a common response to broken families, serious mental or physical illness, or economic destitution. The hapless individual is placed under the responsibility of a trustee or guardian, who is charged to look out for the best interests of that person. In a commercial context, bankruptcy codes accomplish a similar purpose, providing a transitional period under which those unable to conduct business relations are given a second chance at economic viability. It is time that the United Nations consider such a response to the plight of failed states.[39]

State failure and human rights abuses are illnesses. A global liberal order must manage these issues, just like the state can institutionalize those who are a danger to themselves and society—even if these solutions remove all agency, sovereignty, and power from the actors in question.

One might wonder what the genealogy of this connection between state failure and rights is. This is a complicated genealogy. On the one hand, human rights were built into the early definitions and discussions of state failure literature in the early 1990s. Helman and Ratner's article shows this discursive move clearly. On the other hand, this connection between state capacity and state failure is a much longer one that is endemic to liberal thought since the early-modern period. Its operationalization in contemporary liberal discourses is most pronounced in the era after the Cold War. Thomas Hobbes and John Locke, for instance—each widely credited as progenitors of liberal ideology—saw state capacity as fundamentally linked to rights. For Hobbes, this was the right to self-preservation: the lack of moral order in a society leads to a world where self-preservation is nearly impossible. For Locke, state capacity was tied into natural right—the state as the arbitrator of justice was necessary for the maintenance of individual rights to life, liberty, and property.[40] Beyond the term *state failure*, the broader discursive connection between the failure of governing institutions and the threat to rights is a long one.

Another origin to this story is a discursive shift that began in the 1980s and was further elaborated in the 1990s. The emergence of a "capabilities" approach to the study and implementation of justice connected the capacity of governing institutions directly to fundamental human rights, this time couched in a language about what humans are "capable of."[41] These intellectual changes interfaced directly with policy. The Human Development Index (HDI), for instance—a way to measure the development of a particular society with an eye toward the development of human capabilities—inspired Amartya Sen's development of his capabilities theory. In the 2016 HDI report, the United Nations Development Program (UNDP) makes clear the connections between state failure and human capabilities/rights: "Broader peace, stability, and security are linked not only to the end of wars and conflicts, but also to the end of violence within societies and human security in personal and community life."[42] This is not to say that this assessment is empirically incorrect; however, it demonstrates the pervasiveness of arguments that make rights and state capacity inseparable. While these specific arguments emerge in the early 1990s with the beginnings of the state-failure discourse, their broader contours were built into liberal thinking about the state from the beginning of liberalism.

This legacy continues in contemporary liberal IR theory as well. For liberals, proper "authority structures would ensure a society that is peaceful, protects human rights, has a consultative mechanism, and honors the rule of law based on a shared understanding of justice."[43] Failed states are failed *precisely* because they lack the institutional structures that define a modern, liberal, democratic polity. Furthermore, these demands on state capacity are often unrealistic and go beyond the evaluation of a state's capacity to govern. Under this definition, states like North Korea or Iran have weak authority structures, and are failing states, when that is far from the case. For liberals today, state failure is synonymous with illiberalism.

Nor has liberal IR theory shied away from integrating these conceptual arguments into larger pleas for international policy change. Krasner, in the previously referenced article, argues that because of the problem of state failure, great powers and international organizations should consider "sharing sovereignty" with failed states in order to help them bring their governing capacity to a level of adequacy. In a telling phrase from the piece, Krasner states, "Domestic sovereignty does not involve a norm or a rule, but is rather a description of the nature of domestic authority structures [. . .]."[44] Bruce Gilley found himself in hot water over an article in *Third World Quarterly* giving the "case for colonialism."[45] While Gilley's argument was offensive, and ignored the massive violence and horrors of colonialism, he was correct in demonstrating that such arguments are not new in IR. Even Fearon and Laitin's 2004 piece criticizing policies of "neotrusteeship" points to some benefits in certain policy areas, particularly monitoring of institutional effectiveness and the collection of taxes.[46] Rather than serve as a critique of foreign policy practices that mirror colonialism, liberal IR has provided the social scientific justification for such policies—using euphemistic languages like "trusteeship" or "shared sovereignty" to advocate for an interventionist foreign policy.

State failure discourses, as I have shown, are relatively new discourses—emerging only after the Cold War. But there are comparisons and connections between these ideas and earlier forms of emancipatory liberalism. On the one hand, for instance, state-failure discourses mirror civilizational rhetoric about the evils of barbarism, and the (racial) contrasting of Western liberal states and societies in the colonial periphery. Furthermore, the policy solutions are similar: arguments deriving from academic/policy discussion about "trusteeships" are deeply indebted to mandate-era discourses of colonialism and paternalism. Nonetheless, two differences are significant. First, post–Cold War ideas of state failure often focus on the effects of state failure on the *individual*, especially in the way that state failure is tied to human rights. This was not entirely true in civilizational discourses, which focused on societies as a whole. Second, state-failure discourses are often avowedly anti-colonialist,[47] moving the legitimacy of internationalist solutions to the problems posed by such states into a realm of discourse *outside* of colonialism, obscuring its imperial genealogies.

"The Roots of Muslim Rage": Liberalism, Orientalism, Terror

Human rights are not only linked to state failure in post–Cold War liberal imaginaries; they are also linked directly to issues of terrorism and stability. These imaginaries are positioned in what we might term a "liberal orientalism": a form of racial and spatial ordering based on a distinction between a civilized, reasoned "West" and an uncivilized, violent "East."[48] These languages, developing in earnest in the 1990s, differ from earlier forms of racism related to emancipatory liberalism's vision of world order for at least two reasons. First, languages like "barbarian," or languages that draw specifically on images of blatant inferiority are no longer front and center in these discourses. Racism, and ethnocentrism, are hidden behind mechanisms of expertise, social science, and some broader forms of understanding about the world that promise to move above what writers in this genre might consider more crude understandings of the relationships between civilizations and ethnicities. Second, these languages rarely imply a distinction in terms of political right. While John Stuart Mill saw Indians, for instance, as possessing fewer rights than the British, liberals writing within the context of liberal orientalism carry a universal understanding of rights quite at odds with empire and interwar understandings of race, identity, and difference. It is the case that Muslims, as liberal orientalists argue, should be recipients of universal rights and protections; this is precisely why social science or historians should determine the origins of Muslim violence—to protect and promote human rights and security in those areas.

These discourses do carry similarities. On the one hand, liberal orientalists in the 1990s through to the contemporary era often talk about civilizational differences, and even (in the case of writers like Huntington) civilizational development, in a way that is similar to empire theorists.[49] On the other hand, writers have invoked policy solutions to the problems of liberalism's "Other" by drawing on justifications for violence and intervention that were central to the arguments made in previous periods. One specific commonality is with the development discourses of the Cold War period, wherein modernization theory suggested that "backward countries" were behind the curve on modernizing processes due to cultural and political idiosyncrasies. It is little surprise, then, that a significant number of the liberal orientalists of the contemporary period got their careers started as influential modernization theorists—Huntington being a prime example.

Thus, we can see differences in this discourse from early imperial discourses, as well as similarities. Thinking about contemporary liberal orientalism as merely a continuation of 150-year-old discursive tropes, however, is dangerous. It misses key nuances, and especially differences that have to do with the veritable explosion in the 1990s of literature on human rights, underdevelopment, globalization, and terrorism. Similarly, seeing this discourse as simply a continuation of modernization theory is also ahistorical. It overlooks the fact that modernization theory itself had to grapple with the phenomenon of postcolonial development in ways that the original theorists (including Huntington, Rostow, et al.) could not adequately envision in the Cold War context. There were new enemies, new battlegrounds, and new ways of imagining unilateral and institutional solutions to the problems facing an increasingly fragile liberal world order.

One of the most notable of these theorists is Huntington himself, whose work "The Clash of Civilizations?" from a 1993 edition of *Foreign Affairs* exemplified both a liberal orientalism and a connecting of terror, human rights, and threat. Huntington's article is precisely about a distinction between liberal states and other states in the developing world. Huntington notes early on in the piece that "Western ideas of individualism, liberalism, constitutionalism, human rights, equality, liberty, the rule of law, democracy, free markets, the separation of church and state, often have little resonance in Islamic, Confucian, Japanese, Hindu, Buddhist or Orthodox cultures."[50] For Huntington, one of the things that makes the West unique is that it is a civilization of liberty. Notice in the above quote that liberalism and liberty are both listed in the first clause. Whether this is sloppy writing or purposeful emphasis, it is notable that one of the characteristics that Huntington sees as constituting the identity of the liberal state ("civilization," in his term) is this adherence to values associated with liberalism—values that are incommensurate with values in other states.[51]

While Huntington's liberal orientalism, and his view of Western liberal identity, are used to justify statements throughout his piece of the bumper-sticker variety— including "the West vs. the Rest"[52] and "Islam has bloody borders"[53]— Huntington's own conceptualization of what the liberal West is to do is a bit more contingent. At the end of the article, Huntington suggests that states must balance this threat through military power and force, while also arguing that Western civilization needs to learn about, and engage with, other civilizations; "we will have to learn to coexist," he writes in the final lines of the piece.[54] On precisely whose terms this coexistence will be built is opaque in Huntington's formulation. In the periods of empire and internationalism charted in chapters 3 and 4, theorists and policy makers were clear about the goals and duties of Western liberal states in dealing with other civilizations. Huntington, writing in a period of universal rights and global justice, an age of globalized politics, does not use the language of conquest and intervention; but the piece does not rule out force, either.

Bernard Lewis, a prominent academic orientalist, developed many of these themes explored by Huntington, though beginning even earlier. In his famous 1990 article titled "The Roots of Muslim Rage," Lewis makes similar arguments to Huntington's later assertions about a Clash of Civilizations. He argues that Islamic civilization has tended toward rage and violence, and that this is related to the way that Islamic culture refuses the separation between faith and politics. Lewis makes, however, the connections between Western civilizational identity and liberalism even more explicit than Huntington, beginning and ending his article with quotes by, and commentary of, Thomas Jefferson's call for a clear separation between church and state.[55] The problem with Islamic civilization today, for Lewis, is the lack of liberal understandings of government. Quoting Jefferson in the last lines of the piece, he writes, "Mind should be free as the light or of the air."[56] While a professional historian, Lewis saw his duty as more than documenting the history of the "roots of Muslim rage." Lewis became a strong advocate for regime change in countries like Iraq. Writing in an opinion piece for the *Wall Street Journal*, for instance, Lewis argues:

> In the same way, the dictatorships that rule much of the Middle East today will not, indeed cannot, make peace, because they need conflict to justify their tyrannical oppression of their own people, and to deflect their peoples' anger against an external enemy. As with the Axis and the Soviet Union, real peace will come only with their defeat or, preferably, collapse, and their replacement by governments that have been chosen and can be dismissed by their people and will therefore seek to resolve, not provoke, conflicts.[57]

Lewis's argument, in contrast to the hedging of Huntington, was that Western liberal countries would need to intervene.

These formulations would prove to be not just those of a history professor safe in his ivory tower. These arguments were deeply influential with members of US President George W. Bush's administration, particularly in the way that the administration thought about intervention in Iraq. For example, Vice President Dick Cheney, in an interview with *Meet the Press*, clearly demonstrated the depth of Lewis's influence on administration thinking: "I firmly believe," Cheney states, "along with men like Bernard Lewis, who is one of the great students of that part of the world, that strong, firm, US response to terror and to threats to the United States would go a long way, frankly, toward calming things in that part of the world."[58] Liberal orientalism as a textual formulation, backed by claims of social scientific knowledge (in Huntington's case), and historical expertise (in Lewis's case), made its way not just into the policy world, but also was directly implicated in the deployment and operation of violence and intervention in the Middle East.

Despite Lewis's dichotomy between reason and faith, he was now a holy warrior in the struggle for Western liberalism's global dominance.

Liberalism and the Public after the Cold War

These discourses about the relationship between state failure and human rights, terrorism, development, and illiberalism, made their way from academic, philosophic, and policy discourses into the public realm with relative speed. Major newspapers like the *New York Times* in the United States, or the *Guardian* in the UK, were publishing editorials, op-eds, and feature stories that mirrored these discourses. By the mid-to late 1990s, it was commonplace and commonsensical to equate state failure with a discourse about human rights; by the early 2000s, especially following September 11, public outlets ran articles that contained the same sorts of liberal orientalism as that found in the writings of scholars like Bernard Lewis and Samuel Huntington. In the post–Cold War order, liberal political culture was built upon two dichotomies: the dichotomy between the developed liberal state and the failed state, replete with human rights abuses, and the dichotomy between the reasoned West and terrorism/underdevelopment in the third world.

One of the pivot points for this discourse in public media was in the coverage and commentary on the United Nations Mission in Haiti (UNMIH), which was sent to Haiti with the goal of peacekeeping following a series of turbulent years in the 1990s. The British liberal-leaning newspaper the *Independent* ran a series of investigative and opinion articles on the conflict in the mid-1990s, most of which were penned by Peter Pringle, documenting the politics of the intervention and providing perspective on the events. Pringle consistently identifies Haiti as a "'rogue' and 'failed' state."[59] In a column on Clinton's successes in Haiti, columnist Patrick Cockburn compares the UN intervention in Haiti with the liberation of France in 1944.[60] The *Independent* was not idiosyncratic in this way. On the other side of the Atlantic, the *New York Times,* in reflecting on the end of the UN mission in 1997, directly tied human-rights issues to state failure in Haiti, arguing that the mood of the time was "of frustration at the difficulties of making a failed state work."[61] The article praises the United States for its commitment to liberalism and human rights, including the successes of the intervention in giving "Haiti a more democratic government." Haiti was a failure, however, because of the UN's attempt to too "rapidly" change the political environment of Haiti. If there were limits to nation building, for popular outlets like the *New York Times,* these limits were not in the *aims* of such interventions, but in their methods. Curing state failure and its symptoms takes time.

Countries like Cambodia,[62] Zaire,[63] Yemen, Rwanda, and Azerbaijan[64] were regularly labeled with such terms as well. In an opinion piece in the *Washington Post,* journalist Blaine Harden writes of Liberia as suffering from what he calls "failed state syndrome," blaming the United States for the country being "blasted backward into a Hobbesian state of nature."[65] The specter of Thomas Hobbes is evoked to describe a failed state—in line with intellectual arguments by liberals about state failure, but also with the implication that failed states are those states that challenge individuals' natural right to self-preservation. "Hobbesian" is not sloppy use of a cliché adjective; it is directly connecting a failed-state discourse with human rights, development, and forms of constitutional government. The difference is that this text, and other popular texts like it, were making this argument and these discourses recognizable to a broader public.

Liberal orientalism exited the academy and landed on the opinion pages of major news outlets. This discourse operated to remove terrorism from the realm of the political altogether, drawing on tropes of liberal orientalism to argue against an alleged "metaphysics" or anti-liberalism in the fight against terrorism. In an opinion piece appearing in the *Guardian* soon after 9/11, Harvard professor Michael Ignatieff exemplified this shift in language, suggesting, "What we are up against is apocalyptic nihilism." He further writes that "The apocalyptic nature of their goals makes it absurd to believe that they are making political demands at all."[66] Ignatieff uses this framing of the Other to justify Western intervention, in what would aptly be described by Doyle as a liberal "crusade."[67] Ignatieff argues, "the obligations we owe are to ourselves alone, to the moral identity that gives justice to the cause."[68] This framing illustrates the ultimate goals of liberal orientalism: portraying the Other as so fundamentally different as to be beyond the realm of politics altogether, and to use this to justify war in defense of freedom. Ignatieff's use of the phrase "gives justice to the cause" frames this in the starkest of religious imageries: that of incompatible, and irreconcilable, metaphysical narratives.

Beyond news, other forms of public media—including film and television shows—also demonstrated the strong cultural embeddedness of ideas associated with liberal orientalism. Film functions as a form of promotion of social and political ideas, and even as a way of "embedding liberalism" in aesthetic contexts.[69] One example of this was the veritable explosion of films documenting the beginnings and middles of the war on terror, often portraying terrorists as not just the enemy of a state and a society, but also enemies of liberty itself. The oft-cited example of post–September 11 aesthetic culture, the television action/adventure show *24*, develops themes related to the response to terrorism aimed at the enemies of the West. The show itself came under fire from critics for its portrayal of torture techniques by the hero of the show, Jack Bauer, who each season finds himself under the time restraints of a 24-hour window in which to stop a terrorist attack. Cultural critic Slavoj Žižek compares the ethics of *24* to other intellectual currents in American politics, and is largely correct in drawing an analogy between the ethic of torture as developed in shows like *24* and those developed by scholars like Alan Dershowitz, who famously argued that the dictates of liberal political ethics—humanitarianism, human rights, and constitutionalism—do not apply to terrorists, and, therefore, "enhanced interrogation techniques" are necessary.[70] Like the liberal orientalism of Lewis and Huntington, *24* and Dershowitz's ethics work to reify difference, and paint the Other as beyond the pale of reason and outside the boundaries of liberal world order altogether.

Liberal orientalism, and the way it ties together discourses of terrorism, race, development, and liberal internationalism, exists in intellectual, policy, and public forms and is part and parcel of a post–September 11 political culture. More than that, it helped to characterize the way that states and their agents justified, practiced, and rationalized the use of force.

Emancipatory Liberalism and the Afghanistan War

The Afghanistan intervention by a US-led coalition in 2001 was preceded by a civil war in the country. The Taliban political movement gained control of Kabul in 1996, founding the Islamic Emirate of Afghanistan in place of the existing government. Despite the government's formation of the Northern Alliance to combat the influence of the Taliban in the state, the latter had significant financial and military assistance from the Saudi and Pakistani governments, as well as al-Qaeda.[71] Afghanistan became a haven for al-Qaeda operatives—including Osama bin Laden, who fled to the country in 1996 following his expulsion from Sudan that year.[72] Bin Laden would claim responsibility for the September 11 terrorist attacks on the United States, where nearly three thousand people were killed. This event became pivotal in the forthcoming intervention in Afghanistan, which set the United States' sights on Afghanistan as a haven for bin Laden and Al-Qaeda, and the focal point of the West's emerging "War on Terror."[73]

Following the attacks, and unsuccessful US attempts to get the Taliban to surrender bin Laden, the US Congress passed a joint resolution authorizing the president to commit US armed forces to be used against the perpetrators of the attacks and those who harbored them.[74] The initial deployment of force began as a covert mission; the US inserted CIA operatives into Afghanistan on September 26, 2001, and within less than a month had also deployed Special Forces to the region to coordinate with Northern Alliance fighters in a bid to overtake several Taliban-controlled cities. A full-scale military intervention began on October 7, with the United States launching airstrikes in Kabul, Kandahar, and Jalalabad. By November, the UK, along with Canada and Australia, had deployed troops to Afghanistan, beginning a long coalition intervention in the country. By the end of the year, the United Nations had created the International Security Assistance Force (ISAF) in an effort at peacekeeping in Kabul. A portion of the operation fell under NATO command two years later.[75] The intervention was transformative in its aims—purposed with regaining control from the Taliban government and restructuring the institutions of the country—and marked the beginning of an emancipatory intervention policy in the post-9/11 world.

Though self-defense was a central justification for war in Afghanistan, this motive was tied very closely to justifications and rationalizations for war that were connected to discourses about state failure, human rights, and terror. The first of these justifications had to do with Afghanistan as a failed state, and the role that the United States, and its allies, would play in state-building in the country.[76] In an address to the nation after ordering the first strikes of the intervention, President Bush made this justification most clear: "We defend not only our precious freedoms, but also the freedom of people everywhere to live and raise their children free from fear."[77] In conceptualizing liberty as a cure for terror, Bush justified and rationalized intervention and state-building as a means to an emancipatory end. The UN made this connection more explicit in UNSCR 1386, which was passed on December 20, 2001. The document states that the Security Council is "Welcoming developments in Afghanistan that will allow for all Afghans to enjoy inalienable rights and freedom unfettered by oppression and terror."[78] The text further authorizes the ISAF to assist in the "maintenance of security" in the capital.[79] This early commitment to providing security in order to make available rights and protections in the context of terrorism mirrors the international emancipatory discourses of the period.

Second, the US took pains to couch the justification for intervention in post–Cold War vocabularies of human rights and state failure. Notable in this regard was the use of women's rights as a way to mobilize support for the war.[80] Perhaps most famous was First Lady Laura Bush's November 2001 radio address, where she argued that the War on Terror was "also a fight for the rights and dignity of women."[81] The US State Department released the same month a document titled "The Taliban's War against Women." The document makes the argument that women's rights were central to the struggle for Afghanistan, suggesting, "The regime systematically repressed all sectors of the population and denied even the most basic individual rights. Yet the Taliban's war against women was particularly appalling."[82] This intersection between human rights and the Taliban's campaign of terror operated as a means of convincing the public that the intervention was justified. It was the duty of the United States as a nation committed to liberal values to intervene to rebuild a fractured society that mistreats women. Liberal state identity claims were brought to bear in these justifications.

This rhetorical strategy was effective and sparked significant debate in the public sphere about the connection between state failure, terror, and human rights (particularly those of women) in Afghanistan. The editorial pages of the *New York Times,* for instance, welcomed intervention for this reason, suggesting "America did not go to war in Afghanistan so that women there could once again feel the sun on their faces, but the reclaimed freedom of Afghan women is a collateral benefit that Americans can celebrate."[83] Another article went as far as to say that the Bush administration should urgently request that Congress appropriate new funds to build infrastructure in Afghanistan, stating, "Afghanistan requires substantial help to avoid returning to the lawlessness that opened the door to the Taliban a decade ago."[84] Afghanistan was a prime case for demonstrating the perils of state failure, how it leads to terror, and how it affects the rights of individuals. In constructing these justifications, the United States superimposed an emancipatory liberal narrative onto the conflict in Afghanistan.

Even during President Barack Obama's administration, the selling of the intervention in Afghanistan developed these popular tropes connecting state failure, terror, and human rights. In a 2009 speech justifying a troop surge in Afghanistan, Obama argued that the return of the Taliban, and the dismantling of the Afghan government, would have disastrous consequences. It would "condemn the country to brutal governance, international isolation, a paralyzed economy, and the denial of basic human rights to the Afghan people, especially women and girls."[85] The personification of these conceptual issues through the use of human rights for women and girls was an effective tactic, meant to put a human face on nation building and war in Central Asia.

Just as much as the use of force was connected to the protection of human rights in the context of terrorism and state failure, it was also tied directly to state identity. One such example was in early justifications for the war, including those made by the British government, which argued that intervention in Afghanistan was both vital to the preservation of Western identity and exemplary of liberal values. In a speech to parliament immediately following the 9/11 attacks, Prime Minister Tony Blair made this position clear in his justification for war in his concluding remarks:

> We will act because for the protection of our people and our way of life, including confidence in our economy, we need to eliminate the threat Bin

Laden and his terrorism represent. We act for justice. We act with world opinion behind us. And we have an absolute determination to see justice done, and this evil of mass terrorism confronted and defeated.[86]

These comments are noteworthy for two reasons. In the first place, the use of the phrase "our way of life" points to common rhetorical justifications for the war that went beyond physical security, and into the realm of ontological security—security of the fundamental values of a liberal Western state. In the second place, war itself is placed not in the context of self-defense, or physical security, but is framed as a fight over metaphysics—a realization of Ignatieff's argument about opposition to an "apocalyptic nihilism" that must be met with the resolve of a crusading liberalism. Justice must be served; Western liberalism must root out the evil of terror.

The justifications for the Afghanistan intervention and appeals to legitimacy were not just made to domestic publics. They were also placed in the context of institutional legitimacy, and particularly aimed at building a large coalition of international support for the invasion. This was not solely for material assistance; the US and the UK bore the brunt of casualties in the initial invasion, and in the post-invasion context.[87] Placing the use of force within institutional contexts gave added legitimacy to the intervention. The history of institutional involvement with the war is mixed. The UN was the principle organization appealed to by the US in justifying the war. There was no Security Council (UNSC) resolution authorizing the war, though there were later resolutions, particularly UNSC Resolution 1386 of December 20, 2001, which gave legitimacy to post-intervention nation-building operations, "welcoming developments in Afghanistan that will allow for all Afghans to enjoy inalienable rights and freedom unfettered by oppression and terror."[88] NATO would also be an important institutional forum to engage with, particularly in the context of post-intervention dynamics.

Despite lack of initial formal authorization of the war, the Bush administration set its sights on engaging directly with the UN in making the argument for intervention in Afghanistan. These arguments appealed to common discursive tropes within emancipatory liberalism that would have made sense to members of the General Assembly and the UNSC—particularly arguments that dealt with human rights and state failure, a set of policy issues the UN had been at the forefront of addressing.[89] Speaking to the Assembly on November 10, 2001, Bush made the human rights argument clear and prominent: "Women are executed in Kabul's soccer stadium. They can be beaten for wearing socks that are too thin. Men are jailed for missing prayer meetings."[90] While the speech itself often takes on a religious tone (invoking terms like "evil" and quoting scripture), and appeals to the United States' right to self-defense, it also raises a duty to intervene based on the horrors of state failure, human rights abuses, and underdevelopment. For example, near the end of the speech, Bush lays out the role of the United Nations in this fight, arguing that "the dreams of mankind are defined by liberty, the natural right to create and build and worship and live in dignity. When men and women are released from oppression and isolation, they find fulfillment and hope, and they leave poverty by the millions."[91] The conflation of several narratives and concepts—liberty, natural right, oppression, poverty, and underdevelopment—makes sense in the institutional and discursive contexts of emancipatory liberalism of that period. Emancipatory liberalism imagined the deep connection between human rights, state failure, and terror in such a way that the rhetoric of the administration at the UN was an effective way for the US to argue for the justness of its cause.

These were not just idle words or "spin." Justifications like this worked. At the very least, they impacted the deliberative context of the war at institutions like the United Nations. UN Secretary General Kofi Annan made similar arguments about the duty to intervene in Afghanistan on October 8, one month before the US address to the UN, arguing that not only did the US have a right to intervene based on self-defense, but that institutions like the UN had a duty to provide aid, humanitarian assistance, and actively promote a representative government in Afghanistan.[92] Annan's Nobel Prize address one month later would draw on similar themes about liberty, underdevelopment, and terror in ways similar to Bush's argument. While the speech itself had as its aim to cast light on the need to "fight poverty, prevent conflict, and cure disease," Afghanistan is mentioned five separate times in the speech. Afghanistan became, following September 11, the dominant mythscape for the realization of emancipatory liberal aims.

Identity politics built upon emancipatory discourses also framed the relationships between nation-builders and local actors after the initial intervention. States often disagreed, however, about the efforts of nation building in Afghanistan. The reason for this has to do with the broad goals of post-interventionary efforts, which focused their attention on the wholesale reconstruction of the Afghani governing apparatus. Emancipatory liberal goals associated with development, "curing" state failure, and resolving human rights abuses were operationalized in a variety of ways, often resulting in NATO allies working at cross-purposes. In short, emancipatory aims were so broad in their goals of reconstructing a failed state like Afghanistan that NATO operations in the country have been characterized with confusion. One particularly strong example of this was the implementation of Provincial Reconstruction Teams (PRTs), which were designed as civil-military units that had as their primary goals the penetration of government authority from the center into the frontiers of the country. PRTs were put under the remit of individual NATO countries, however, who had varied aims associated with reconstruction. Institutional involvement, in this case, resulted in diverse outcomes because different countries had different interpretations of post-intervention goals.[93]

While institutions like the UN affected the way that justifications were framed and articulated for the intervention in Afghanistan, institutional contexts provided schema for the operations on the ground. The primary structural component of UN involvement in peacebuilding was in the form of the United Nations Assistance Mission in Afghanistan (UNAMA), which was established on March 28, 2002, with the aim of assisting in building a lasting peace and infrastructure in the country. The authorizing resolution for the Mission lays out several of the same themes developed in the connection between state failure, human rights, and development by applying them to the political situation in Afghanistan. For example, the institution would be based on the principles of democratic and local governance in the post-intervention setting, with the condition that such governance "contribute[d] to the maintenance of a secure environment and demonstrate[d] respect for human rights."[94] From the beginning of UN involvement in peacebuilding, the connection between these ideas built the bases of on the ground operations. Existing discourses developed in the literatures and policy discussions about state failure and human rights found their way into official UN policy in Afghanistan.

In the context of post-intervention dynamics, the coalition forces deployed a variety of expert knowledges that helped to constitute administrative and peacebuilding operations on the ground after the initial invasion. One of these initiatives was known as the "Human Terrain Systems" project, which was an attempt to help commanders and policy makers better interface with the Afghan people. The deployment of academic anthropologists into the field had its basis in understandings about the emancipatory mission in Afghanistan, and particularly in the way that anthropologists might provide insight into local dynamics—especially local cultures, practices, and social structures—in a way that might better help the military in its peacekeeping operations. The military itself believed that this would appeal to domestic US audiences. As one anthropologist, who was opposed to the program, pointed out, the program was but an example of "a propaganda tool for convincing the American public—especially those with liberal tendencies—that the US-led occupations of Iraq and Afghanistan were benevolent missions [. . .]. It appeared to demonstrate how US forces were engaged in a kinder, gentler form of occupation."[95]

While the Human Terrain Systems project was dismantled in 2015,[96] it represented two crucial ways that emancipatory discourses, expertise, and post-intervention peacebuilding intersected during the Afghanistan War. First, it was built on a set of assumptions based in a liberal orientalism—that the Afghan people were so fundamentally different than Western liberal citizens that a "translation" process would be necessary. Bringing in anthropologists could give soldiers and administrators a way to understand a vastly different Other. Second, it illustrated an attempt to paint the intervention itself as a humanitarian mission, aimed at saving the people of Afghanistan through nation building and development. The role of anthropologists operated as a way to demonstrate—both for the American public, and in the mind of the post-intervention administrators—that the intervention required an interfacing with the local population. After all, that population is who the interveners are serving, helping, pulling out of the wretches of state failure and desperation.

Justification for war, and the deployment of violence on the ground in a peacebuilding setting, was not without its critics. In the US and Europe, even alternative currents in liberal thinking questioned the veracity of emancipatory claims that violence was the only answer against the enemies of a modern liberal world order. Libertarians, like the Cato Institute's John Mueller, took particular aim at the Afghanistan War and the larger context of the "War on Terror" as a pretext to attack liberties rather than spread them. Mueller argued, for example, that the War on Terror is an overreaction, committing Americans to war, and also using fear to gain support for the taking away of civil liberties.[97] This sentiment was echoed by members of the Libertarian Party itself. One prominent instance was public condemnation of the Obama administration's justifications for escalating the war via troop surge strategies in 2009. Wes Benedict, the Executive Director of the Libertarian Party, issued a press release that compared Obama's policy to his predecessor's, and argued that he was fulfilling the wishes of conservative media voices like Rush Limbaugh in escalating the war; Benedict tied the escalation directly to conservativism, calling Obama's liberal credentials into question.[98]

Resistance was not limited to contrary imaginings of liberal world order. Resistance was also a part of the politics "on the ground." Political actors, insurgents, and intellectuals in Afghanistan mounted ideational offenses against the

US-led coalition's intervention in the country. One outspoken example of such resistance came from women's movements inside Afghanistan, which rejected the premises of both the intervention itself as well as the motives couched in liberal human rights discourses. One such organization, the Revolutionary Association of the Women of Afghanistan (RAWA), made these objections clear with direct opposition to the war, including threats to sue the US government over the unauthorized use of a photograph owned by RAWA. The group's concern was that the replacement of the Taliban with a new government—and especially the involvement of the Northern Alliance in postwar settlement—would be just as bad for women as the former government.[99] While often not existing at the apex of debates about Afghanistan, such arguments (resistances) to dominant narratives about intervention and war in Afghanistan to nation-build as well as root out terrorists were vibrant, and offered a powerful alternative to the arguments made by emancipatory liberals.

These attempts at resisting dominant narratives of the intervention were disciplined by emancipatory discourses. Emancipatory liberal discourses challenged the legitimacy of discourses from Afghanistan itself, arguing that certain views of "emancipation" were the wrong interpretation of liberty. The issue of the treatment of women and girls is a prime example of this delegitimation. One common rhetorical trope was simply to ignore nuanced arguments about women's freedom made by groups like RAWA, and instead construct the alternative argument as simply the rejection of women's rights altogether. In lauding the successes of the Afghanistan intervention on the rights of women and girls, US Senator Hillary Clinton framed the "critics" as arguing "that to promote equal rights for women and a role for women in Afghan government and society amounts to cultural imperialism [. . .]."[100] This was certainly not the argument of other critics, like RAWA, who believed that the intervention did not provide the tools necessary for women's rights to be realized. Emancipatory liberalism used strategies of integration and exclusion in order to draw and police the boundaries of legitimate political discourse in relation to the Afghanistan conflict.

Afghanistan is a telling case for this period. Interventions like the 2003 invasion of Iraq mirrored, in their justifications and on the ground political dynamics, emancipatory discourses of the post–Cold War period. Even deployments of force that were decidedly illiberal used emancipatory liberal vocabularies as a way to justify intervention. This happened in the 2014 Russian invasion of Ukraine, which provides a fascinating glimpse at the ways these discourses became hegemonic both within and outside of liberal world order.

CHAPTER SIX

The crisis in Ukraine began in November 2014, when the president of Ukraine, Viktor Yanukovych, ceased the implementation of an agreement with the European Union (EU) that promised closer integration. This prompted widespread protests, leading to the eventual ousting of Yanukovych on February 22, 2014.[101] Social unrest in pro-Yanukovych areas of the country—particularly in Crimea—began following the former president's escape from Ukraine, setting the stage for Russia to take advantage of simultaneous social upheaval and pro-Russian sentiment.[102]

Russian intervention comprised two main parts. The first was intervention in, and annexation of, Crimea. This was the function of both internal armed groups in the area as well as the alleged intervention of unmarked Russian special operations forces. The latter overtook the Crimean parliament building, leading to the announcement of the Crimean political leadership that it would hold a public referendum on whether it should secede from the Ukraine and become part of the Russian Federation; this referendum was passed in mid-March 2014.[103] Second was Russian intervention in the Donbass region of Ukraine, where Russian paramilitary—making up, by some accounts, a majority of the combatants—and anti-government groups engaged in a separatist conflict against the Ukrainian government.[104] On August 22, Russian troops directly invaded Ukraine.[105]

Like liberal states, Russia rationalized/justified intervention in ways that meshed with the emancipatory political culture of the post–Cold War era. This was primarily through focusing on elements of state instability and nation building. President Vladimir Putin, for example, framed the intervention in terms of instituting stability in the Ukraine, and guarding against the problems of state failure. As the *Wall Street Journal* notes, "Mr. Putin claimed there is no legitimate authority in Ukraine, which puts those living in the predominantly ethnic-Russian region under threat."[106] Russian Foreign Minister Sergey Lavrov seconded this justification, suggesting Russian occupation "until the normalization of the political situation."[107] Like nation building by NATO in Bosnia and Afghanistan, Russia envisioned its project as responding to the potential for state failure—whether this was a warranted concern or not.

In terms of identities and goals, the Russian government explicitly placed itself within the identity of Western liberal states—that is, having an emancipatory goal for the Ukraine. Putin's government used language of humanitarianism and positive liberty to frame its goals and aims in the Ukraine, appropriating language from existing liberal discourses. For instance, Russian Ambassador to the United Nations Vitaly Churkin stated, "The United States do not have a monopoly on humanism, you know? We are all human. So if you are trying to question our humanism, I would resent that."[108] This appeal to the alleviation of suffering through intervention and nation building is a common theme in Western interventions during the post–Cold War period, and the Russian government closely connected its own goals and identities as part of an international society through an appeal to those values.

Though Russia used emancipatory liberal vocabularies to justify the intervention, the justificatory discourse simultaneously positioned Russian intervention against the West. For example, Putin noted, in response to proposed sanctions by Europe:

> What are the so-called European values then? Support for an armed coup, suppression of opponents with armed forces—so these are "European values"? I believe our colleagues should be reminded of their own ideals.[109]

Rather than aligning himself with "European values," Putin simultaneously draws on emancipatory vocabularies that Western states will recognize—and that appear legitimate—while at the same time drawing stark lines between a Western world order and a Russian one.

Conclusion

This chapter has argued that emancipatory liberalism after the Cold War focused its sights on human rights and state failure. Both of these concerns were tied to an emerging discourse centered on "terror" as a threat to a global liberal world order. Two trends were central here. In the first place was the merging of a failed-state discourse with a human-rights discourse. This discourse positioned the identities of Western liberal states as fundamentally opposed to other states that did not reflect liberal democratic institutions. These arguments were expressed earliest in social science literature on political development beginning in the 1990s, and found their way into both the policy making realm and the public sphere. The case of the Afghanistan War exemplifies how these discourses intersected with violence and intervention; states used justifications based on the connection between failed states and human rights that were developed throughout the post–Cold War period.

In the second place, the concept of "terrorism," though of much older vintage than "state failure," came to characterize the new enemies of liberal world order. Rather than overturning existing discursive tropes, however, the discourse of terrorism would become closely integrated into concerns about state failure, capacity, and human rights. The image of the terrorist, and the way this image was contrasted with the image of the Western liberal individual in particular, became a site for new ways of writing war. The Afghanistan case illustrates these processes on the ground as well. Afghanistan was framed as a fight against terror, and terrorists. A fight that was inseparable from other aims like nation building and protecting human rights.

The final chapter of the book takes the lessons of the empirical chapters and develops an alternative theorization of an international liberal order—one that is characterized by minimalism—to provide the bases for rethinking liberalism and its relationship to the use of force in international society.

CHAPTER SEVEN

Conclusion

Toward a Minimalist Liberalism

The Scarecrow: *There goes some of me again.*
Dorothy: *Does it hurt you?*
The Scarecrow: *Oh, no. I just keep picking it up and putting it back in again.*

—*The Wizard of Oz* (MGM, 1939)

THE STORY OF INTERNATIONAL LIBERALISM'S development is a dual one. On the one hand, liberalism has contributed to mechanisms of collective action, cooperation, and a sense of community that is unparalleled in international history. On the other hand, liberalism has a relationship to the use of force. It discursively mobilizes nations to arms, and it (re)produces patterns and practices of conflict, violence, and intervention. International liberalism represents not just a salvation from the "barbarism" of earlier ages, but a tremendous hope about its ability to emancipate the world from what ails it. Just like the Scarecrow's continual act of reassembling himself when his straw comes loose, liberal optimism (since the mid-nineteenth century) has seen nothing, including its own "dismantling," as beyond its emancipatory potential.

This concluding chapter wraps up the book on two fronts. First, I address the general implications of this study for the field of IR theory as an empirical enterprise. This book, I argue, holds general implications for the way IR deals with ideas and discourse, as well as the study of violence and military intervention. Second, in providing a critical history that shows liberalism's connection to international violence, the book has thus far left unanswered: what is to be done? The final part of this chapter briefly elaborates the starting point for an alternative—what I have termed "minimalism," based on an understanding of global democracy as a "consensual democracy" grounded in pragmatist democratic theory.

A Critical History of Liberal Violence: Confronting International Relations Theory

In this book, I have argued that the development of international liberalism, and particularly the emancipatory liberalism examined herein, is closely connected to violence in international politics. I have shown that changes in the practices of violence and intervention waged by liberal states are intimately connected to the historical trajectory of emancipatory liberalism. This argument holds several contributions to both the study of the development of international liberalism as well as the study of violence within the context of IR. Though this book develops a historical narrative about the connection between discourses of emancipatory liberalism and interventionism, force, and violence, it holds several broader implications for the endeavor of IR theory.

Research within the vein of social constructivism focuses on the ways that ideas constitute social reality in international politics.[1] In particular, constructivist research has tended to focus on the role of social norms for creating the possibility for state action in IR.[2] Constructivist understandings of norms, however, are conceptually limited in examining the norm-as-consensus.[3] For example, normative agreement about the nonuse of nuclear weapons creates the conditions whereby states consider their use "taboo," and therefore do not consider them as a tactical option.[4] The present study rejects this standard conceptualization of norms in constructivist research, and instead focuses on the varied ways that discourses are integrated into international society in different periods of time. All four periods under study show that consensus in the ideational politics of international liberalism is hard to find. Though we can talk about broader cultures of emancipatory liberalism that structured the possible iterations of discourse, there has always been normative contestation.

A broadly genealogical approach, as employed here, allows for a macro-historical study of the development of emancipatory liberalism, examining not just the periods of relative consensus, but also the ways in which ideas about liberty in international politics have been sites of conflict, competition, and debate. As I argue in chapter 5, this conflict, particularly between development liberals and anti-totalitarian liberals, had an impact on the way that intervention practices and patterns were configured, especially in the face of the increased importance of media coverage of military intervention. Additionally, a discursive approach to ideas challenges contemporary understandings of the relationship between ideology, norms, and state action by situating norms within the broader political and social context from which they arise: namely, the production of distinct discursive systems that affect the structure of social action for states. Thus, though there were few international norms that prescribed appropriate behavior for intervention practices in the empire period, a common discourse about civilizational development patterned practices of violence in ways that were comprehensible and defensible from the perspective of state actors.

This book, further, touches on aspects of the institutionalist literature in international politics. Chapter 2 argues that one of the pathways connecting emancipatory liberalism to practices of violence and intervention relates to the way that discourses interact with institutions. Chapter 4, for instance, demonstrates this in relation to the League of Nations mandate system, and how it affected the way that states intervened in the periphery for the purpose of civilizational development. This mechanism contributes not only to our understanding of institutional design and change—that is, a historical institutionalist approach to international politics—but also to understanding the effects that institutions have on the use of force more generally. Much institutionalist literature focuses on the way that liberal institutions restrain the use of force;[5] yet, this is a complicated relationship, as the study of the US-led intervention in Afghanistan in chapter 6 demonstrates.

Finally, this study contributes to classic insights of IR theory about the relationship between morality, power, and international politics. In making the argument that discourses about liberal values and morality have an impact on the way that states exercise power and deploy violence, this book continues a long tradition of IR theory that is theoretically and empirically skeptical of a triumphalist liberal internationalist narrative about the development of international society. Reinhold Niebuhr argued that "politics will, to the end of history, be an area where conscience and power meet, where the ethical and coercive factors of human life will interpenetrate and work out their tentative and uneasy compromises."[6] This "interpenetration" is precisely what this study has demonstrated in a genealogical analysis of the concomitant evolution of a liberal morality in international society, and the changing patterns/practices of transformative intervention.

E. H. Carr, too, highlights this issue in his own contention that utopianism, by nature, tries to disconnect from the political, but in doing so tries to make politics conform to those very utopian understandings.[7] The agents of international liberalism have consistently put their visions of an alternative "free" world order as an aim that is outside the political—an aim that is endowed with a higher moral universalism. The use of force is the operationalization of a moral framework to re-create a world order that fits within a dominant discourse about emancipation. In this sense, the irony of liberalism's claim to independence from the political is simultaneously representative of the most political act there is: the distinction of "us" and "them."[8]

As a study focusing on violence and the use of force, this book also contributes to a growing literature on the violent foreign imposition of domestic institutions[9] by forwarding new mechanisms for understanding historic changes in the practices of such interventions, as well as literatures on peace building.[10] While institutionalization has become an important factor in the study of intervention politics, its position as an element that mediates between broader discourses and intervention is one that has not been thoroughly explored in studies of foreign imposition.

A discursive approach contributes to the theoretical study of violence and intervention in two additional ways. First, it provides a more precise theorization of the way that ideas affect such interventions. Though much of the literature on foreign imposition of domestic institutions focuses on these two factors, many questions are left unanswered about where such beliefs come from, and about the cohesiveness of ideology.[11] Methodologically, a genealogical focus on intervention practice overcomes many of the issues that earlier studies encounter in addressing the phenomenon of violent interventions. A "sovereignty bias" in the intervention literature has caused a general neglect of the role that imperialism has played in the history and change of intervention practices in the modern world—a fact that calls into question certain fundamental claims about the spatial and ideational causes of intervention.[12] Though the Cold War is consistently a focus of the intervention literature, critical historical analysis allows us to see the radical differences between the Cold War period and others. Furthermore, though the post–Cold War period is seen as qualitatively new in relation to intervention, it carries along similar patterns related to development politics that stretch back to the mid-nineteenth century. Genealogical study allows us to look at broad patterns, and to see the substantive changes and continuity in the discursive politics of intervention

A final benefit of the study to the examination of practices of violence is a call for IR theory to engage more closely with political theory in the exploration of the causes, consequences, and normative value of military intervention. Literature in political theory has begun to develop such arguments about humanitarian intervention,[13] and critical literature has theoretically engaged with the problems of violence and interventionism;[14] however, this study combines insights from both fields with the aim of developing a sustained analysis of military intervention patterns and their connection with political, social, and policy thought since the mid-nineteenth century.

How should IR scholars continue to study this connection between the rise of liberalism and the use of violence, while avoiding the problems associated with a triumphalism that characterizes existing narratives? There is much more intellectual work to do. Further research should examine the ways that liberalism and force are related to one another. First, we might ask, How has liberalism informed the way that states have waged war? This literature is growing, albeit at the margins—and often as an appendix to democratic peace theory.[15] Part of this is a function of the only recent attention that mainstream IR theory has given to the importance of ideology. But, more than anything else, it is a function of the influence of triumphalism in liberal international theory. While intervention is an ideal topic for such research, great power war, intrastate violence, and other forms of force could also provide promising avenues for study.

Second, in what ways is liberalism connected to other forms of political violence? The neoliberalism literature, in particular, has addressed this issue from the perspective of "structural violence,"[16] and security studies has investigated how democracies, particularly, use covert force.[17] Drone strikes, torture, and other forms of violence are worth studying in more detail in the context of a liberalizing international society. Third, in what ways do liberal vocabularies affect processes of securitization?[18] Though some studies exist in this vein, more genealogical work in the field of securitization studies might lead to a greater understanding of the role that liberal discourses play in the use of force. Concepts like "civilization," "totalitarianism," "terror," and "state failure" are historically important in relation to war and intervention. Locating these ideas within the context of liberal discursive structures gives us insight into the ways that words and ideas affect international violence.

An Alternative: Pragmatism, Global Consensual Democracy, and a New "Minimalism"

Building on a critical approach to the origins of liberal violence in world politics, how do we deal with the problem of violence from a normative perspective? In developing a critical history of emancipatory liberalism, and outlining its historic connection to violence and intervention, I argue for a rethinking of international political theory from the lens of a pragmatic, consensual understanding of global democracy—what I term "minimalism."

Pragmatism's general critique of liberalism is one that challenges both its understanding of the self, and the way that the individual relates to society. Most particularly, this critique can be divided into two strands. On the one hand, pragmatism challenges paternalism—the idea that some autonomy should be given up by an actor for her own good[19]—through an appeal to consensual democracy. On the other hand, pragmatism focuses on remaking the liberal subject in the context of small communities, striking a balance between a radical individualism and a deep social embeddedness.

If pragmatist social thought has a running thematic, it is related to that of *consensual democracy*. By *consensual democracy*, I mean the development of a socially constituted "process" of democracy, whereby agonism and conflict lead to the construction, and defense, of a common good.[20] This is in contrast to two alternative visions of democracy. The first is an institutionalist understanding of liberal democracy as a means to constrain individual passions (that is, as a constitutional mechanism to protect a society from the excesses of individualism).[21] The second is a poststructural conception of democracy as a "denaturalization of everyday understandings of space, place, and nature."[22] In contrast to the former, consensual democracy sees democracy as processes of social action, constitutive of the self and a democratic society. In contrast to the latter, consensual democracy sees the aims of a radical, agonistic democracy as a means to develop a *consensus* surrounding the public good, rather than viewing the deconstruction of the good as an end in and of itself.

Pragmatism, and particularly pragmatist theories of action, focus our attention on the social nature of human relationships; this carries over into a social theory of active democratic participation. George Herbert Mead's understanding of a democratic society as a communicative process "of putting one's self in the place of the other person's attitude" conceptualizes consensual democracy as a form of social interactionism.[23] Jürgen Habermas's communicative action, Axel Honneth's "mutual recognition," and Dewey's focus on developing the self in relation to community are also illustrative of this action-centered understanding of democracy.[24] Pragmatism's democratic theory is arrived at through a close engagement with two social-theoretic concerns shared by its thinkers. The first is the social construction of the self through interaction. The second is its mirror image: a society that is a product of the interaction, communication, and negotiation of identities between its constitutive members.[25] For pragmatists, democracy is the means by which the self can self-actualize within the context of an interdependent society.[26]

Furthermore, this understanding of consensual democracy is an agonistic one.[27] Rather than highlighting the social aspect of democracy to simply demonstrate the process whereby multiple selves come to consensus within the context of interdependence, pragmatist accounts of democracy highlight the role that conflict plays in the development of the public good. Honneth, in discussing the social "struggle for recognition," argues that the struggle moves community from underdevelopment to more mature relationships.[28] The maturity of a consensual democracy lies in the ability for conflict to result in the development of a more democratized society that is able to reconcile its differences through a communicative process of recognition and respect. Richard Bernstein, too, highlights this agonism in his "engaged fallibilistic pluralism," which is a "willing[ness] to listen to others without denying or suppressing the otherness of the other." Social conflict, for pragmatists, is a key component of a robust democratic process.[29]

These interventions take apart paternalism in two ways. First, a social conception of democratic action is one that is egalitarian and places agency in the context of the community. As Michael Barnett notes, paternalism in liberal theory is based on a desire, even a duty, to engage without consent in affecting an agent's freedom, power, and personal integrity.[30] For pragmatists, the conflict between self-realization and community, which is embodied in paternalism's function of determining "what is best" for individuals within the community, is overcome through the democratization of modern society. The pragmatist understanding of democracy, then, values democracy as a "higher spiritual expression in which the individual realizes himself in others through that which he does as peculiar to himself."[31] Second, pragmatists point to the agonistic features of democracy that encourage conflict as a key component of creativity and recognition, which paternalism impedes through a limitation on choice. Honneth and John Farrell develop such a point at length in a reconstruction of Dewey's democratic philosophy by suggesting that:

> Dewey goes so far as to conceive of the process of public will formation as a large-scale experimental process in which, according to the criteria of the rationality of past decisions, we continually decide anew how state institutions are to be specifically organized and how they are to relate to one another in terms of their jurisdiction.[32]

This social feature of democracy developed within the pragmatist tradition connects both republican and proceduralist conceptions of radical democracy by focusing on the ways that communities can come together in the public sphere to govern themselves through debate and civil conflict.[33] This is an argument directly against liberal paternalism in relation to the way that interests are constituted. In a radical democratic conception, like Dewey's and Honneth's, communities in an agonistic public sphere decide upon the common good, and collective interests, through a communicative and collaborative process of experimentation. It is a form of collective, creative, governance. Paternalism, however, interferes with this process in two ways.

First, it can (potentially) remove decision-making power from those whose interests are affected. Humanitarians, for example, have been charged with not acting in the interests of what their beneficiaries want, and instead intervening based on apparently self-evident and obvious needs.[34] Second, paternalism may affect individuals "whose interests are not in question."[35] In a radical democratic process, the negotiation of policy through a communicative and agonistic public sphere is one in which the community comes to a determination of its collective interest. Individual autonomy is developed in the context of community. The problem of paternalism's distribution of interests is overcome in a pragmatist conception, because of its understanding of democracy as "a deep sense of the realization of the other in one's self."[36]

In short, pragmatist thought carries within it—from its social theoretic foundations—an advocacy for consensual democracy. Furthermore, such a conception is a critique of liberal paternalism. The question remains, however: what does a radical democratic community look like? How does pragmatism overcome the problem of democracy's potential erasure of the individual through a focus on the community? On the face of it, pragmatists seem to disagree on how to resolve the latter issue. Dewey, for example, places a large emphasis on the community's role in self-realization, while theorists like Richard Rorty see this as a way of violating an individual's negative liberty. As one prominent pragmatist suggests, any attempt at a conception of positive liberty in relation to participation would be antithetical to democracy: imposing a single view of self-actualization on a citizen without recognizing the potential plurality of understandings about personal meaning.[37] This contradiction can be resolved, however—as others have argued—through "splitting the difference" between Dewey's communitarianism and Rorty's individualism by focusing on small democratic communities.[38]

What is a "small community"? Small communities have two features. First, small communities are arenas where true interpersonal interaction can take place in a way that provides for meaningful deliberation, conflict, and cooperation. Second, and in mirror image, small communities must be networked, and influential, so that they can be embedded and have an effect on much larger social and political processes.[39] Richard Shusterman uses the idea of the university as one such example of a small community, but this concept might be extended to other areas of social organization as well. For example, associational life may be a form of small community. While bowling leagues might not fulfill the "influential" test,[40] NGOs with well-funded, and well-respected, advocacy campaigns might. Regional deliberative bodies, too, might be considered small communities.

The idea of a global public, which is present in much of the IR literature on public spheres, is problematic from an ethical perspective. While for Aristotle, the politics of the public square represented a small community, the "global citizenry" of billions, or an exclusive sphere of the elite,[41] does not fulfill the pragmatic vision of a small-community conception of the public sphere. Where is the university community equivalent in global democratic politics? Nancy Fraser, in a perceptive agenda-setting piece, asks us to start thinking about how transnational and global public spheres might constitute a new realm of consideration for the problems of deliberative democracy: "What sorts of changes (institutional, economic, cultural and communicative) would be required even to imagine a genuinely critical and democratizing role for transnational public spheres under current conditions?"[42] Fraser does not flesh out answers to these questions; however, our consideration of consensual democracy on a global scale should take these sorts of questions seriously.

The best way to conceptualize this issue is by rethinking the global public sphere not just as multiple, networked, and overlapping public spheres. Rather, conceptualizing the global public as a series of agonisms across micro-communities moves us away from an understanding of the public sphere as norm-creating to debate-creating.[43] Such a disaggregation of the public sphere from a site of consensus to one of agonism does two things. First, it creates a space for continual dissent and debate. Democracy is not a tool *just* for consensus; it is a method by which claims are articulated and battled over. It is an arena wherein the fundamental struggle of recognition is played out in an iterative process. Interests are defined, battle lines are drawn, and meaningful debate about identities, ideas, and global processes can be developed.

Second, it preserves the self in the face of a developing world society. If Rorty was concerned with the threat to individual liberty that a "bourgeois liberalism" posed, this issue is magnified in the conceptualization of a global public, where the individual not only has to surrender pieces of his/her identity to a collective, but to the whole of humanity. Small communities are a way to reconcile these issues by disaggregating the public sphere into arenas where individual interests can interact with fundamental questions about the global good(s).

A key aspect of this rethinking of the liberal subject that an engagement with pragmatism allows is an appreciation for and concern with the problem of human agency. Agency is deeply intertwined with both consensual democracy *and* small communities. Anthony Lang defines agency as "the status of individuals in a public space that gives them the ability to engage each other."[44] There are two aspects of this definition that deserve further elaboration.

First, individuals are agents. Even when we consider states to be a proxy for individuals, states are—at most—*collective* agents.[45] Focusing on individuals as agents, endowed with rights and responsibilities, reveals the problems with liberal paternalism most clearly. A truly consensual democracy that places the deliberative process of global democracy in the hands of a global citizenry is built on an understanding of political actors as autonomous, thinking, but also socially embedded subjects. "Admitting the importance of self-hood and agency," Colin Wight writes, "does not preclude the fact that structural factors often impact human action in profound ways."[46] What it does do, though, is focus our attention on the fact that international politics is the governing of humans, actors, agency, and subjects for whom paternalism, transformation, and imposition are not always well suited.

Second, the concept of a public space is an important component of an agentic understanding of global democracy. Small communities—the deep recursivity between the autonomous self and the socially embedded self—provide such a space. Large communities are aggregated at such a high level that the ability of agents to engage effectively is limited simply by numbers. For example, the ability of a single individual, or group, to exercise sufficient influence in a broader global public sphere is difficult. Studies that have demonstrated the normative power of individuals and organizations, in fact, have shown that these efforts are often most effective within the context of smaller groups. Martha Finnemore details this in her study of the role that conferences played in changing norms of intervention surrounding sovereign debt.[47] Jennifer Mitzen, too, has shown through a study of the European concert system that public debate, and the arrival of consensus in the context of a small community, created the conditions for a long peace in the nineteenth century.[48]

A focus on agency in the milieu of small communities and consensual democratic politics is a step in resolving significant global political issues. First, it returns the "political" to international politics. Constructivists have, for over two decades now, shown that an empirical examination of agency in world politics can help us return a study of global phenomena to a study of "politics." Finnemore, for instance, argues that "[constructivists] must also focus on the origins and dynamics of [. . .] norms, a focus which inevitably takes us into the realm of agents."[49] Second, it gives voice to subaltern, or otherwise marginalized, claims. Third, it re-centers our understanding of global democracy from its institutional context to its participants. Norms and institutions are not the only things that matter in thinking about the global public sphere; the voices that participate within the context of global communities also matter.

Following from this general critique, pragmatic democracy offers three interventions in the realm of international theory, and particularly in the realms of international security, conflict, and violence. The first of these is an interrogation of liberal violence, challenging the paternalism of liberal interventionism and demanding mechanisms of international and transnational accountability. The second is a conception of global democracy in the context of small, agonistic, public spheres. Third—and perhaps most ambitiously—the pragmatic critique of liberalism offers a point of departure for a new conceptualization of liberal world order through the idea of a "minimalist" international liberalism: a liberalism that is democratic, pluralist, and embracing of difference.

As this book has shown, liberalism has historically been closely related to practices of violence in international society. This is related to a propensity for international liberal orders to be founded upon discourses, identities, and cultures related to paternalism and positive liberty. The dichotomy between reasoned European states and the "barbarians" of the periphery during the age of imperialism was constituted by liberal discourses, which constructed roles for European states to use force for the purported aim of civilizational development (see chapter 3)—this is evident, for instance, in the way that British officials imagined their roles in Iraq in the 1920s as a paternalist endeavor through which the Iraqis would eventually be prepared for self-government after a period of British tutelage. Variation in intervener identity conceptions are a result of the way in which liberal ideology grants certain rights and responsibilities on intervening states. This is a process whereby citizenship in international society is historically (re)defined vis-à-vis changing understandings of international liberalism.

These discourses of liberal paternalism are prominent in the twentieth and twenty-first centuries as well—old wine in new bottles, as chapters 4 through 6 demonstrate. For example, US intervention in the Dominican Republic was made meaningful as a means to prevent the further spread of totalitarian political order into the Western Hemisphere. This affects the way the moral function of force is imagined by first constituting the structure of international liberal political order, and then constructing the dilemmas that intervention is tasked with resolving. International liberalism, in this sense, creates a vision of international order, associated disorder, and the means of resolving the conflict between the two. This vision is often constructed around a paternalism that—though working in the name of a liberal international society—is anti-democratic.

The most glaring problem with a paternalist international liberalism is the lack of accountability that its agents are held to. As Barnett notes, "the final characteristic of a strong paternalism is the lack of accountability mechanisms that give local populations some way to restrain the actions of paternalizers."[50] Paternalism by its nature is not accountable, because the very premise of the idea—that some should be able to make decisions for others in the name of "their own good"—requires relaxing standards of consent, accountability, and democratic decision making. This did not go unnoticed in modern political thought, with theorists like J. S. Mill arguing forcefully that interfering with someone's liberty "for his own good, either moral or physical, is not a sufficient warrant for the exercise of power."[51] This form of power, however, is the basis for the justification of many forms of force, including military intervention, annexation, and a myriad of violence in between.

A pragmatic, consensual-democratic critique of international paternalism attacks this practice of power in three primary ways. First, these practices lack accountability to the people whose interests are affected. This propensity to favor great power, or corporate/donor interests is apparent in the literature on intervention. For example, the interests of Western liberal states and the interests of postconflict societies do not always align. Oftentimes, liberalizing interventions in such areas can exacerbate existing conflicts and create new ones.[52] Furthermore, peacebuilding interventions operate within ideological environments that are not always in sync with facts on the ground. The ideological underpinnings of intervention in the Democratic Republic of Congo, for instance, "made it possible for foreign interveners to ignore the micro-level tensions that often jeopardized macro-level settlements."[53] International paternalism often ignores the interests of the individuals they aim to "help"; any consensual-democratic understanding of global citizenship should be sharply critical of the lack of local agency in intervention settings.

Second, pragmatic understandings of consensual democracy alert us to the problems in liberal paternalist violence in denying the legitimacy of the "struggle for recognition." Liberal international theory is premised on the idea that the struggle for recognition is vital to the creation of global political community; however, the lack of democratic agency that individuals often have in relation to intervention politics stifles this political process of recognition. Alexander Wendt, for example, sees international history as moving toward a world state based on the assumption that the struggle for recognition is creating the context for a global conception of rights.[54] But such a theory is problematic when recognizing that the forces of liberalism supposedly driving this struggle are its primary obstacles. In postwar Iraq, for example, journalist George Packer quotes an Iraqi citizen: "[The Americans] are not caring much for the simple Iraqi citizen. They care for a chief of a tribe here, a religious man here, a militia man here, head of a party there."[55] If America, the hegemon of a global liberal order, knew what was best for the Iraqis, it certainly did not seem as if the latter were active participants in a deliberative democratic process.

If international liberalism has paternalist strands, the way that this is executed is not only an "inside-out" problem of democratic accountability. It is also a "top-down" problem.[56] The way that force is used in international society is increasingly democratizing due to normative pressures for multilateralism.[57] This process of democratization, however, opens the sphere of debate to only a select few—namely, international governmental organizations, highly influential NGOs that can shame state actors into certain policies, and officials from powerful states who may have a normative effect on state policies. Though the liberalization of world politics is supposedly leading to a more cosmopolitan international system, much of the influence that weaker actors have had on foreign policy has given way to global institutional structures; international democracy suffers from an elite problem.

A rethinking of global deliberative bodies from the perspective of "small communities" leads to two propositions. First, smaller deliberative bodies allow for more sustained and interpersonal debate and engagement. Some scholars have argued that large international institutions are heavily socialized and interpersonal, but there are limits to this. Persuasion and socialization are most likely, and most effective, in institutions that have small memberships.[58] More than persuasion, the processes of debate, argumentation, and agonistic engagement may be more effective when membership is small. One contemporary example of the failure of larger organizations to deliberate with effectiveness (though not an example from the realm of violence/security) is climate change. According to the World Economic Forum, climate change governance has largely failed because large institutions do not lack a universal legitimacy from the wide range of actors who are affected by proposed policies.[59] This can create one of the greatest barriers to global democracy: a failure to engage in the first place.

Second, deliberations are more effective, and more productive, when those who are engaged share common lifeworlds, or at least (as John Rawls would put it) a common background political culture.[60] Not only are smaller communities important, but these communities must share something fundamental about values for debate to even happen. The climate change example is important here: different states have vastly different issues, histories, and legacies related to the use of fossil fuels. A disaggregating of climate change institutions may provide a more productive first cut for getting certain interest blocs to debate these issues. Democracy is served best by debate; that is hard to accomplish when you cannot begin a conversation.

One way of thinking about small communities in world politics is to consider the importance/effectiveness of regional organizations and regional deliberative bodies. There is an emerging literature in IR on regional organizations and institutions. Peter Katzenstein, for instance, argues that regionalism makes a consideration of a broader global governance system doomed to failure. As he states, these smaller normative orders "are unlikely to be assimilated fully into one normative global order."[61] This disaggregation of institutions into small communities is precisely because of the fact that there is no single global background culture from which democratic politics can launch. Katzenstein illustrates this point clearly in arguing that global legal norms "will remain politically contested."[62] When norms about procedure become sites of disagreement, then where is the space for global debate about substantive, issue-based, problems? And what if these issues are life or death issues of war vs. peace?

Minimalism: Linking Pluralism, Anti-Paternalism, and an Agonistic Global Public

While international liberalism is often a universal, paternalistic, and positive liberalism, another tradition offers an alternative liberal ethic in international politics. This tradition helps to answer the question of how we can develop a liberal international society while minimalizing the violence and force that is associated with an emancipatory vision.

Minimalism is a form of liberalism that is pluralistic, pragmatic, and democratic. It embraces difference and consensual democracy and recognizes the problems with universalism and paternalism. In particular, such a minimalism is one that is *radically democratic*. It is a central contention that a liberal democracy requires an understanding of liberalism that not only celebrates difference, but requires it for the creation of a world society that can stand up to the problems associated with power. If an emancipatory liberal internationalism, throughout history, is united by a relatively coherent set of principles, which—though varying in operationalization—represent an important factor in the evolution of military force, then dissent, deliberation, and defection are the only means available for challenging it.

Prototypes of minimalism have been present throughout the development of a liberal international society, and provide historical models on which to reflect.

Anti-imperialist movements in America in the late nineteenth and early twentieth centuries stressed the need for America to reject a European imperial worldview, though this was hardly a celebration of difference (see chapter 3). Pluralism during the Cold War was dissent against a development discourse, but was closely tied to emancipatory liberal concerns with totalitarianism—so much so, as chapter 5 illustrates, that the interaction between Cold War pluralism and development liberalism had causative effects on intervention. "Facts on the ground" and alternative liberal imaginaries, including the libertarian movement, in the post–Cold War era provided powerful critiques of intervention and state building, though such lines would often become blurred in practice (see chapter 6). Minimalism is a utopian radical democratic vision, but one that should guide a pragmatic ethics of the international. Pragmatists would recognize (as discussed above) the consensual democratic aspects of minimalism, as well as its pluralism, and focus on small communities.

There are three interventions minimalism can make in liberal international theory. First, it introduces a consensual-democratic element into liberal international theory that is often either assumed or entirely absent. While the civilizing process literature focuses on liberalizing elements in the development of international society, less emphasis is given to the importance of global democracy—defined as consistent discursive agonism and contestation—in constituting international society. Liberalism's connection to violence is one that has often occurred in the name of spreading liberty, while simultaneously being closed to vigorous contestation within the public sphere. A most striking example, in chapter 3, is the use of liberalism to justify war in the imperial periphery during the age of empire. Paternalism is a value that democracy is meant to guard against.

Second, minimalism is a way to integrate pluralism and small communities into liberal-democratic international theory. Often, pluralist critiques of liberalism happen from outside the liberal tradition, but minimalism is grounded in a value pluralism based in public-sphere engagement with the foundational principles of a liberal international society. Intervention for domestic institutional change in the name of liberalism, for example, is antithetical to pluralism. It assumes universal principles, acts upon them by using military force to establish certain governance structures, and does not consider difference in motivation and justification. This is problematic for a liberal-democratic conception of global politics.

Third, a focus on minimalism shifts our attention from a triumphalist version of international liberal society to one that shows the distinction, difference, and debate that have historically existed between protominimalisms and more emancipatory, universalist versions of international liberalism. Minimalism is not the only possible political solution to the excesses of a liberal paternalist politics. Other possibilities include the rejection of the liberal world order altogether, or a passive acceptance of the status quo. Minimalism's benefit, however, is an engagement with liberalism from the *inside*, offering a liberal-democratic alternative to an emancipatory international liberalism.

While pragmatism provides the basis of a democratic critique of a universalist, and emancipatory, international liberalism, more work is needed to develop this critique into a liberal democratic alternative that is pluralist, embraces difference, and places a premium on democratic values in the global public sphere.

Conclusion

Violence is a constitutive feature of international politics, just as it is a feature of any other social order. Much of human history can be interpreted as iterated attempts at dealing with the issues posed by violence, harm, and the use of force. This book has presented a new narrative of the history of the development of international liberalism, and its relationship to violence and intervention. In so doing, it has touched on themes that are relevant to the fields of security studies, international organization, world history, and political theory. It is with modesty—though also a sincere optimism—that I hope this research will spark further critical inquiry into the relationship between emancipatory liberalism(s) and the use of force in modern international relations.

This book began with an anecdote about Jacques-Pierre Brissot's call for war "against the enemies of humanity." As a history of liberalism's encounter with intervention demonstrates, this war has been an enduring one—one that has become enmeshed, in important ways, with a liberal international society, especially after the 1840s. While Brissot's story would end with a disillusionment with violence, and the sharp blade of a guillotine, Western liberalism continued beyond the French Revolution to profoundly shape international politics in ways that its progenitors could hardly imagine. And, though humanity has overcome the boundaries of civilizational thought, defeated the threats of "totalitarianism," and contemporaneously confronts terrorism and the abuse of human rights, the discourse and practice of liberal interventionism continues to be reshaped, repurposed, and reimagined as a means toward the end of a global political revolution.

NOTES

Chapter One

1. Whatmore, "War, Trade, and Empire," 172.
2. Whatmore, "War, Trade, and Empire," 173.
3. Fukuyama, *End of History*, xi.
4. Tesón, "Liberal Case for Humanitarian Intervention," 93–129.
5. Bayly, *Birth of the Modern World*, 439.
6. Mill, "Few Words on Non-Intervention," 368–84. For a recent consideration of Mill's arguments about intervention, see Doyle, *Question of Intervention*.
7. "Transcript: George Bush's speech on Iraq," *Guardian*, October 7, 2002, http://www.guardian.co.uk/world/2002/oct/07/usa.iraq.
8. The literature on discourse in IR is large and growing. For a taste of important contributions, see Bartelson, *Genealogy of Sovereignty*; Hansen, *Security as Practice*; P. T. Jackson, *Civilizing the Enemy*; Epstein, *Power of Words in International Relations*; and Kinsella, *Image before the Weapon*.
9. Jahn, *Liberal Internationalism*, 4.
10. Thomas, "Why Don't We Talk about 'Violence' in International Relations?," 1815.
11. For an argument about this, see Adcock, *Liberalism and the Emergence of American Political Science*.
12. Mills, *Black Rights/White Wrongs*, 12.
13. For a particularly illustrative study in this regard, see Dominco Losurdo, *Liberalism*.
14. See Mills, *Black Rights/White Wrongs* for an argument about the possibilities of reform *within* liberalism. See Mehta, *Liberalism and Empire*, for an argument about why racism, empire, and exclusion are part and parcel of the liberal project.
15. Bell, "What is Liberalism?"
16. Mehta, *Liberalism and Empire*, 46.
17. Bell, *Reordering the World*, 93.
18. Bell, *Reordering the World*, 93.
19. Morefield, *Covenants without Swords*, 16.
20. See Owen, *Liberal Peace, Liberal War*.
21. Ikenberry, *Liberal Leviathan*, 6.
22. Sørensen, *Liberal World Order in Crisis*.
23. Sørensen, *Liberal World Order in Crisis*, 5.

24. Robert Kagan's controversial book about American power's role in maintaining a global liberal order focuses on hegemony in much the same way, though with a decidedly more optimistic outlook than others. See *World America Made*.

25. Michael Hardt and Antonio Negri's work is important here. See their *Empire*, *Multitude*, and *Commonwealth*.

26. Duffield, *Global Governance and the New Wars*. See also Kaldor, *New and Old Wars*.

27. See Mueller, *Remnants of War*; and Pinker, *Better Angels of Our Nature*.

28. MacMillan, *On Liberal Peace*. The broader literature on Liberal Peace Theory often does not go as far as arguing that liberal states are necessarily less peaceful, but that liberal democracies have constructed their own zone of peace. For an overview of these arguments, see Russett and Oneal, *Triangulating Peace*.

29. Linklater, *Problem of Harm in World Politics*, 111.

30. Doyle, "Liberalism and World Politics."

31. Wendt, "Why a World State is Inevitable."

32. Thomas, "Why Don't We Talk about 'Violence' in International Relations?," 1815.

33. Campbell and Dillon's *Political Subject of Violence* is one of the few notable attempts in IR to grapple with these issues.

34. See, most notably, Wheeler, *Saving Strangers*; and Finnemore, *Purpose of Intervention*.

35. Many ways of dividing up liberalism, conceptually, have been attempted. Some have focused on the differences between liberal constitutionalism and libertarianism: see Holmes, *Passion and Constraint*. Others have addressed divisions between American liberalisms that are characterized as either a "Hebraic separatism" or a "Christian universalism": see: Hartz, *Liberal Tradition in America*; and Holland, "Hartz and Minds," 230. For a liberalism of order vs. justice, see Bull, *Anarchical Society*. For classical liberalism vs. new liberalism, see Richardson, "Contending Liberalisms." And for a liberalism of imposition vs. restraint, see Sørensen, *Liberal World Order in Crisis*. Isaiah Berlin's differentiation of positive and negative liberty is perhaps the most famous: see Berlin, *Liberty*.

36. Dworkin, "Paternalism."

37. This may seem to be commonsensical, but this was not always the case. Early liberal-republican thought was pluralistic in relation to proper domestic institutions. See, for instance, Montesquieu, *Spirit of the Laws*.

38. This dichotomy is borrowed from Foucault, *Birth of Biopolitics*.

39. Berlin, *Liberty*.

40. Berlin, *Liberty*, 200.

41. Epstein, in *The Power of Words in International Relations*, defines discourse clearly and operationalizes the concept in her study of anti-whaling movements. The idea of discourse as representing a "symbolic order" is drawn from Walker, "Culture, Discourse, Insecurity."

42. For an overview, see Vucetic, "Genealogy as a Research Tool in International Relations"; and Tatum, "Discourse, Genealogy, and Methods."

43. See, inter alia, Price and Tannenwald, "Norms and Deterrence"; Kinsella, *Image before the Weapon*; and Epstein, *Power of Words in International Relations*.

44. Berger and Luckmann, *Social Construction of Reality*, 39.

45. Epstein, "Who Speaks?," 17. Epstein draws on Judith Butler's work. See, in particular, *Psychic Life of Power*.

46. Swidler, "Culture in Action."

47. For the clearest summary of this idea, see Martin, Gutman, and Hutton, *Technologies of the Self*, 16–49.

48. This is in contrast to common explanations about hypocrisy in world politics. See, inter alia, Krasner, *Sovereignty*; and Finnemore, "Legitimacy, Hypocrisy."

49. Foucault, *"Society Must Be Defended,"* 15.

50. Foucault, *"Society Must Be Defended,"* 16.

51. Derrida, *Of Grammatology*, 158.

52. Michael Sandel offers a very different meaning of *minimalism*. See his *Liberalism and the Limits of Justice*.

53. Laclau and Mouffe, *Hegemony and Socialist Strategy*. This idea of radical democracy can be traced back to Jean-Jacques Rousseau; see Inston, *Rousseau and Radical Democracy*.

Chapter Two

1. Quoted in Eldar, "France in Syria," 489.

2. Smuts, *League of Nations*, 21.

3. "Dominican Sequel," *New York Times*, May 5, 1965.

4. For recent, synthetic approaches, see Bell, *Reordering the World*; Jahn, *Liberal Internationalism*.

5. See, for example, Wheeler, *Saving Strangers*; Finnemore, *Purpose of Intervention*; Simms and Trimm, *Humanitarian Intervention*.

6. See chapter 1 for extensive references to this literature.

7. Gilles Deleuze suggests that Foucault was notable not simply a theorist of discourse, but a theorist of the way that discourse interacted with the nondiscursive. See: *Foucault*, 23–44.

8. O'Mahoney, "Why Did They Do That?," 231–62.

9. Mearsheimer, *Why Leaders Lie*.

10. In social theory, see, inter alia, Searle, *Speech Acts*. In international relations theory, see, most notably, Kratochwil, *Rules, Norms, and Decisions*.

11. Cf. Fukuyama, *End of History and the Last Man*.

12. Milliken, "Study of Discourse in International Relations," 229.

13. For this formulation, see Walker, "Culture, Discourse, Insecurity," and Epstein, "Who Speaks?" The latter borrows this terminology from Jacques Lacan; see *Ecrits*.

14. Milliken, "Study of Discourse in International Relations," 242.

15. Thacker, "Foucault and the Writing of History," 30.

16. Deleuze makes this argument in his *Foucault*.

17. Foucault, *History of Sexuality, vol. 1*.

18. Howarth, *Discourse*, 41. This discussion is related to Derrida's conception of discourse and iterability; see "Signature, Event, Context," 1–23.
19. See Epstein, "Who Speaks?"
20. Doyle, "Liberalism and World Politics," 1152.
21. Derrida, *Archive Fever*, 77.
22. Connolly, *Identity/Difference*.
23. For a full development of this argument, see Bauman, *Modernity and Ambivalence*.
24. Morefield, *Covenant without Swords*.
25. See Hall, Evans, and Nixon, *Representation*.
26. This is a key argument from structuralist and some strains of post-structural linguistics. See Derrida, *Writing and Difference*, for a critique of the former set of arguments and an elaboration of the latter.
27. Evrigenis, *Fear of Enemies and Collective Action*.
28. Creppell, "Concept of Normative Threat," 450–87.
29. There is a literature, for example, within the continental tradition about the dually positive/negative role of the Other. This literature is voluminous, but see, notably, Levinas, *Time and the Other*.
30. Towns, *Women and States*.
31. Most notably is Gong, *Standard of Civilization in International Society*.
32. Harré, "Discursive Production of Selves," 57–58.
33. See Deleuze, *Foucault*, 47–69. Also see Foucault, *Discipline and Punish*.
34. Hook, "Genealogy, Discourse, 'Effective History,'" 9 (italics in original).
35. Schmidt, "Discursive Institutionalism, 303–25.
36. This is a central argument in Reus-Smit, *Moral Purpose of the State*.
37. P. Y. Martin, "Gender as a Social Institution," 1249–73.
38. For example, Ikenberry, *Liberal Leviathan*.
39. Goldstein and Keohane, *Ideas and Foreign Policy*, 20.
40. See Morefield, *Covenant without Swords*.
41. For example, Carr, *Twenty Years' Crisis*.
42. On persuasion vis-à-vis international institutions, see Schimmelfennig, "Community Trap," 47–80.
43. Krebs and Jackson, "Twisting Tongues and Twisting Arms," 35–56.
44. Dodge, *Inventing Iraq*, is a great account of this.
45. Foucault, *History of Madness*.
46. See Finnemore, *Purpose of Intervention*.
47. Milliken, "Study of Discourse in International Relations," 229 (italics in original).
48. Austin, *How to Do Things with Words*.
49. Bueger and Gadinger, "Play of International Practice," 451.
50. Borren, "'A Sense of the World,'" 225–55.
51. Said, *Orientalism*, 3
52. Milliken, "Study of Discourse in International Relations," 237.
53. Huysmans, "Security! What Do You Mean?," 228.
54. Huysmans, "Security! What Do You Mean?," 228.

55. Gramsci, *Prison Notebooks*.

56. Taylor, *Michel Foucault*, 173.

57. Bjola, "Legitimating the Use of Force in International Politics," 269. The literature on the legitimation of the use of force is large. For a classic formulation, see Hurd, "Legitimacy and Authority in International Politics," 379–408.

58. The literature on hypocrisy in IR is vast. For two classic treatments, see, respectively, Krasner, *Sovereignty*, and Finnemore, "Legitimacy, Hypocrisy, and the Structure of Unipolarity."

59. Dodge, "Iraq," 189.

60. Gadinger, "On Justification and Critique," 193.

61. On the use of these languages, see Morefield, *Covenants without Swords*.

62. This literature is now vast. See Neumann, "Returning Practice to the Linguistic Turn," 627–51. For a broad review of the current literature, see Bueger and Gadinger, "Play of International Practice."

63. On liberalism and peacebuilding, see Chandler, *Peacebuilding*.

64. Political science scholarship has developed this insight in several contexts. For one of the best treatments of expertise knowledge, see T. Mitchell, *Rule of Experts*.

65. Toby Dodge's work points out well why the deployment of these expert knowledges were "doomed to failure." See *Inventing Iraq*.

66. This conflict was not always the case. As chapter 5 demonstrates, these traditions often overlapped.

67. See Jahn, *Liberal Internationalism*, for a critique of the "disjuncture" arguments.

68. This is a nod to Foucauldian genealogy, which has shown just how important a methodological reflection on disjunctures, change, and contestation is in the study of discourses and institutions.

69. Foucault, "Nietzsche, Genealogy, History," 139.

70. Niemann and Schillinger, "Contestation 'All the Way Down'?," 43.

71. For a classic work addressing the concept of critical juncture, see Thelen, "Historical Institutionalism in Comparative Politics," 369–404.

72. Barnett and Finnemore, "The Politics, Power, and Pathologies of International Organizations," 699–732; and Wendt, "Driving with the Rearview Mirror," 1019–49.

73. Bevir, "What is Genealogy?," 268.

74. While an in-depth examination of decolonization and voices from the Global South is beyond the scope of the present study, it is a subject worthy of more intensive examination by scholars of liberalism, intervention, and global violence.

75. This is a major claim in mainstream constructivist scholarship. See Ruggie, "Continuity and Transformation in the World Polity"; Wendt, *Social Theory of International Politics*; Reus-Smit, *Moral Purpose of the State*; and Finnemore, *Purpose of Intervention*.

76. Vucetic, "Genealogy as a Research Tool in International Relations," 1295.

77. For a closer examination of genealogy's method in this regard, see Deleuze, *Foucault*.

78. Foucault, "Nietzsche, Genealogy, History," 88.

79. On the methodological deployment of the concept of "critical history" in international relations, see Kinsella, *Image before the Weapon*.

80. Deleuze, *Foucault*, 4.

81. Deleuze uses this term to aptly describe the creations of new assemblages of power; see *Foucault*, 23–44.

82. See Kinsella, *Image before the Weapon*.

83. See, for example, Bartelson, *Genealogy of Sovereignty*.

84. Said, in *Culture and Imperialism*, makes an argument about the connection between popular discourses and culture.

85. See, for instance, Krebs, *Narrative and the Making of US National Security*.

86. On this approach in genealogy, see Tatum, "Discourse, Genealogy, and Methods." On the problems of selection bias in historical/historiographical research, see Lustick, "History, Historiography, and Political Science."

87. C. Mitchell, "Case Studies," 239. See also McKeown, "Case Studies and the Limits of the Quantitative Worldview."

88. On constitutive arguments in international relations, see Wendt, "On Constitution and Causation in International Relations."

Chapter Three

1. Wright, *"New Imperialism."*

2. Fieldhouse, *Economics and Empire*, 3.

3. D. Bell, "Empire and International Relations," 289.

4. Matena, *Alibis of Empire*.

5. This literature is voluminous, but a recent updating of this literature can be found in Duncan Bell's *Reordering the World*.

6. An important study of this change is Eric Hobsbawm's *Age of Revolution*.

7. Many authors trace the acceptance of such principles by broader publics and political actors to an even earlier period. Reus-Smit, in *The Moral Purpose of the State*, writes: "By the end of the eighteenth century, the new preoccupation with the individual extended well beyond the confines of economic and political thought" (125), while Neier, in *The International Human Rights Movement*, suggests that the anti-slavery movement of the late eighteenth century represents the operationalization of these ideas into international political practice (26–36).

8. Richardson, "Contending Liberalisms," 14–15.

9. Simpson, "Two Liberalisms," 546–47.

10. Simpson, "Two Liberalisms," 546–47. See also Gong, *The Standard of Civilization in International Society*. These discourses were as much technical as they were political. See Nelson, "Civilizational Complexes and Inter-Civilizational Relations," 79–105.

11. Barnett, "International Paternalism and Humanitarian Governance," 485–521.

12. On the reasons for the failure of such revolutions in Britain, see Chase, *Chartism*.

13. For a brief discussion of this dispute, see Bossche, *Carlyle and the Search for Authority*, 128.

14. Mill, *Principles of Political Economy*, 166.
15. D. Bell, "John Stuart Mill on Colonies," 37.
16. Spencer, *Essays*, 284.
17. Spencer, *Essays*, 324.
18. Whelan, *Edmund Burke and India*, 23. On Burke's relationship with classical liberalism, see Lakoff, "Tocqueville, Burke, and the Origins of Liberal Conservativism."
19. Claeys, *Imperial Skeptics*, 260–61.
20. Narayan, "Colonialism and Its Others," 135.
21. MCM Simpson, *Correspondence and Conversations of Alexis de Tocqueville*, 2:127.
22. cf. Said, *Orientalism*.
23. MCM Simpson, *Correspondence and Conversations of Alexis de Tocqueville*, 188–89.
24. MCM Simpson, *Correspondence and Conversations of Alexis de Tocqueville*, 189.
25. MCM Simpson, *Correspondence and Conversations of Alexis de Tocqueville*, 120.
26. MCM Simpson, *Correspondence and Conversations of Alexis de Tocqueville*, 156.
27. I appropriate this term from Duncan Bell (see "Mythscapes").
28. This trend characterizes much of the liberal empire literature. In fact, it has spawned sub-literatures interested in interrogating which theorists were "pro" or "anti" empire. See, inter alia, Claeys, *Imperial Skeptics*; and Cullinane, *Liberty and American Anti-Imperialism*. Duncan Bell's recent work attempts to show that intellectuals in Britain were not uniformly advocates of empire, spending much of his discussion mediating between who was/was not a justifier of settler colonialism. See *Reordering the World*.
29. Sager, "A Nation of Functionaries, a Colony of Functionaries," 152.
30. Roche, *Frédéric Bastiat*, 162.
31. Bastiat, *Economic Harmonies*, 485.
32. See Jahn, "Barbarian Thoughts," on Mill's civilizational development narrative.
33. Bastiat, *Economic Harmonies*, 537.
34. Bastiat, *Economic Harmonies*, 537.
35. Bastiat, *Economic Harmonies*, 534.
36. Bastiat, *Economic Harmonies*, 477.
37. Bastiat, *Economic Harmonies*, 481.
38. Bastiat, *Economic Harmonies*, 486.
39. Jahn's "Barbarian Thoughts" comes closest to this.
40. The edition cited here is from *Collected Works of John Stuart Mill*, vols. 2 and 3, ed. J. M. Robinson; this edition includes revisions to later editions.
41. Zastoupil, *John Stuart Mill and India*, 2.
42. Jahn, "Barbarian Thoughts."
43. Mill, *Principles of Political Economy*, 21.
44. Mill, *Principles of Political Economy*, 247.
45. Mill, *Principles of Political Economy*, 247.
46. Mill, *Principles of Political Economy*, 104.
47. This is most fully developed, theoretically, in John Stuart Mill's *System of Logic*. As Terrence Ball points out, however, much of the rest of Mill's systematic works were

applied studies in his attempt at a science of ethology. See Ball, "Formation of Character." For a more in-depth discussion of how Mill's ethology related to his understanding of identity, nationality, and difference, see Varouxakis, *Mill on Nationality*.

48. Mill, *System of Logic*, 873.

49. See Schmitt, *Concept of the Political*.

50. Prager, "Intervention and Empire," 628–29.

51. This terminology comes from Giorgio Agamben's *State of Exception*. For an application of Agamben's conceptual apparatus to military intervention, see Fassin and Pandolfi, *Contemporary States of Emergency*.

52. Mill, quoted in Prager, "Intervention and Empire," 629–30.

53. This terminology is not an accident. The word *barbarian* was used to describe a spatial difference between Greek (and later Roman) civilization and any society that was not Greek (or Roman).

54. Mill, *Principles of Political Economy*, 211.

55. Mill, *On Liberty and the Subjugation of Women*, 180.

56. Mill, *On Liberty and the Subjugation of Women*, 24–25.

57. Mill, "Few Words on Non-Intervention." For a contemporary reinterpretation of Mill's views on intervention, see Doyle, *Question of Intervention*.

58. *Times* (London), Jul 4, 1864 (issue 24915).

59. *Times* (London), Nov 5, 1852 (issue 24915).

60. *Times* (London), Jan 15, 1848 (issue 19760).

61. *Times* (London), Jan 15, 1848 (issue 19760).

62. Herring, *From Colony to Superpower*, 320.

63. Herring, *From Colony to Superpower*, 322; Linn, *Philippine War, 1899–1902*, chap. 3. See also Linn, *US Army and Counterinsurgency in the Philippine War, 1899–1902*, for a detailed account of the counterinsurgency operations.

64. Miller, *Benevolent Assimilation*.

65. On the anti-imperialists, see Beisner, *Twelve against Empire*; Welch, *Response to Imperialism*; and Cullinane, *Liberty and American Anti-Imperialism*.

66. Muthu, in *Enlightenment against Empire*, points to this conclusion.

67. On the causes and course of the first conflict, see Blackburn, *Defeat of Ava*. On the Treaty of Yandabo, see Allot, *End of the First Anglo-Burmese War*, which includes the full text of the treaty; and Myint-U, *Making of Modern Burma*, 20.

68. The treaty became practically ineffective by 1840, when deteriorating relations between the Burmese and the British resulted in the removal of the British resident in Burma that year. See Pollack, "Origins of the Second Anglo-Burmese War," 486.

69. For a discussion of these processes, see Myint-U, *Making of Modern Burma*, 20–23.

70. Pollack, "Origins of the Second Anglo-Burmese War," 489–90.

71. Pollack, in "Origins of the Second Anglo-Burmese War" (496–501), provides a detailed account of Lambert's escalation of the conflict. For a good discussion of the aftermath of the escalation in Britain, see Pollack, "Mid-Victorian Coverup."

72. Myint-U, *Making of Modern Burma*, chap. 8.

73. Myint-U, *Making of Modern Burma*, 4.

74. See, particularly, Webster, *Debate on the Rise of the British Empire*, 162–63. Also see Webster's *Gentlemen Capitalists* and "Business and Empire" for this argument.

75. Snodgrass, *Narrative of the Burmese War*, 1

76. Snodgrass, *Narrative of the Burmese War*, 2

77. Snodgrass, *Narrative of the Burmese War*, 287.

78. Snodgrass, *Narrative of the Burmese War*, 292–93.

79. *Times* (London), May 31, 1852. Quoted in Laurie, *Our Burmese Wars and Relations with Burma*, 442–43.

80. Furnivall, *Colonial Policy and Practice*, 6.

81. On the history of humanitarian intervention as a method for protecting oppressed (namely religious) populations, see Simms and Trim, *Humanitarian Intervention*.

82. Hall was in the Indian Civil Service for more than twenty-five years in India and Burma, but spent most of his service in Burma.

83. Hall, *Soul of a People*, 87.

84. Bayly, *Birth of the Modern World*.

85. Snodgrass, *Narrative of the Burmese War*. Quoted in Cheesman, "Seeing 'Karen' in the Union of Myanmar," 206–7.

86. Turku, *Isolationist States in an Interdependent World*, 78. For a complete account of the putting down of these rebellions, see Smith, *Burma*.

87. Cortazzi and Webb, *Kipling's Japan*, 251n15.

88. Horace Spearman (British Burma Foreign-Department), *Administration Report for 1868–69*, 18–19, http://www.myanmar-law-library.org/law-library/legal-journal/reports-on-the-administration-of-british-burma/report-on-the-administration-of-british-burma-1868-1869.html.

89. Spearman (British Burma Foreign-Department), *Administration Report for 1868–69*, 21.

90. Orwell, "Shooting an Elephant."

91. William Gladstone, "Speech to Britain's House of Commons" (April 8, 1840), in vol. 3 of The Mirror of Parliament for the Third Session of the Fourteenth Parliament of Great Britain and Ireland [. . .]: Session of 1840, ed. John Henry Barrow (London: Longman et al., 1840).

Chapter Four

1. I borrow this term from James Thompson ("Democracy," 475). Though "democracy talk" saw a revolution in the 1800s, it was not until the early twentieth century that liberals began to seriously engage with the issues of globalization of democracy.

2. The historical literature on the emergence of IR as a discipline is vast. For a broad view of early imaginings, see Bell, *Reordering the World*. For a critical review of recent work, see Thakur, Davis, and Vale, "Imperial Mission, 'Scientific Method.'"

3. The best book-length study of this phenomenon in British political thought is Morefield, *Covenants without Swords*.

4. Mueller, *Remnants of War*.

5. Norman Angell, *Great Illusion*.
6. Zimmern, *League of Nations and the Rule of Law*.
7. Anderson, in *Imagined Communities* (85–86) makes this point about the nation-ness of nineteenth-century imperial states by suggesting that though nationalism was an important feature of this period, empire often demanded a certain anti-national structure.
8. This is a central argument in Morefield, *Covenants without Swords*.
9. For a discussion of the concept of self-determination, see Kapitan, "Self-Determination and the International Order."
10. Manela, *Wilsonian Moment*.
11. Morefield, *Covenants without Swords*, 16.
12. Koskenniemi, *Gentle Civilizer of Nations*, chap. 2.
13. Morefield, *Covenants without Swords*, 10.
14. Woodrow Wilson, "Address to a Joint Session of Congress on the Conditions of Peace," January 8, 1918, The American Presidency Project, posted by Gerhard Peters and John T. Woolley, https://www.presidency.ucsb.edu/documents/address-joint-session-congress-the-conditions-peace-the-fourteen-points.
15. On the development of the mandate system, see Callaghan, *Mandates and Empire*; and Anghie, "Colonialism and the Birth of International Institutions." For a connection between League mandates and contemporary trusteeship, see Bain, *Between Anarchy and Society*.
16. Smuts, *League of Nations*, 21. For a further discussion of this thematic in the mandate system in general, see Grant, *Civilized Savagery*, chap. 5; and Dubow, "Smuts, the United Nations, and the Rhetoric of Race and Rights."
17. The discussion of rationalism and colonial governance is more fully developed in the fields of sexuality, race, and family studies. For a taste, see Stoler's, *Carnal Knowledge and Imperial Power* and *Race and the Education of Desire*. For a theoretical treatment of this method of analysis, see Huffer, *Mad for Foucault*.
18. Morefield, *Covenants without Swords*, 113.
19. Long and Schmidt, *Imperialism and Internationalism*.
20. Sarraut, *Grandeur et servitude coloniales*, 43–50.
21. For an interpretive biography of Addams, see Elshtain, *Jane Addams and the Dream of American Democracy*.
22. For an excellent introduction to the WILPF in the context of both the international peace movement and the women's movement, see Foster, *Women and the Warriors*. On Addams and the peace movement, see, inter alia, Knight, *Jane Addams*.
23. Agnew, "Will to Peace," 6.
24. Addams, *Peace and Bread in Time of War*, 174–76.
25. Tyrell and Sexton, introduction to *Empire's Twin*, 9.
26. Addams, "Potential Advantages of the Mandate System," 71.
27. Addams, "Potential Advantages of the Mandate System," 72.
28. Addams, "Potential Advantages of the Mandate System," 73.
29. The best biographical work on Hobhouse can be found in Hobhouse Balme, *Agents of Peace*. On her friendship with Smuts, see Marks, "White Masculinity."

30. I highlight this language here in order to show the way it is mobilized by writers like Hobhouse. For a more in-depth analysis, see Krebs, *Gender, Race, and the Writing of Empire*, 64.

31. Emily Hobhouse, "The Story of My Visit to Germany, June 7–June 24, 1916, During the Great War," in Balme, *Agent of Peace*.

32. Guyot, *Causes and Consequences of the War*, 107.

33. Guyot, *Causes and Consequences of the War*, 203.

34. Guyot, *Causes and Consequences of the War*, 203.

35. Guyot, *Causes and Consequences of the War*, 302.

36. These ideas are most fully developed in a 1913 essay. See Durkheim and Mauss, "Note on the Notion of Civilization." For an interpretation and contextualization, see Swedberg, "Note on Civilizations and Economies." Swedberg ties these ideas into a comparison with Max Weber's sociological approach to civilizations as well.

37. See, particularly, Durkheim, *Suicide*, which looks at European "races" from a civilizational perspective. For an analysis, see Riley, *Social Thought of Emile Durkheim*, 110–11.

38. Fenton, *Durkheim and Modern Sociology*, 123–25.

39. See Swedberg, "Note on Civilizations and Economies," for a brief discussion of this distinction in Durkheim's work.

40. Lehmann, "Question of Caste in Modern Society," 570.

41. For a collection of Durkheim's lectures on self-determination and moral education, see Durkheim, *Moral Education*. For an analysis of these writings, see Peterson, "Quest for Moral Order."

42. Wallas, "Eastern Question," 348.

43. Lugard, *Dual Mandate in British Tropical Africa*, 50

44. Brailsford, "League and Its Mandates," 107.

45. Goldschmidt, *Concise History of the Middle East*, 204–5.

46. The timing of the development of Syrian nationalism is debated in the historiography. On these debates, see Provence, *Great Syrian Revolt*.

47. The mandate was *officially* recognized by the League of Nations in 1923.

48. Mardam Bey, *Syria's Quest for Independence*, 7–8.

49. Quoted in Eldar, "France in Syria," 489.

50. Eldar, "France in Syria," 487–89.

51. This crisis resulted in the ultimate suspension of the Syrian Congress.

52. Mardam Bey, *Syria's Quest for Independence*, 9–10. Due to concerns about public opinion, French troops did not overtake Damascus. See Eldar, "France in Syria," 500.

53. Quoted in Neep, *Occupying Syria*, 70.

54. Neep, *Occupying Syria*, 75.

55. On the evolution of the concept of banditry in the Middle East, see Brown, "Brigands and State Building."

56. Koskenniemi, "Idealism and Ignorance," 33.

57. "French Mandate for Syria and Lebanon," *American Journal of International Law* 17, no. 3 [supplemental documents] (1923): 177.

58. "French Mandate for Syria and Lebanon," 178.

59. Louis Aubert, "France and the League of Nations," *Foreign Affairs*, July 1, 1925, 644–45.
60. Quoted in "Syria Appeals to the League," *Times* (London), July 21, 1920, 13.
61. Quoted in Neep, *Occupying Syria*, 39.
62. Lange, "'Bedouin' and 'Shawaya,'" 202.
63. The social construction of a nomadic, or semi-nomadic, Other as the antithesis of modern state identity in the Middle East is not unique to Syria. In fact, it played a central role in the politics of nation building throughout much of the twentieth century. For one remarkable account, see Chatty, *Mobile Pastoralists*.
64. Abisaab, "Warmed or Burnt by Fire?," 300.
65. Lorca, "Petitioning the International," 508.
66. Lorca, "Petitioning the International," 508.
67. Provence, *Great Syrian Revolt*, 56.
68. Though Dodge, in *Inventing Iraq*, argues that the revolt actually began in early July of that year (8).
69. Charles Tripp, *History of Iraq*, 30.
70. Marr, *Modern History of Iraq*, 21.
71. Dodge, *Inventing Iraq*, 2. Dodge also makes the argument that the revolt, itself, helped determine the outcome of British debates about Iraq—namely, that the British government should maintain influence in the country, but the primary goal was to "ensure the state be constructed as efficiently as possible" (9).
72. Cox, "Historical summary."
73. Cox, "Historical summary."
74. Dodge, *Inventing Iraq*, 15–17.
75. G Bell, "Letter to Florence Bell and Hugh Bell."
76. Dodge, *Inventing Iraq*, 2.
77. See the discussion above, and also Morefield, *Covenants without Swords*.
78. See Callaghan, *Mandates and Empire*.

Chapter Five

1. Strauss, *City and Man*, 5.
2. Shklar, "Liberalism of Fear."
3. Arendt, *Origins of Totalitarianism*, 466.
4. Fukuyama, *End of History and the Last Man*.
5. A. Anderson, "Character and Ideology," 214.
6. A. Anderson, "Character and Ideology," 228.
7. Fukuyama, "End of History?," 3.
8. Early efforts included Keohane and Nye, *Power and Independence*. Most significantly was the turn to interests and open economy politics; see Moravcsik, "Taking Preferences Seriously."

9. See, most notably, Mueller, *Remnants of War*; Linklater, *Problem of Harm in World Politics*; and Pinker, *Better Angels of Our Nature*.

10. Yack, *Liberalism without Illusions*.

11. Müller, "Fear and Freedom," 48.

12. Chappel, "Catholic Origins of Totalitarianism Theory."

13. Gleason, *Totalitarianism*, 3.

14. Koestler is most notable for his anti-totalitarian novel, *Darkness at Noon*. Koestler had a major impact on Orwell's thought—as the latter makes clear throughout his critical essay on the former's works.

15. Orwell, "Arthur Koestler," 305.

16. Orwell, "Arthur Koestler." Orwell is often studied from the point of view of socialist ideology. I have included a brief discussion of Orwell, however, because his writings are exemplary of the power of this discourse to span the spectrum of emancipatory liberalism from the Center to the Left.

17. An emerging literature on Berlin's relationship to Cold War intellectual battles exists. For a taste, see Kelly, "Political Thought of Isaiah Berlin"; and A. Anderson, "Character and Ideology."

18. Berlin, "Two Concepts of Liberty," 167.

19. Berlin was certainly not alone in this view. Most prominent, also, were intellectuals like Karl Popper and Raymond Aron. Even American writers, including the southern novelist Lillian Smith, were—in many ways—proponents of a certain value pluralist liberalism developed in the shadow of Cold War totalitarianism. Smith would go as far as expressing this fear vis-à-vis her own participation in the civil rights movement, and the association of Soviet totalitarianism with the stifling of individual aesthetic development in the American South. She even suggests that southerners were the biggest threat to American liberalism—as they were used to living under totalitarian conditions. On Popper and Aron, see Müller, "Fear and Freedom." On Smith, see Haddox, "Lillian Smith, Cold War Intellectual," 55.

20. This idea would be a central one in the thought of Israeli historian Jacob Talmon. See below for a more detailed discussion.

21. This is true even despite Orwell's apparent defenses of the British Empire—which are illustrated, perhaps most provocatively, in his 1949 essay "Reflections on Gandhi."

22. Berlin, "Originality of Machiavelli," 76. Even French liberals, like Raymond Aron, made these discursive moves in connecting the spread of Soviet communism with totalitarianism. See his *Démocratie et totalitarisme*.

23. Losurdo, "Towards a Critique of the Category of Totalitarianism," 30. For a similar critique of the use of the term *totalitarianism* in political discourse, see Žižek, *Did Somebody Say Totalitarianism?*

24. See Campbell, *Writing Security*, for one study in this regard.

25. Dean Rusk, interviewed by Paige E. Mulhollan, September 26, 1969, interview 2, Oral History transcript, LBJ Presidential Library, Austin, TX, https://www.discoverlbj.org/item/oh-ruskd-19690926-2-74-245-b.

26. George Brown, quoted in "Britain Denounces Charges by Zambia at UN," *Times* (London), December 10, 1966. Obviously, these justifications were ways of rationalizing British racism in Rhodesia/Zimbabwe. The appropriation of this discourse, however, is striking.

27. For examples, see Mehta, "Liberal Strategies of Exclusion"; and Morefield, *Covenants without Swords*.

28. This association of the Soviet Union with earlier totalitarian regimes was a common rhetorical act during the Cold War. See Guilhot, *Democracy Makers*, chap. 1, for a brief discussion.

29. Harold Wilson, "Leaders Speech," Blackpool, UK, January 10, 1968, British Political Speech Archive, http://www.britishpoliticalspeech.org/speech-archive.htm?speech=166. He states: "We reject equally the apostles of authoritarian violence on the one hand and negative violence on the other. Both are essentially and profoundly antidemocratic. Both seek to destroy. The Conservatives at home and abroad seek to destroy the defences we have built for the weak against those who abuse economic and social power. The nihilists in their despair seek to destroy the very fabric of organised society."

30. For more on Talmon's pessimistic liberalism, see Tatum, "Liberal Pessimism"; and Tatum, "Pessimistic Liberalism."

31. Jacoby, *Picture Imperfect*, 60.

32. Dubnov, "Priest or Jester?," 134.

33. This term originates from Judith Shklar's work; see "Liberalism of Fear."

34. Hacohen, "Jacob Talmon between Zionism and Cold War Liberalism," 147.

35. See Hacohen, "Jacob Talmon between Zionism and Cold War Liberalism," 150.

36. Talmon, *Romanticism and Revolt*, 100.

37. Dubnov, "Anti-Cosmopolitan Liberalism," 564.

38. Ricoeur, *Freud and Philosophy*.

39. Ricoeur, *Freud and Philosophy*, 32 (this is where the idea is introduced; the focus of the book is most specifically on Freud). For more on this, see Stewart, "Hermeneutics of Suspicion."

40. Bevir, "What is Genealogy?"

41. Ricoeur, *Freud and Philosophy*, 33.

42. Dubnov, "Tale of Trees and Crooked Timbers," 224.

43. Talmon, *Romanticism and Revolt*, 23.

44. Talmon, *Origins of Totalitarian Democracy*.

45. Talmon, *Origins of Totalitarian Democracy*, 6.

46. Talmon, *Origins of Totalitarian Democracy*, 2.

47. Talmon, *Origins of Totalitarian Democracy*, 1.

48. Marso, "Simone de Beauvoir and Hannah Arendt," 175.

49. Beauvoir, "Personal Freedom and Others," 302. Beauvoir had an ambivalent relationship with liberalism; however, her philosophy engaged in similar themes developed here.

50. See Beauvoir's discussion throughout part II of *Ethics of Ambiguity*.

51. See Gaddis, *Cold War*, 180–84.

52. For example, see Wolin, *Politics and Vision*.

53. Ciepley, *Liberalism in the Shadow of Totalitarianism*.

54. Vidal, "Theodore Roosevelt." He writes, with characteristic wit, "Now that war is once more thinkable among the thoughtless, Theodore Roosevelt should enjoy a revival. Certainly, the New Right will find his jingoism appealing, though his trust-busting will give less pleasure to the Honorable Society of the Invisible Hand. The figure that emerges from the texts of both Mr. McCullough and Mr. Morris is both fascinating and repellent. Theodore Roosevelt was a classic American sissy who overcame—or appeared to overcome—his physical fragility through 'manly' activities of which the most exciting and ennobling was war. [. . .] As a politician-writer, Theodore Roosevelt most closely resembles Winston Churchill and Benito Mussolini. Each was as much a journalist as a politician. Each was a sissy turned showoff. The not unwitty Churchill—the most engaging of the lot—once confessed that if no one had been watching him he could quite easily have run away during a skirmish in the Boer War. Each was a romantic, in love with the nineteenth-century notion of earthly glory, best personified by Napoleon Bonaparte, whose eagerness to do in *his* biological superiors led to such a slaughter of alpha-males that the average French soldier of 1914 was markedly shorter than the soldier of 1800—pretty good going for a fat little fellow, five foot four inches tall—with, to be fair, no history of asthma" (371–72).

55. Gore Vidal, interview by David Sheff, *Playboy* 34, no. 12 (December 1987).

56. M. Barnett, *Empire of Humanity*, 101.

57. Hirschman, *Essays in Trespassing*, 3–5. The literature on the history of international development is vast, and this section—necessarily—is simultaneously narrow in focus, and broad in theme. For a good overview, see Rist, *History of Development*.

58. T. Mitchell, *Rule of Experts*, chap. 3.

59. Fassin, *Humanitarian Reason*.

60. "Mutual Security Adrift," *Washington Post*, September 3, 1957.

61. "Mutual Security Adrift."

62. See M. Barnett, *Empire of Humanity*, 97–106, for a brief account.

63. John F. Kennedy, "Special Message to the Congress on Foreign Aid," March 22, 1961, The American Presidency Project, posted by Gerhard Peters and John T. Woolley, https://www.presidency.ucsb.edu/node/236184.

64. Kennedy, "Special Message."

65. Rostow, *Stages of Economic Growth*. The subtitle, "A Non-Communist Manifesto," is especially telling, considering it positions "modernization" in direct contrast to communist ideology.

66. Ish-Shalom, "Theory Gets Real."

67. On the alliance, see Taffet, *Foreign Aid as Foreign Policy*.

68. John F. Kennedy, "On the Alliance for Progress," March 13, 1961, *The Department of State Bulletin XLIV*, no. 1136 (April 3, 1961): 471–74, in Internet Modern History Sourcebook, https://sourcebooks.fordham.edu/mod/1961kennedy-afp1.asp.

69. Allcock, "Becoming 'Mr. Latin America,'" 1029.

70. This term is Thomas Mann's. See Allcock, "Becoming 'Mr. Latin America,'" 1034.

71. Tad Szulc, "US Mission is Flying to Chile to Speed Lagging Aid Program," *New York Times*, March 5, 1962.

72. Szulc, in "US Mission is Flying," goes on to say, "Washington, it is held, cannot expect too much too fast from the right-of-center Government . . . ," suggesting that development in Chile may be an uphill battle, though clearly one worth fighting.

73. Adlai Stevenson, "What is Their Purpose? And Ours?," *New York Times*, November 4, 1962.

74. Bernard Nossiter, "Whether It's Altruism, Self-Interest, or Politics: Foreign Aid is Alive and Well in Other Countries," *Washington Post*, November 15, 1971.

75. By neoliberalism, I refer to "an emerging new form of capitalism—post-Fordist, 'disorganized,' transnational." See Fraser, "Feminism, Capitalism, and the Cunning of History," 98.

76. P. T. Bauer and Cranley Onslow, "Making Sure Overseas Aid Goes Where It Is Needed," *Times* (London), November 15, 1977. The authors make it clear that this issue is intimately tied to the issue of totalitarianism, stating, "We are sure it cannot be in the interest of either the West, or the ordinary people of the Third World, that aid should be engulfed by an international tide of totalitarian collectivism."

77. President Jimmy Carter, in his 1979 State of the Union Address, hints at this changing sentiment in commenting that, in regard to global problems, "Abroad, few of them can be solved by the United States alone." Quoted in Edward Walsh, "Limits Here and Abroad: Carter Asks Americans' Help in Building 'New Foundation,'" *Washington Post*, January 24, 1979.

78. World Bank, *World Development Report 1978* (Washington, D.C.: World Bank Group, 1978), 12.

79. D. Williams, "Development, Intervention, and International Order," 1217.

80. "Statement by Principal Deputy Press Secretary Speakes on United States Assistance for the Nicaraguan Democratic Resistance," June 23, 1986,

https://www.reaganlibrary.gov/archives/speech/statement-principal-deputy-press-secretary-speakes-united-states-assistance.

81. For an overview of this episode, see Calder, *Impact of Intervention*. The best treatment of the intervention from within IR theory can be found in Saunders, *Leaders at War*.

82. See Rabe, *Eisenhower and Latin America*, 134–69, for a detail of this. Herring, in *From Colony to Superpower*, provides a brief overview (689). There is little recent historical research on the Dominican intervention—which means that many recently unclassified documents have yet to be analyzed by historians. Therefore, much of this case study relies on archival documentation to supplement the existing historiography. These documents are collected in the US State Department's *Foreign Relations of the United States*, 1964–1968, Volume XXXII, Dominican Republic; Cuba; Haiti; Guyana, ed. Daniel Lawler and Carolyn Yee (Washington, DC: Government Printing Office, 2005). [Hereafter referred to as *FRUS*.]

83. Herring, *From Colony to Superpower*, 717. There's indication that the administration was just as pleased with the seemingly "apolitical" nature of the new regime as it was

with its anti-communist leanings. See "Special National Intelligence Estimate: Instability and the Insurgency Threat in the Dominican Republic" (SNIE 86.2-64), January 17, 1964, *FRUS*, document 1. Lack of consolidation of power proved to be a major headache for the US, however: "Telegram from the Embassy in the Dominican Republic to the Department of State," May 21, 1964, *FRUS*, document 5.

84. As early as February 1965, the administration was becoming keenly aware of the problems Bosch posed even while in exile in Puerto Rico: "Letter from the Ambassador to the Dominican Republic (Bennett) to the Assistant Secretary of State for Inter-American Affairs (Mann)," February 2, 1965, *FRUS*, document 18. Reid's resignation came on April 25, wherein a military junta was placed in charge of the country with hopes of preventing further bloodshed: "Telegram from the White House Situation Room to President Johnson at Camp David," April 25, 1965, *FRUS*, document 21.

85. For a review of the run-up to intervention, see Slater, *Intervention and Negotiation*; and Lowenthal, *Dominican Intervention*. As phone records between Johnson and the State Department indicate, however, intervention was already being considered by April 26, the day after Reid stepped down: "Telephone Conversation between the Under Secretary of State for Economic Affairs (Mann) and President Johnson," April 26, 1965, *FRUS*, document 22.

86. Memorandum from William G. Bowdler of the National Security Council Staff to the President's Special Assistant for National Security Affairs (Bundy), April 27, 1965, *FRUS*, document 25.

87. "Telephone Conversation," April 26, 1965, *FRUS*, document 22.

88. "Telegram from the Embassy in the Dominican Republic to the Director of the National Security Agency (Carter)," April 28, 1965, *FRUS*, document 29; "Transcript of Teleconference between the Department of State and the Embassy in the Dominican Republic," April 28, 1965, *FRUS*, document 33.

89. "Memorandum of Telephone Conversation between the Under Secretary of State for Economic Affairs (Mann) and President Johnson," April 28, 1965, *FRUS*, document 38.

90. Senator William Fulbright, quoted in Felten, "Path to Dissent," 1010.

91. "Minutes of Meeting: Meeting with Congressional Leadership on Dominican Republic in Attendance," April 28, 1965, *FRUS*, document 35.

92. "Minutes of Meeting," April 28, 1965, *FRUS*, document 35.

93. "Dominican Sequel," *New York Times*, May 5, 1965.

94. "Rockefeller Voices Doubt on Dominican Role of the US," *New York Times*, May 5, 1965.

95. Felten, "Path to Dissent," 1013–14.

96. Felten, "Path to Dissent," 1014.

97. Felten, "Path to Dissent," 1015.

98. Transcript of Tape No. 10: "I Don't Want to Be an Intervenor," May 23, 1965, 5:10 p.m., in *Lyndon Johnson and the Dominican Intervention of 1965*, ed. David Coleman (National Security Archive, Electronic Briefing Book No. 513), https://nsarchive2.gwu.edu/NSAEBB/NSAEBB513/ [hereafter *National Security Archive*].

99. Transcript of Tape No. 10.

100. Transcript of Tape No. 6: "This Is Going to Be Bad in Our Country," April 29, 1965, 4:26 p.m., *National Security Archive*.

101. Transcript of Tape No. 10.

102. Transcript of Tape No. 10.

103. Transcript of Tape No. 11: "We've Tried to Save That Country," August 27, 1965, 11:30 a.m., *National Security Archive*.

104. Transcript of Tape No. 11.

105. For a full text of the initial announcement, see Lyndon B. Johnson, "Statement by the President on the Situation in the Dominican Republic," April 30, 1965, The American Presidency Project, posted by Gerhard Peters and John T. Woolley, https://www.presidency.ucsb.edu/documents/statement-the-president-the-situation-the-dominican-republic-0.

106. Lyndon B. Johnson, "Report on the Situation in the Dominican Republic," May 2, 1965, https://millercenter.org/the-presidency/presidential-speeches/may-2-1965-report-situation-dominican-republic.

107. Johnson, "Report on the Situation in the Dominican Republic."

108. "Editorial Note," *FRUS*, document 43.

109. "Memorandum from the President's Special Assistant for National Security Affairs (Bundy) to President Johnson," October 6, 1965, *FRUS*, document 137.

110. See Rostow, *Stages of Economic Growth*.

111. "National Intelligence Estimate: Prospects for Stability in the Dominican Republic" (NIE 86.2–66), April 28, 1966, *FRUS*, document 171.

112. Committee on US and Latin American Relations, "Revolution of 1965 Shaped Resistance in the Dominican Republic and US," April 4, 2015, https://cuslar.org/2015/04/24/revolution-of-1965-shaped-resistance-in-dominican-republic-us/.

113. "Telegram from the Department of State to the Embassy in the Dominican Republic," FRUS, p. 265.

Chapter Six

1. Ghani and Lockhart, *Fixing Failed States*, 3.

2. A Google NGram search—which charts the frequency of word or phrase usage in published books—shows that the term *failed state* experiences a veritable explosion of usage beginning in 1992, preceded by a conspicuous absence of the term altogether.

3. The literature on such processes of "securitization" is vast. See Huysman, "Security! What Do You Mean?"; M. Williams, "Words, Images, Enemies"; Vuori, "Illocutionary Logic and Strands of Securitization"; Hansen, "The Politics of Securitization and the Muhammad Cartoon Crisis"; M. Williams, "Securitization and the Liberalism of Fear"; and Abulof, "Deep Securitization and Israel's 'Demographic Demon.'"

4. There are several excellent histories of the evolution of the international human rights movement. For a taste, see Hunt, *Inventing Human Rights*; Ishay, *History of*

Human Rights; Neier, *International Human Rights Movement*; and Moyn, *Human Rights and the Uses of History*.

5. Dietrich, "US Human Rights Policy in the Post-Cold War Era," 272. See also the argument in Fukuyama, *End of History and the Last Man*.

6. For a classic study of the influence of transnational human rights groups, see Keck and Sikkink, *Activists beyond Borders*.

7. Hitchcock, "The Rise and Fall of Human Rights?," 100.

8. See Thérien and Joly, "'All Human Rights for All.'"

9. For a discussion of ethnic conflict and human rights debates, particularly in relation to refugees, see Newland, "Ethnic Conflict and Refugees."

10. William J. Clinton, "Proclamation 6584—Helsinki Human Rights Day, 1993," August 1, 1993, The American Presidency Project, posted by Gerhard Peters and John T. Woolley, https://www.presidency.ucsb.edu/documents/proclamation-6584-helsinki-human-rights-day-1993.

11. Paddy Ashdown, "Leader's Speech," Torquay, 1993, British Political Speech Archive, http://www.britishpoliticalspeech.org/speech-archive.htm?speech=53.

12. "Blood Tide Rising," *New York Times*, June 8, 1992.

13. "Blood Tide Rising."

14. On recognition, see Honneth, *Struggle for Recognition*.

15. Fukuyama, *End of History and the Last Man*, xix.

16. Huntington, "Clash of Civilizations?," 29.

17. Englehart, "State Capacity, State Failure, and Human Rights," 176.

18. Mary Manjikian, in "Diagnosis, Intervention, and Cure" (349), discusses the way that the "curing" metaphor associated with state failure is connected to intervention.

19. B.G. Jones, "'Good Governance' and 'State Failure,'" 62.

20. Ali, "Books vs. Bombs?," 544.

21. International Commission on Intervention and State Sovereignty, *The Responsibility to Protect* (Ottawa, ON: International Development Research Centre, 2001), 5, quoted in B. G. Jones, "'Good Governance' and 'State Failure,'" 63.

22. This is in contrast to Mark Duffield's arguments about the merging of security and development after the Cold War. See Duffield, *Global Governance and the New Wars*.

23. Stuckey and Ritter, "George Bush, 'Human Rights,' and American Democracy."

24. The White House, *The National Security Strategy of the United States of America* (March 2006), https://www.comw.org/qdr/fulltext/nss2006.pdf, 27. Note that this was a common connection drawn in Bush and Blair rhetoric: Hameiri, "Failed State or a Failed Paradigm?," 122.

25. Angel Gurría, "Accelerating Development in Fragile States: The Role of the OECD Development Assistance Committee," *UN Chronicle* XLV, no. 1 (2008), http://unchronicle.un.org/article/accelerating-development-fragile-states-role-oecd-development-assistance-committee/

26. "Sudan's Other Crisis," *New York Times*, May 3, 2010.

27. David Rose, "Neo Culpa," *Vanity Fair*, December 2006, http://www.vanityfair.com/news/2006/12/neocons200612.

28. Lisa Wedeen, "Yemen: State Fragility, Piety, and the Problems with Intervention," *Noref Report* no. 6, March 2010, https://ciaotest.cc.columbia.edu/wps/noref/0018450/f_0018450_15803.pdf.

29. "Political Indicators: P3: Human Rights and Rule of Law" in Fund for Peace, *Fragile States Index,* https://fragilestatesindex.org/indicators/p3/.

30. "The Fragile States Index Rankings 2014," in Fund for Peace, *Fragile States Index 2014,* https://fundforpeace.org/2014/06/24/failed-states-index-2014-the-book/.

31. Gros, "Towards a taxonomy of failed states in the New World Order," 455.

32. See, respectively, Locke, *Political Writings*, 324–27; and Rousseau, *Social Contract and Other Later Political Writings*.

33. See, particularly, the work of Jeffrey Herbst. For example, "War and the State in Africa," and *States and Power in Africa*.

34. Herbst, "War and the State in Africa," 124.

35. Tilly, "Reflections on the History of European State-Making," 38.

36. R Jackson, *Quasi-States*.

37. Helman and Ratner, "Saving Failed States."

38. Helman and Ratner, "Saving Failed States."

39. Helman and Ratner, "Saving Failed States."

40. See, respectively, Hobbes, *Leviathan*; and Locke, *Political Writings*.

41. See, inter alia, Nussbaum and Glover, *Women, Culture, and Development*; and Sen, *Development as Freedom*.

42. "Human Development Report," *United Nations Development Program* (2016): p. 37.

43. Krasner, "Sharing Sovereignty," 88.

44. Krasner, "Sharing Sovereignty," 88.

45. Gilley, "Case for Colonialism."

46. Fearon and Laitin, "Neotrusteeship and the Problem of Weak States."

47. Herbst, *State and Power in Africa,* for example, ties the causes of state failure directly to colonialism and arbitrary border making.

48. The classic writing on Orientalism is Said, *Orientalism* For a contemporary evaluation of Orientalism in US policy discourses, see Lockman, *Contending Visions of the Middle East*.

49. For a similar comparison of imperial discourses with contemporary authors, see Morefield, "Empire, Tragedy, and the Liberal State in the Writings of Niall Ferguson and Michael Ignatieff."

50. Huntington, "Clash of Civilizations?," 40.

51. This is not to say that Huntington was a "liberal" in the sense of international relations theory, but his writings exemplified liberal ideology about civilization in the post–Cold War era.

52. Huntington, "Clash of Civilizations?," 41. This is not his term. It is borrowed from Kishore Mahbubani ("The West and the Rest").

53. Huntington, "Clash of Civilizations?," 35.

54. Huntington, "Clash of Civilizations?," 49.

55. Lewis, "Roots of Muslim Rage," 47, 60.

56. Lewis, "Roots of Muslim Rage," 60.

57. Bernard Lewis, "Time for Toppling," *Wall Street Journal*, September 27, 2002, https://www.wsj.com/articles/SB1033089910971012713. He would later recant (or otherwise conveniently ignore?) these statements in an interview: Evan Goldstein, "'Osama bin Laden Made Me Famous': Bernard Lewis Looks Back," *The Chronicle of Higher Education*, April 22, 2012, https://www.chronicle.com/article/Osama-bin-Laden-Made-Me/131584.

58. Quoted in Goldstein, "'Osama Bin Laden Made Me Famous.'"

59. Peter Pringle, "UN Ready to Endorse Haiti Invasion," *Independent*, July 29, 1994, https://www.independent.co.uk/news/world/un-ready-to-endorse-haiti-invasion-1417053.html.

60. Patrick Cockburn, "Better Clinton than Cedras: The US might yet succeed in Haiti where it failed in Somalia, argues Patrick Cockburn," *Independent*, October 10, 1994, https://www.independent.co.uk/voices/better-clinton-than-cedras-the-us-might-yet-succeed-in-haiti-where-it-failed-in-somalia-argues-1442270.html.

61. "The Limits of Nation-Building," *New York Times*, December 11, 1997, https://www.nytimes.com/1997/12/11/opinion/the-limits-of-nation-building.html.

62. David E. Sanger, "Pain, and Dreams, Greet Christopher in Cambodia," *New York Times*, August 5, 1995, https://www.nytimes.com/1995/08/05/world/pain-and-dreams-greet-christopher-in-cambodia.html.

63. Howard W. French, "Zaire City a Symbol of Nation's Chaos," *New York Times*, December 13, 1996, https://www.nytimes.com/1996/12/13/world/zaire-city-a-symbol-of-nation-s-chaos.html.

64. Christopher Bellamy, "The End of War—and Peace," *Independent* June 13, 1996, https://www.independent.co.uk/news/the-end-of-war-and-peace-1336902.html.

65. Blaine Harden, "Who Killed Liberia? We Did," *Washington Post*, May 26, 1996, https://www.washingtonpost.com/archive/opinions/1996/05/26/who-killed-liberia-we-did/925168e5-e388-436b-b122-a403b96c7e35.

66. Michael Ignatieff, "It's war—but it doesn't have to be dirty," *Guardian*, September 30, 2001, https://www.theguardian.com/world/2001/oct/01/afghanistan.terrorism9.

67. Doyle, "Liberalism and World Politics."

68. See Ignatieff, "It's War."

69. Aitken, "Provincializing Embedded Liberalism."

70. Slavoj Žižek, "Jack Bauer and the Ethics of Urgency," *In These Times*, January 27, 2006, http://inthesetimes.com/article/2481/jack_bauer_and_the_ethics_of_urgency. Also see Dershowitz, *Why Terrorism Works*.

71. For an overview of the early rise of the Taliban in Afghanistan, see Matinuddin, *Taliban Phenomenon*. For a treatment of the civil war more generally, see Nojum, *Rise of the Taliban in Afghanistan*.

72. On this period, see Scheuer, *Osama Bin Laden*, chap. 5.

73. In fact, President George W. Bush's first use of the term identified its origin in the context of the Taliban's harboring of Al-Qaeda. He states, "Our war on terror begins with Al-Qaeda, but it does not end there." See George W. Bush, "Address before a

Joint Session of the Congress on the United States Response to the Terrorist Attacks of September 11," September 20, 2001, http://www.washingtonpost.com/wp-srv/nation/specials/attacked/transcripts/bushaddress_092001.html.

74. Joint Resolution to authorize the use of United States Armed Forces against those responsible for the recent attacks launched against the United States, Pub. L. No. 107–40, 115 STAT. 224 (September 18, 2001), https://www.gpo.gov/fdsys/pkg/PLAW-107publ40/pdf/PLAW-107publ40.pdf.

75. A large academic and journalistic literature exists on the Afghanistan war. See, for a taste, S. Jones, *In the Graveyard of Empires*; and Gall, *Wrong Enemy*.

76. Michael Williams, in "Securitization and the Liberalism of Fear," makes the argument that the entire war on terror, in fact, was framed as a fight between "liberty and tyranny."

77. George W. Bush, "Presidential Address to the Nation," October 7, 2001, http://georgewbush-whitehouse.archives.gov/news/releases/2001/10/20011007-8.html.

78. UN Security Council, Resolution 1386, on the Situation in Afghanistan, S/RES/1386, 1 (December 20 2001), http://www.refworld.org/docid/3c4e94571c.html, 1.

79. UN Security Council, Resolution 1386, 2, ¶ 1.

80. On this process, see Schlag and Heck, "Securitizing Images."

81. Laura Bush, "The Weekly Address Delivered by the First Lady," November 17, 2001, The American Presidency Project, posted by Gerhard Peters and John T. Woolley, https://www.presidency.ucsb.edu/documents/the-weekly-address-delivered-the-first-lady.

82. Bureau of Democracy, Human Rights and Labor, R, "Report on the Taliban's War Against Women," November 17, 2001, https://2009-2017.state.gov/j/drl/rls/6185.htm.

83. "Liberating the Women of Afghanistan," *New York Times,* November 24, 2001.

84. "Winning the Peace in Afghanistan," *New York Times,* November 21, 2002.

85. Barack Obama, "President Obama's Remarks on New Strategy for Afghanistan and Pakistan," March 29, 2009, https://www.nytimes.com/2009/03/27/us/politics/27obama-text.html, quoted in Woodward, *Obama's Wars*, 113.

86. Tony Blair, "Speech to Parliament," October 4, 2001, https://www.theguardian.com/world/2001/oct/04/september11.usa3.

87. Data on deployments and casualties were drawn from Andrew Rafferty, "The War in Afghanistan: By the Numbers," *NBC News,* August 21, 2017, https://www.nbcnews.com/politics/politics-news/war-afghanistan-numbers-n794626.

88. UN Security Council, Resolution 1386, on the Situation in Afghanistan, S/RES/1386, 1 (December 20 2001), http://www.refworld.org/docid/3c4e94571c.html, 1.

89. On the UN's human rights mission, see Mertus, *United Nations and Human Rights*. On the UN and state failure, see Ghani and Lockhart, *Fixing Failed States*.

90. George W. Bush, "Speech to the United Nations," November 10, 2001, http://www.cnn.com/2001/US/11/10/ret.bush.un.transcript/index.html.

91. Bush, "Speech to the United Nations."

92. Kofi Annan, "Statement on Military Strikes in Afghanistan," October 8, 2001, http://avalon.law.yale.edu/sept11/un_005.asp.

93. For a summary of these efforts, see Vincent Morelli and Paul Belkin, "NATO in Afghanistan: A Test of the Transatlantic Alliance," *Congressional Research Service Report*, July 2, 2009, 11–13, https://digital.library.unt.edu/ark:/67531/metadc26247/m1/1/high_res_d/RL33627_2009Jul02.pdf.

94. UN Security Council, Resolution 1401, S/RES/1401 (March 28, 2002), 2 ¶ 4, http://unscr.com/en/resolutions/doc/1401.

95. Roberto Gonzalez, quoted in Scott Jaschik, "Embedded Conflicts," *Inside Higher Ed*, July 7, 2015, https://www.insidehighered.com/news/2015/07/07/army-shuts-down-controversial-human-terrain-system-criticized-many-anthropologists.

96. The program itself faced much professional criticism throughout its development and deployment. See the 2007 American Anthropological Association's statement on the practice as representative of the tone of this criticism: http://www.americananthro.org/ConnectWithAAA/Content.aspx?ItemNumber=1626.

97. John Mueller, "Terrorphobia," *The American Interest* 3, no. 5 (May 1, 2008), https://www.the-american-interest.com/2008/05/01/terrorphobia/. Also see Mueller's book-length treatment, *Overblown*.

98. US Libertarian Party, "Libertarians opposed to new war plans for Afghanistan," December 2, 2009, https://www.lp.org/news-press-releases-libertarians-opposed-to-new-war-plans-for-afghanistan/.

99. See Brodsky, *With All Our Strength*, for a detailed background on the organization. See, especially, chap. 3, for an overview of the group's response to intervention.

100. Hillary Clinton, "New Hope for Afghanistan's Women," *Time*, November 24, 2001, http://content.time.com/time/nation/article/0,8599,185643,00.html.

101. Andrew Higgins, "With President's Departure, Ukraine Looks toward a Murky Future," *New York Times*, February 23, 2014.

102. Steven Lee Myers, "Growing Crisis in Backyard Snares Russia," *New York Times*, February 27, 2014.

103. For an account of these events, see Ewan MacAskill, "Does US evidence prove Russian special forces are in eastern Ukraine?," *Guardian*, April 22, 2014, http://www.theguardian.com/world/2014/apr/22/-sp-does-us-evidence-prove-russian-special-forces-are-in-eastern-ukraine; "Russian parliament approves troop deployment in Ukraine," *BBC News*, March 1, 2014, http://www.bbc.com/news/world-europe-26400035; and "Ukraine crisis: 'Russians' occupy Crimea airports," *BBC News*, February 28, 2014, http://www.bbc.com/news/world-europe-26379722.

104. See Gabriela Baczynska and Aleksandar Vasovic, "Pushing locals aside, Russians take top rebel posts in east Ukraine," *Reuters*, July 27, 2014, http://www.reuters.com/article/us-ukraine-crisis-rebels-insight-idUSKBN0FW07020140727.

105. Michael Gordon, "Russia Moves Artillery Units into Ukraine, NATO Says," *New York Times*, August 22, 2014.

106. Lukas I. Alpert, "5 Reasons Putin Gave for Annexing Crimea," *Wall Street Journal*, March 18, 2014, http://blogs.wsj.com/briefly/2014/03/18/5-reasons-vladimir-putin-gave-for-annexing-crimea/.

107. Quoted in Brittany Greenquist, "Russia Justifies Its Invasion of Ukraine as Protection of Compatriots," *Ryot,* February 21, 2014, http://www.ryot.org/russia-justifies-invasion-ukraine-protection-compatriots/588997.

108. Quoted in Simon Shuster, "Russia Lashes Out at US 'Monopoly' on Humanitarianism with Aid Convoy to Ukraine," *Time,* August 24, 2014, http://time.com/3166682/russia-ukraine-trucks-putin/.

109. Quoted in "Putin: Impossible to say when political crisis in Ukraine will end," RT, August 31, 2014, https://www.rt.com/news/184040-ukraine-putin-peace-plan/.

Chapter Seven

1. See Wendt, *Social Theory of International Politics* for a seminal study. For an overview of early developments, see Adler, "Seizing the Middle Ground."

2. See Finnemore and Sikkink, "International Norm Dynamics and Political Change."

3. Critiques of the focus of the norms literature on norms-as-consensus have been made. These critiques have focused on the importance of contestation in normative universes. See, inter alia, Weiner, "Contested Compliance" and "Dual Quality of Norms and Governance beyond the State"; and Sandholtz, "Dynamics of International Norm Change."

4. Tannenwald, "The Nuclear Taboo."

5. See Ikenberry, *After Victory.*

6. Niebuhr, *Moral Man and Immoral Society,* 4.

7. Carr, *Twenty Years' Crisis,* 19.

8. For this famous conception, see Schmitt, *Concept of the Political.*

9. See, most significantly, Duffield, *Global Governance and the New Wars*; Owen, "Foreign Imposition of Domestic Institutions"; Saunders, "Transformative Choices" and *Leaders at War*; and Downes and Monten, "Forced to Be Free?"

10. For critical perspectives on peacebuilding, see Autesserre, *Trouble with the Congo* and *Peaceland*; and Chandler, *Peacebuilding.*

11. This is a central problem in Owen, "Foreign Imposition of Domestic Institutions."

12. See Reus-Smit, "Concept of Intervention," for a sustained critique.

13. This literature is vast. See, for an introduction to ethical approaches, Holzgrefe and Keohane, *Humanitarian Intervention.*

14. See Fassin and Pandolfi, *Contemporary States of Emergency*; and Chandler, *Peacebuilding.*

15. See, for example, Downes and Lilley, "Overt Peace, Covert War?"

16. For example, Turshen, *Gender and the Political Economy of Conflict in Africa.*

17. See Downes and Lilley, "Overt Peace, Covert War?"

18. On securitization, see M. Williams, "Securitization and the Liberalism of Fear."

19. On paternalism more generally, see Dworkin, "Paternalism."

20. This is similar to Mansbridge's "unitary democracy," with the exception of a greater emphasis on agonism as producer of consensus. See Mansbridge, *Beyond*

Adversary Democracy. On pragmatism more generally, see Menand, *Metaphysical Club*. On pragmatism in international theory, see Cochran, *Normative Theory in International Relations*.

21. Holmes, *Passion and Constraint*.
22. Barnett and Bridge, "Geographies of Radical Democracy," 1023. Also see Massey, "Thinking Radical Democracy Spatially."
23. Mead, *Mind, Self, Society*, 327.
24. See, respectively, Habermas, *Theory of Communicative Action*; Honneth, *Struggle for Recognition*; and Dewey, *Ethics*, 302–6.
25. See Mead, *Mind, Self, Society*, for the clearest formulation of both accounts.
26. Shusterman, "Pragmatism and Liberalism between Dewey and Rorty," 400–3.
27. On agonistic democracy from a different perspective, see Laclau and Mouffe, *Hegemony and Socialist Strategy*.
28. Honneth, *Struggle for Recognition*, 17.
29. Bernstein, "Pragmatism, Pluralism, and the Healing of Wounds," 15.
30. Barnett, *Empire of Humanity*, 35.
31. Mead, *Mind, Self, Society*, 289.
32. Honneth and Farrell, "Democracy as Reflexive Cooperation," 778.
33. Honneth and Farrell, "Democracy as Reflexive Cooperation," 763–65.
34. Barnett, *Empire of Humanity*, 35.
35. Dworkin, "Paternalism," 68.
36. Mead, *Mind, Self, Society*, 288.
37. Shusterman, "Pragmatism and Liberalism between Rorty and Dewey," 401.
38. Shusterman, "Pragmatism and Liberalism between Rorty and Dewey," 406.
39. Shusterman, "Pragmatism and Liberalism between Rorty and Dewey," 406.
40. Putnam, "Bowling Alone," 65–78.
41. On elite public spheres, see Mitzen, "Reading Habermas in Anarchy."
42. Fraser, "Transnationalizing the Public Sphere," 19.
43. See, inter alia, Risse, "Let's Argue!"; Schimmelfennig, "Community Trap."
44. A. Lang, *Agency and Ethics*, 8.
45. For example, Wendt, "State as Person in International Theory."
46. Wight, *Agents, Structures, and International Relations*, 210.
47. Finnemore, *Purpose of Intervention*, chap. 2.
48. Mitzen, "Reading Habermas in Anarchy."
49. Finnemore, *National Interests in International Society*, 137.
50. Barnett, "International Paternalism and Humanitarian Governance," 505–6.
51. Mill, *On Liberty and Utilitarianism*, 14.
52. Paris, *At War's End*, 6.
53. Autessere, *Trouble with Congo*, 11.
54. Wendt, "Why a World State is Inevitable." See also Fukuyama, *End of History and the Last Man*.
55. Packer, *Assassins' Gate*, 409.
56. Cochran, "Democratic Critique of Cosmopolitan Democracy."

57. For example, Finnemore, *Purpose of Intervention*.
58. Johnston, "Treating International Institutions as Social Environments," 509.
59. World Economic Forum, "Global Agenda Council on Geopolitical Risk," Davos-Klosters, Switzerland (2012), 2, https://www.weforum.org/agenda/2012/01/global-institutions-ineffective-amid-the-rise-of-regionalism/.
60. Rawls, *Justice as Fairness*.
61. Katzenstein, "World of Regions," 65.
62. Katzenstein, "World of Regions," 82.

BIBLIOGRAPHY

Primary documents (newspaper articles, speeches, government reports, and archival documents, etc.) are not included in the bibliography. These sources are referenced in the text as endnotes.

Abisaab, Malek. "Warmed or Burnt by Fire? The Lebanese Maronite Church Navigates French Colonial Policies, 1935." *Arab Studies Quarterly* 36, no. 4 (2014): 292–312.

Abulof, Uriel. "Deep Securitization and Israel's 'Demographic Demon.'" *International Political Sociology* 8 (2014): 396–415.

Adcock, Robert. *Liberalism and the Emergence of American Political Science: A Transatlantic Tale*. Oxford: Oxford University Press, 2014.

Addams, Jane. *Peace and Bread in Time of War*. New York: MacMillan Company, 1922.

Addams, Jane. "The Potential Advantages of the Mandate System." *The Annals of the American Academy of Political and Social Science* 96 (1921): 70–74.

Adler, Emanuel. "Seizing the Middle Ground: Constructivism in World Politics." *European Journal of International Relations* 3, no. 3 (1997): 319–63.

Agamben, Giorgio. *State of Exception*. Translated by Kevin Attell. Chicago: University of Chicago Press, 2005.

Agnew, Elizabeth. "A Will to Peace: Jane Addams, World War I, and 'Pacifism in Practice.'" *Peace & Change* 42, no. 1 (2017): 5–31.

Aitken, Rob. "Provincializing Embedded Liberalism: Film, Orientalism, and the Reconstruction of World Order." *Review of International Studies* 37, no. 4 (2011): 1695–1720.

Ali, Nosheen. "Books vs. Bombs?: Humanitarian Development and the Narrative of Terror in Northern Pakistan." *Third World Quarterly* 31, no. 4 (2010): 541–59.

Allcock, Thomas Tunstall. "Becoming 'Mr. Latin America': Thomas C. Mann Reconsidered." *Diplomatic History* 38, no. 5 (2014): 1017–45.

Allot, Ana. *The End of the First Anglo-Burmese War: The Burmese Chronicle Account of How the 1826 Treaty of Yandabo Was Negotiated*. Bangkok: Chulalongkorn University Press, 1994.

Anderson, Amanda. "Character and Ideology: The Case of Cold War Liberalism." *New Literary History* 42, no. 1 (2011): 209–29.

Anderson, Benedict. *Imagined Communities: Reflections on the Origin and Spread of Nationalism*. London: Verso, 2006.

Angell, Norman. *The Great Illusion*. New York: Cosimo Classics, 2010.

Anghie, Antony. "Colonialism and the Birth of International Institutions: Sovereignty, Economy, and the Mandate System of the League of Nations." *NYU Journal of International Law and Politics* 34, no. 3 (Spring 2002): 513–633.
Arendt, Hannah. *On Violence*. New York: Harcourt, 1970.
Arendt, Hannah. *The Origins of Totalitarianism*. Enlarged ed. Cleveland: Meridian, 1958.
Aron, Raymond. *Démocratie et totalitarisme*. Paris: Gallimard, 1965.
Austin, JL. *How to Do Things with Words*. 2nd ed. Cambridge: Harvard University Press, 1975.
Autesserre, Séverine. *Peaceland: Conflict Resolution and the Everyday Politics of International Intervention*. Cambridge: Cambridge University Press, 2014.
Autesserre, Séverine. *The Trouble with the Congo: Local Violence and the Failure of International Peacebuilding*. Cambridge: Cambridge University Press, 2010.
Bain, William. *Between Anarchy and Society: Trusteeship and the Obligations of Power*. Oxford: Oxford University Press, 2003.
Ball, Terence. "The Formation of Character: Mill's 'Ethology' Reconsidered." *Polity* 33, no. 1 (2000): 25–48.
Barnett, Clive, and Gary Bridge. "Geographies of Radical Democracy: Agonistic Pragmatism and the Formation of Affected Interests." *Annals of the Association of American Geographers* 103, no. 4 (2013): 1022–40.
Barnett, Michael. *Empire of Humanity: A History of Humanitarianism*. Ithaca: Cornell University Press, 2011.
Barnett, Michael. "International Paternalism and Humanitarian Governance." *Global Constitutionalism* 1, no. 3 (2013): 485–521.
Barnett, Michael, and Martha Finnemore, "The Politics, Power, and Pathologies of International Organizations." *International Organization* 53, no. 4 (1999): 699–732.
Bartelson, Jens. *A Genealogy of Sovereignty*. Cambridge: Cambridge University Press, 1995.
Bastiat, Frédéric. *Economic Harmonies*. 1850. Translated by W. Hayden Boyers. Edited by George B. de Huszar. Introduction by Dean Russell. Irvington-on-Hudson: Foundation for Economic Education, 1996.
Baum, L. Frank. *The Treasury of Oz*. Radford, VA: Vilder Publications, 2007.
Bauman, Zygmunt. *Modernity and Ambivalence*. Cambridge: Polity Press, 1991.
Bayly, C. A. *The Birth of the Modern World, 1780–1914*. Oxford: Blackwell, 2004.
Beauvoir, Simone de. "Personal Freedom and Others." In *Phenomenology: Critical Concepts in Philosophy*, edited by Dermont Morgan and Lester Embree, 297–317. London: Routledge, 2004.
Beauvoir, Simone de. *The Ethics of Ambiguity*. 1948. Translated by Bernard Frechtman. New York: Citadel Press, 1976.
Beisner, Robert. *Twelve against Empire: The Anti-Imperialists, 1898–1900*. New York: McGraw Hill, 1968.
Bell, Duncan. "Empire and International Relations in Victorian Political Thought." *The Historical Journal* 49, no. 1 (2006): 281–98.
Bell, Duncan. "John Stuart Mill on Colonies." *Political Theory* 38, no. 1 (2010): pp. 34–64.

Bell, Duncan. "Mythscapes: Memory, Mythology, and National Identity." *British Journal of Sociology* 54, no. 1 (2003): 63–81.
Bell, Duncan. *Reordering the World: Essays on Liberalism and Empire*. Princeton: Princeton University Press, 2016.
Bell, Duncan. "What is Liberalism?" *Political Theory* 42, no. 6 (2014): 682–715.
Bell, Gertrude. "Letter to Florence Bell and Hugh Bell." In *The Letters of Gertrude Bell*, vol. 2, edited by Lady Bell, D.B.E. New York: Boni and Liveright, 1927. http://gutenberg.net.au/ebooks04/0400461h.html.
Berger, Peter, and Thomas Luckmann. *The Social Construction of Reality: A Treatise in the Sociology of Knowledge*. New York: Anchor Books, 1966.
Berlin, Isaiah. *Liberty*. 2nd ed., edited by Henry Hardy. Oxford: Oxford University Press, 2002.
Berlin, Isaiah. "The Originality of Machiavelli." In *Against the Current: Essays in the History of Ideas*. 2nd ed., 33–100. Princeton: Princeton University Press, 2013.
Berlin, Isaiah. "Two Concepts of Liberty." In *Four Essays on Liberty*, 121–164. Oxford: Oxford University Press, 1969.
Bernstein, Richard. "Pragmatism, Pluralism, and the Healing of Wounds." *Proceedings and Addresses of the American Philosophical Association* 63, no. 3 (1989): 5–18.
Bevir, Mark. "What is Genealogy?" *Journal of the Philosophy of History* 2 (2008): 263–75.
Bjola, Cornelieu. "Legitimating the Use of Force in International Politics: A Communicative Action Perspective." *European Journal of International Relations* 11, no. 2 (2005): 266–303.
Blackburn, Terence. *The Defeat of Ava: The First Anglo-Burmese War, 1824–1826*. New Dehli: APH Publishing, 2009.
Borren, Marieke. "'A Sense of the World': Hannah Arendt's Hermeneutic Phenomenology of Common Sense." *International Journal of Philosophical Studies* 21, no. 2 (2013): 225–55.
Bossche, Chris Vanden. *Carlyle and the Search for Authority*. Columbus: Ohio State University Press, 1991.
Brodsky, Anne. *With All Our Strength: The Revolutionary Association of the Women of Afghanistan*. London: Routledge, 2003.
Brown, Nathan. "Brigands and State Building: The Invention of Banditry in Modern Egypt." *Comparative Studies in Society and History* 32, no. 2 (1990): 258–81.
Bueger, Christian, and Frank Gadinger. "The Play of International Practice." *International Studies Quarterly* 59, no. 3 (2015): 449–60.
Bull, Hedley. *The Anarchical Society: A Study of Order in World Politics*. New York: Columbia University Press, 1978.
Butler, Judith. *The Psychic Life of Power: Theories in Subjection*. Palo Alto: Stanford University Press, 1997.
Calder, Bruce. *The Impact of Intervention: The Dominican Republic during the United States Occupation, 1916–1924*. Austin: University of Texas Press, 1984.
Callaghan, Michael. *Mandates and Empire: The League of Nations and Africa, 1914–1931*. Brighton, UK: Sussex Academic Press, 1999.

Campbell, David. *Writing Security: United States Foreign Policy and the Politics of Identity*. Minneapolis: University of Minnesota Press, 1998.
Campbell, David, and Michael Dillon, eds. *The Political Subject of Violence*. New York: Manchester University Press, 1993.
Carr, E. H. *The Twenty Years' Crisis*. 1939. Reissued with a new introduction by Michael Cox. New York: Palgrave MacMillan, 2001.
Chandler, David. *Peacebuilding: The Twenty Years' Crisis, 1997-2017*. London: Palgrave MacMillan, 2017.
Chappel, James. "The Catholic Origins of Totalitarianism Theory in Interwar Europe." *Modern Intellectual History* 8, no. 3 (2011): 561–590.
Chase, Malcolm. *Chartism: A New History*. Oxford: Manchester University Press, 2008.
Chatty, Dawn. *Mobile Pastoralists: Development Planning and Social Change in Oman*. New York: Columbia University Press, 1996.
Cheesman, Nick. "Seeing 'Karen' in the Union of Myanmar." *Asian Ethnicity* 3, no. 2 (2002): 199–220.
Ciepley, David. *Liberalism in the Shadow of Totalitarianism*. Cambridge: Harvard University Press, 2007.
Claeys, Gregory. *Imperial Skeptics: British Critics of Empire, 1850–1920*. Cambridge: Cambridge University Press, 2010.
Cochran, Molly. "A Democratic Critique of Cosmopolitan Democracy." *European Journal of International Relations* 8, no. 4 (2002): 517–548.
Cochran, Molly. *Normative Theory in International Relations: A Pragmatic Approach*. Cambridge: Cambridge University Press, 1999.
Connolly, William. *Identity/Difference: Democratic Negotiations of Political Paradox*. Minneapolis: University of Minnesota Press, 2002.
Cortazzi, Hugh, and George Webb, eds. *Kipling's Japan: Collected Writings*. London: Bloomsbury, 1988.
Cox, Percy. "Historical summary [in honor of Gertrude Bell]" [1927]. In *The Letters of Gertrude Bell*, vol. 2, edited by Lady Bell, D.B.E. New York: Boni and Liveright, 1927. http://gutenberg.net.au/ebooks04/0400461h.html.
Creppell, Ingrid. "The Concept of Normative Threat." *International Theory* 3, no. 3 (2011): 450–487.
Cullinane, Michael. *Liberty and American Anti-Imperialism, 1898–1909*. London: Palgrave MacMillan, 2012.
Deleuze, Gilles. *Foucault*. Translated by Séan Hand. Minneapolis: University of Minnesota Press, 1986.
Derrida, Jacques. *Archive Fever: A Freudian Impression*. Translated by Eric Prenowitz. Chicago: University of Chicago Press, 1996.
Derrida, Jacques. *Of Grammatology*. Translated by Gayatri Chakravorty Spivak. Baltimore: Johns Hopkins University Press, 1976.
Derrida, Jacques. "Signature, Event, Context." In *Limited Inc*, 1–23. Evanston: Northwestern University Press, 1988.

Derrida, Jacques. *Writing and Difference*. Translated by Alan Bass. Chicago: University of Chicago, 1978.
Dershowitz, Alan. *Why Terrorism Works: Understanding the Threat, Responding to the Challenge*. New Haven: Yale University Press, 2003.
Dewey, John. *Ethics*. Carbondale: Southern Illinois University Press, 1989.
Dietrich, John. "US Human Rights Policy in the Post-Cold War Era." *Political Science Quarterly* 121, no. 2 (2006): 269–94.
Dodge, Toby. *Inventing Iraq: The Failure of Nation Building and a History Denied*. New York: Columbia University Press, 2003.
Dodge, Toby. "Iraq: The Contradictions of Exogenous State-Building in Historical Perspective." *Third World Quarterly* 27, no. 1 (2006): 187–200.
Downes, Alexander, and Mary Lauren Lilley. "Overt Peace, Covert War?: Covert Intervention and the Democratic Peace." *Security Studies* 19, no. 2 (2010): 266–306.
Downes, Alexander, and Jonathan Monten. "Forced to Be Free? Why Foreign Imposed Regime Change Rarely Leads to Democratization." *International Security* 37, no. 4 (2013): 90–131.
Doyle, Michael. "Liberalism and World Politics." *American Political Science Review* 80, no. 4 (1986): 1151–69.
Doyle, Michael. *The Question of Intervention: John Stuart Mill and the Responsibility to Protect*. New Haven: Yale University Press, 2015.
Dubnov, Arie. "Anti-Cosmopolitan Liberalism: Isaiah Berlin, Jacob Talmon, and the Dilemma of National Identity." *Nations and Nationalism* 16, no. 4 (2010): 559–78.
Dubnov, Arie. "Priest or Jester? Jacob L. Talmon (1916–1980) on History and Intellectual Engagement." *History of European Ideas* 34, no. 2 (2008): 133–45.
Dubnov, Arie. "A Tale of Trees and Crooked Timbers: Jacob Talmon and Isaiah Berlin on the Question of Jewish Nationalism." *History of European Ideas* 34, no. 2 (2008): 220–238.
Dubow, Saul. "Smuts, the United Nations, and the Rhetoric of Race and Rights." *Journal of Contemporary History* 43, no. 1 (2008): 45–74.
Duffield, Mark. *Global Governance and the New Wars: The Merging of Development and Security*. New York: Zed Books, 2001.
Durkheim, Emile. *Moral Education: A Study in the Theory and Application of the Sociology of Education*. New York: Simon and Schuster, 1973.
Durkheim, Emile. *Suicide: A Study in Sociology*. Edited by George Simpson. New York: Free Press, 1997.
Durkheim, Emile, and Marcel Mauss. "Note on the Notion of Civilization." *Social Research* 38, no. 4 (1971): 808–13.
Dworkin, Gerald. "Paternalism." *Monist* 56 (1972): 64–84.
Eldar, Dan. "France in Syria: The Abolition of the Sharifian Government, April–July 1920." *Middle Eastern Studies* 29, no. 3 (1993): 487–504.
Elshtain, Jean Bethke. *Jane Addams and the Dream of American Democracy: A Life*. New York: Basic Books, 2002.

Englehart, Neil. "State Capacity, State Failure, and Human Rights." *Journal of Peace Research* 46, no. 2 (2009): 163–180.

Epstein, Charlotte. *The Power of Words in International Relations: Birth of an Anti-Whaling Discourse.* Cambridge: MIT Press, 2008.

Epstein, Charlotte. "Who Speaks?: Discourse, the Subject, and the Study of Identity in International Politics." *European Journal of International Relations* 17, no. 2 (2011): 327–50.

Evrigenis, Ioannis. *Fear of Enemies and Collective Action.* Cambridge: Cambridge University Press, 2008.

Fassin, Didier. *Humanitarian Reason: A Moral History of the Present.* Berkeley: University of California Press, 2011.

Fassin, Didier, and Mariella Pandolfi, eds. *Contemporary States of Emergency: The Politics of Military and Humanitarian Interventions.* New York: Zone Books, 2010.

Fearon, James, and David Laitin. "Neotrusteeship and the Problem of Weak States." *International Security* 28, no. 4 (2004): 5–43.

Felten, Peter. "The Path to Dissent: Johnson, Fulbright, and the 1965 Intervention in the Dominican Republic." *Presidential Studies Quarterly* 26, no. 4 (1996): 1009–18.

Fenton, Steve. *Durkheim and Modern Sociology.* Cambridge: Cambridge University Press, 1984.

Fieldhouse, D. K. *Economics and Empire, 1830–1914.* New York: Palgrave MacMillan, 1984.

Finnemore, Martha. "Legitimacy, Hypocrisy, and the Social Structure of Unipolarity: Why Being a Unipole Isn't All It's Cracked Up to Be." *World Politics* 61, no. 1 (2009): 58–85.

Finnemore, Martha. *National Interests in International Society.* Ithaca: Cornell University Press, 1996.

Finnemore, Martha. *The Purpose of Intervention: Changing Beliefs about the Use of Force.* Ithaca: Cornell University Press, 2004.

Finnemore, Martha, and Kathryn Sikkink. "International Norm Dynamics and Political Change." *International Organization* 52, no. 4 (1998): 887–917.

Foster, Carrie. *The Women and the Warriors: The US Section of the Women's International League for Peace and Freedom, 1915–1946.* Syracuse, NY: Syracuse University Press, 1995.

Foucault, Michel. *The Birth of Biopolitics: Lectures at the Collège de France, 1978–1979.* New York: Palgrave Macmillan, 2008.

Foucault, Michel. *Discipline and Punish: The Birth of the Prison.* Translated By Alan Sheridan. New York: Vintage, 1977.

Foucault, Michel. *The History of Madness.* Translated By Jonathan Murphy. New York: Routledge, 2009.

Foucault, Michel. *History of Sexuality.* Vol. 1. Translated By Robert Hurley. New York: Vintage, 1978.

Foucault, Michel. "Nietzsche, Genealogy, History." In *The Foucault Reader,* edited by Paul Rabinow, 76–100. London: Pantheon, 1984.

Foucault, Michel. "Nietzsche, Genealogy, History." In *Language, Counter-Memory, and Practice: Selected Essays and Interviews*, edited by D. F. Bouchard, 139–164. Ithaca: Cornell University Press, 1977.

Foucault, Michel. *"Society Must be Defended": Lectures at the Collège de France, 1975–1976*. Translated by David Macey. New York: Picador, 2003.

Fraser, Nancy. "Feminism, Capitalism, and the Cunning of History." *New Left Review* 56 (March/April 1999): 97–117.

Fraser, Nancy. "Transnationalizing the Public Sphere: On the Legitimacy and Efficacy of Public Opinion in a Post-Westphalian World." *Theory, Culture, and Society* 24, no. 4 (2007): 7–30.

Fukuyama, Francis. "The End of History?" *The National Interest* 16 (1989): 3–18.

Fukuyama, Francis. *The End of History and the Last Man*. 1992. Reprint, New York: Free Press, 2006.

Furnivall, John. *Colonial Policy and Practice: A Comparative Study of Burma and Netherlands India*. Cambridge: Cambridge University Press, 1948.

Gaddis, John Lewis. *The Cold War: A New History*. New York: Penguin, 2005.

Gadinger, Frank. "On Justification and Critique: Luc Boltanski's Pragmatic Sociology and International Relations." *International Political Sociology* 10, no. 3 (2016): 187–205.

Gall, Carlotta. *The Wrong Enemy: America in Afghanistan, 2001–2014*. New York: Mariner Books, 2014.

Ghani, Ashraf, and Claire Lockhart. *Fixing Failed States: A Framework for Rebuilding a Fractured World*. Oxford: Oxford University Press, 2008.

Gilley, Bruce. "The Case for Colonialism." *Third World Quarterly* 38, no. 4 (2017) [Retracted by journal].

Gleason, Abbott. *Totalitarianism: The Inner History of the Cold War*. Oxford: Oxford University Press, 1996.

Goldschmidt, Arthur. *A Concise History of the Middle East*. 7th ed. Boulder: Westview Press, 2002.

Goldstein, Judith, and Robert Keohane, eds. *Ideas and Foreign Policy: Beliefs, Institutions, and Political Change*. Ithaca: Cornell University Press, 1993.

Gong, Gerrit. *The Standard of Civilization in International Society*. Cambridge: Oxford University Press, 1984.

Gramsci, Antonio. *The Prison Notebooks*. Translated by Antonio Callari. New York: Columbia University Press, 1975.

Grant, Kevin. *A Civilized Savagery: Britain and the New Slaveries in Africa, 1884–1926*. New York: Routledge, 2005.

Gros, Jean-Germain. "Towards a Taxonomy of Failed States in the New World Order: Decaying Somalia, Liberia, Rwanda and Haiti." *Third World Quarterly* 17, no. 3 (1996): 455–71.

Guilhot, Nicolas. *The Democracy Makers: Human Rights and International Order*. New York: Columbia University Press, 2005.

Guyot, Yves. *The Causes and Consequences of the War*. Translated by F. Appleby Holt. New York: Brentano's, 1916.

Habermas, Jürgen. *The Theory of Communicative Action*. Vol. 2. Boston: Beacon Press, 1987.

Hacohen, Malachi. "Jacob Talmon between Zionism and Cold War Liberalism." *History of European Ideas* 34, no. 2 (2008): 146–57.

Haddox, Thomas. "Lillian Smith, Cold War Intellectual." *Southern Literary Journal* 44, no. 2 (2012): 51–68.

Hall, Harold Fielding. *The Soul of a People*. London: MacMillan, 1899.

Hall, Stuart, Jessica Evans, and Sean Nixon, eds. *Representation: Cultural Representations and Signifying Practices*. 2nd ed. London: SAGE, 2013.

Hameiri, Shahar. "Failed State or a Failed Paradigm?: State Capacity and the Limits of Institutionalism." *Journal of International Relations and Development* 10, no. 2 (2007): 122–49.

Hansen, Lene. "The Politics of Securitization and the Muhammad Cartoon Crisis: A Post-Structuralist Perspective." *Security Dialogue* 42 (2011): 357–69.

Hansen, Lene. *Security as Practice: Discourse Analysis and the Bosnian War*. London: Routledge, 2006.

Hardt, Michael, and Antonio Negri. *Commonwealth*. Cambridge: Harvard University Press, 2009.

Hardt, Michael. *Empire*. Cambridge: Harvard University Press, 2000.

Hardt, Michael. *Multitude: War and Democracy in the Age of Empire*. New York: Penguin, 2004.

Harré, Rom. "The Discursive Production of Selves." *Theory and Psychology* 1, no. 1 (1991): 51–63.

Hartz, Louis. *The Liberal Tradition in America*. New York: Harcourt, Brace, and World, 1991.

Helman, Gerald, and Steven Ratner. "Saving Failed States." *Foreign Policy* 89 (1992/1993): 3–20. http://foreignpolicy.com/2010/06/15/saving-failed-states/.

Herbst, Jeffrey. *States and Power in Africa: Comparative Lessons in Authority and Control*. Princeton: Princeton University Press, 2000.

Herbst, Jeffrey. "War and the State in Africa." *International Security* 14, no. 4 (1990): 117–39.

Herring, George. *From Colony to Superpower: US Foreign Relations since 1776*. Oxford: Oxford University Press, 2008.

Hirschman, Albert. *Essays in Trespassing: Economics to Politics and Beyond*. Cambridge: Cambridge University Press, 1981.

Hitchcock, William. "The Rise and Fall of Human Rights?: Searching for a Narrative from the Cold War to the 9/11 Era." *Human Rights Quarterly* 37, no. 1 (2015): 80–106.

Hobbes, Thomas. *Leviathan*. Edited by Edwin Curley. Indianapolis: Hackett, 1994.

Hobhouse Balme, Jennifer. *Agents of Peace: Emily Hobhouse and Her Courageous Attempts to End the First World War*. Stroud: History Press, 2015.

Hobsbawm, Eric. *The Age of Revolution, 1789–1848*. 1st Vintage Books ed. New York: Vintage, 1996.

Holland, Catherine. "Hartz and Minds: The Liberal Tradition after the Cold War." *Studies in American Political Development* 19, no. 2 (2005): 227–33.

Holmes, Stephen. *Passion and Constraint: On the Theory of Liberal Democracy*. Chicago: University of Chicago Press, 1995.

Holzgrefe, J. L., and Robert O. Keohane, eds. *Humanitarian Intervention: Ethical, Legal, and Political Dilemmas*. Cambridge: Cambridge University Press, 2003.

Honneth, Axel. *The Struggle for Recognition: The Moral Grammar of Social Conflicts*. Cambridge: MIT Press, 1995.

Honneth, Axel, and John M. M. Farrell. "Democracy as Reflexive Cooperation: John Dewey and the Theory of Democracy Today." *Political Theory* 26, no. 6 (1998): 763–83.

Hook, Derek. "Genealogy, Discourse, 'Effective History': Foucault and the Work of Critique." *Qualitative Research in Psychology* 2, no. 1 (2005): 3–31.

Howarth, David. *Discourse*. London: McGraw Hill, 2000.

Huffer, Lynn. *Mad for Foucault: Rethinking the Foundations of Queer Theory*. New York: Columbia University Press, 2009.

Hunt, Lynn. *Inventing Human Rights: A History*. New York: W. W. Norton, 2008.

Huntington, Samuel. "The Clash of Civilizations?" *Foreign Affairs* 72, no. 3 (1993): 22–49.

Hurd, Ian. "Legitimacy and Authority in International Politics." *International Organization* 53, no.2 (1999): 379–408.

Huysmans, Jef. "Security! What Do You Mean? From Concept to Thick Signifier." *European Journal of International Relations* 4, no. 2 (1998): 226–55.

Ikenberry, G. John. *After Victory: Institutions, Strategic Restraint, and the Rebuilding of Order after Major Wars*. Princeton: Princeton University Press, 2000.

Ikenberry, G. John. *Liberal Leviathan: The Origins, Crisis, and Transformation of the American World Order*. Princeton: Princeton University Press, 2011.

Inston, Kevin. *Rousseau and Radical Democracy*. London: Continuum, 2010.

Ishay, Michelin. *The History of Human Rights: From Ancient Times to the Globalization Era*. Berkeley: University of California Press, 2008.

Ish-Shalom, Piki. "Theory Gets Real, and the Case for a Normative Ethic: Rostow, Modernization Theory, and the Alliance for Progress." *International Studies Quarterly* 50, no. 2 (2006): 287–311.

Jackson, Patrick Thaddeus. *Civilizing the Enemy: German Reconstruction and the Invention of the West*. Ann Arbor: University of Michigan Press, 2006.

Jackson, Robert. *Quasi-States: Sovereignty, International Relations, and the Third World*. Cambridge: Cambridge University Press, 1990.

Jacoby, Russell. *Picture Imperfect: Utopian Thought for an Anti-Utopian Age*. New York: Columbia University Press, 2007.

Jahn, Beate. "Barbarian Thoughts: Imperialism in the Philosophy of John Stuart Mill." *Review of International Studies* 31, no. 3 (2005): 599–618.

Jahn, Beate. *Liberal Internationalism: Theory, History, and Practice.* London: Palgrave MacMillan, 2013.

Johnston, Alastair. "Treating International Institutions as Social Environments." *International Studies Quarterly* 45, no. 4 (2001): 487–515.

Jones, Branwen Gruffyd. "'Good Governance' and 'State Failure': Genealogies of Imperial Discourse." *Cambridge Review of International Affairs* 26, no. 1 (2013): 49–70.

Jones, Seth. *In the Graveyard of Empires: America's War in Afghanistan.* New York: W. W. Norton, 2010.

Kagan, Robert. *The World America Made.* New York: Vintage Books, 2012.

Kaldor, Mary. *New and Old Wars: Organized Violence in a Global Era.* 3rd ed. Stanford: Stanford University Press, 2012.

Kapitan, Tomis. "Self-Determination and the International Order." *The Monist* 89, no. 2 (2006): 356–70.

Katzenstein, Peter. "A World of Regions: America, Europe, and East Asia." *Indiana Journal of Global Legal Studies* 1, no. 1 (1993): 65–82.

Keck, Margaret, and Kathryn Sikkink. *Activists beyond Borders: Advocacy Networks in International Politics.* Ithaca: Cornell University Press, 1998.

Kelly, Duncan. "The Political Thought of Isaiah Berlin." *British Journal of Politics and International Relations* 4, no. 1 (2002): 25–48.

Keohane, Robert, and Joseph Nye. *Power and Independence: World Politics in Transition.* Boston: Little, Brown, 1977.

Kinsella, Helen. *The Image before the Weapon: A Critical History of the Distinction between Combatant and Civilian.* Ithaca: Cornell University Press, 2011.

Knight, Louise. *Jane Addams: Spirit in Action.* NY: W. W. Norton, 2010.

Koestler, Arthur. *Darkness at Noon.* New York: MacMillan, 1941.

Koskenniemi, Martti. *The Gentle Civilizer of Nations: The Rise and Fall of International Law, 1870–1960.* Cambridge: Cambridge University Press, 2001.

Koskenniemi, Martti. "Idealism and Ignorance." *The Nation*, November 16, 2015, 32–36.

Krasner, Stephen. "Sharing Sovereignty: New Institutions for Collapsed and Failing States." *International Security* 29, no. 2 (2004): 85–120.

Krasner, Stephen. *Sovereignty: Organized Hypocrisy.* Princeton: Princeton University Press, 1999.

Kratochwil, Friedrich. *Rules, Norms, and Decisions: On the Conditions of Legal and Practical Reasoning in International Relations and Domestic Affairs.* Cambridge: Cambridge University Press, 1989.

Krebs, Paula. *Gender, Race, and the Writing of Empire: Public Discourse and the Boer War.* Cambridge: Cambridge University Press, 2004.

Krebs, Ronald. *Narrative and the Making of US National Security.* Cambridge: Cambridge University Press, 2015.

Krebs, Ronald, and Patrick Thaddeus Jackson. "Twisting Tongues and Twisting Arms: The Power of Political Rhetoric." *European Journal of International Relations* 13, no. 1 (2007): 35–56.

Lacan, Jacques. *Ecrits*. Translated by Bruce Fink. New York: W. W. Norton, 2007.

Laclau, Ernesto, and Chantal Mouffe. *Hegemony and Socialist Strategy: Toward a Radical Democratic Politics*. London: Verso, 2001.

Lakoff, Sanford. "Tocqueville, Burke, and the Origins of Liberal Conservativism." *Review of Politics* 60, no. 3 (1998): 435–64.

Lang, Anthony. *Agency and Ethics: The Politics of Military Intervention*. Albany: SUNY Press, 2001.

Lange, Katharina. "'Bedouin' and 'Shawaya': The Performative Constitution of Tribal Identities in Syria during the French Mandate and Today." *Journal of the Economic and Social History of the Orient* 56 (2015): 200–35.

Laurie, William Ferguson Beatson. *Our Burmese Wars and Relations with Burma*. 2nd ed. London: W. H. Allen and Co, 1885.

Lehmann, Jennifer. "The Question of Caste in Modern Society: Durkheim's Contradictory Theories of Race, Class, and Sex." *American Sociological Review* 60, no. 4 (1995): 566–85.

Levinas, Emmanuel. *Time and the Other*. Translated by Robert Cohen. Pittsburgh: Duquesne University Press, 1987.

Lewis, Bernard. "The Roots of Muslim Rage." *The Atlantic*, September 1990, 47–60.

Linklater, Andrew. *The Problem of Harm in World Politics: Theoretical Investigations*. Cambridge: Cambridge University Press, 2011.

Linn, Brian. *The Philippine War, 1899–1902*. Lawrence: University Press of Kansas, 2000.

Linn, Brian. *The US Army and Counterinsurgency in the Philippine War, 1899–1902*. Chapel Hill: University of North Carolina Press, 1989.

Locke, John. *Political Writings*. Indianapolis: Hackett Publishing, 1993.

Lockman, Zachary. *Contending Visions of the Middle East: The History and Politics of Orientalism*. 2nd ed. Cambridge: Cambridge University Press, 2009.

Long, David, and Brian Schmidt, eds. *Imperialism and Internationalism in the Discipline of International Relations*. Albany: SUNY Press, 2005.

Lorca, Arnulf Becker. "Petitioning the International: A 'Pre-History' of Self-Determination." *European Journal of International Law* 25, no. 2 (2014): 497–523.

Losurdo, Domenico. *Liberalism: A Counter-History*. London: Verso, 2011.

Losurdo, Domenico. "Towards a Critique of the Category of Totalitarianism." *Historical Materialism* 12, no. 2 (2004): 25–55.

Lowenthal, Abraham. *The Dominican Intervention*. Cambridge: Harvard University Press, 1972.

Lugard, Frederick. *The Dual Mandate in British Tropical Africa*. 5th ed. London: Frank Crass, 1965.

Lustick, Ian. "History, Historiography, and Political Science: Multiple Historical Records and the Problem of Selection Bias." *American Political Science Review* 90, no. 3 (1996): 605–18.

MacMillan, John. *On Liberal Peace: Democracy, War, and the International Order*. London: IB Tauris, 1998.

Mahbubani, Kishore. "The West and the Rest." *National Interest*, Summer 1992, 3–13.
Manela, Erez. *The Wilsonian Moment: Self-Determination and the International Origins of Anti-Colonial Nationalism*. Oxford: Oxford University Press, 2007.
Manjikian, Mary. "Diagnosis, Intervention, and Cure: The Illness Narrative in the Discourse of Failed States." *Alternatives* 33, no. 3 (2008): 335–57.
Mansbridge, Jane. *Beyond Adversary Democracy*. 2nd ed. Chicago: University of Chicago Press, 1983.
Mardam Bey, Salama. *Syria's Quest for Independence, 1939–1945*. Berkshire, UK: Ithaca Press, 1994.
Marks, Shula. "White Masculinity: Jan Smuts, Race, and the South African War." *Proceedings of the British Academy* 111 (2001): 199–223.
Marr, Phoebe. *The Modern History of Iraq*. 3rd ed. Boulder: Westview Press, 2011.
Marso, Lori. "Simone de Beauvoir and Hannah Arendt: Judgments in Dark Times." *Political Theory* 40, no. 2 (2012): 165–93.
Martin, Luther, Huck Gutman, and Patrick Hutton, eds. *Technologies of the Self: A Seminar with Michel Foucault*. Amherst: University of Massachusetts Press, 1988.
Martin, Patricia Yancey. "Gender as a Social Institution." *Social Forces* 82, no. 4 (2004): 1249–73.
Massey, Doreen. "Thinking Radical Democracy Spatially." *Environment and Planning D: Society and Space* 13, no. 3 (1995): 283–88.
Matena, Karuna. *Alibis of Empire: Henry Maine and the Ends of Liberal Imperialism*. Princeton: Princeton University Press, 2010.
Matinuddin, Kamal. *The Taliban Phenomenon: Afghanistan, 1994–1997*. New York: Diane Publishing, 1999.
McKeown, Timothy. "Case Studies and the Limits of the Quantitative Worldview." In *Rethinking Social Inquiry: Diverse Tools, Shared Standards*, edited by Henry Brady and David Collier, 139–68. Lanham, MD: Rowman and Littlefield, 2004.
Mead, George Herbert. *Mind, Self, and Society from the Standpoint of a Social Behaviorist*. Chicago: University of Chicago Press, 1967.
Mearsheimer, John. *Why Leaders Lie: The Truth about Lying in International Politics*. Cambridge: Oxford University Press, 2011.
Mehta, Uday. "Liberal Strategies of Exclusion." *Politics and Society* 18, no. 4 (1990): 427–54.
Mehta, Uday. *Liberalism and Empire: A Study in Nineteenth Century British Liberal Thought*. Chicago: University of Chicago Press, 1999.
Menand, Louis. *The Metaphysical Club: A Story of Ideas in America*. New York: Farrar, Straus, and Giroux, 2001.
Mertus, Julie. *The United Nations and Human Rights: A Guide for a New Era*. London: Routledge, 2005.
Mill, John Stuart. "A Few Words on Non-Intervention." In *John Stuart Mill: Essays on Politics and Culture,* edited by Gertrude Himmelfarb, 368–84. Garden City, NY: Anchor Books, 1963.

Mill, John Stuart. *On Liberty and the Subjection of Women*. New York: Henry Holt, 1879.
Mill, John Stuart. *On Liberty and Utilitarianism*. New York: Bantam, 1993.
Mill, John Stuart. *Principles of Political Economy*. Vols. 2 and 3 of *The Collected Works of John Stuart Mill*. Edited by J. M. Robinson. Toronto: Toronto University Press, 1965.
Mill, John Stuart. *System of Logic*. Vol. 8 of *The Collected Works of John Stuart Mill*. Edited by J. M. Robinson. Toronto: University of Toronto Press, 1974.
Miller, Stuart. *Benevolent Assimilation: The American Conquest of the Philippines, 1899–1903*. New Haven: Yale University Press, 1982.
Milliken, Jennifer. "The Study of Discourse in International Relations: A Critique of Research and Methods." *European Journal of International Relations* 5, no. 2 (1999): 225–54.
Mills, Charles. *Black Rights/White Wrongs: The Critique of Racial Liberalism*. Oxford: Oxford University Press, 2017.
Mitchell, Clyde. "Case Studies." In *Ethnographic Research: A Guide to General Conduct*, edited by RF Ellen, 237–41. Orlando: Academic Press, 1984.
Mitchell, Timothy. *Rule of Experts: Egypt, Techno-Politics, Modernity*. Berkeley: University of California Press, 2002.
Mitzen, Jennifer. "Reading Habermas in Anarchy: Multilateral Diplomacy and Global Public Spheres." *American Political Science Review* 99, no. 3 (2005): 401–18.
Montesquieu, Charles de. *The Spirit of the Laws*. Translated by Anne Cohler, Basia Miller, and Harold Stone. Cambridge: Cambridge University Press, 1989.
Moravcsik, Andrew. "Taking Preferences Seriously: A Liberal Theory of International Politics." *International Organization* 51, no. 4 (1997): 513–53.
Morefield, Jeanne. *Covenants without Swords: Idealist Liberalism and the Spirit of Empire*. Princeton: Princeton University Press, 2004.
Morefield, Jeanne. "Empire, Tragedy, and the Liberal State in the Writings of Niall Ferguson and Michael Ignatieff." *Theory and Event* 11, no. 3 (2008): 1–20.
Moyn, Samuel. *Human Rights and the Uses of History*. London: Verso, 2014.
Mueller, John. *Overblown: How Politicians and the Terrorism Industry Inflate National Security Threats, and Why We Believe Them*. New York: Free Press, 2009.
Mueller, John. *The Remnants of War*. Ithaca: Cornell University Press, 2004.
Müller, Jan-Werner. "Fear and Freedom: On 'Cold War Liberalism.'" *European Journal of Political Theory* 7, no. 1 (2008): 45–64.
Muthu, Sankar. *Enlightenment against Empire*. Princeton: Princeton University Press, 2003.
Myint-U, Thant. *The Making of Modern Burma*. Cambridge: Cambridge University Press, 2001.
Narayan, Uma. "Colonialism and Its Others: Considerations on Rights and Care Discourses." *Hypatia* 10, no. 2 (1995): 133–40.
Neep, Daniel. *Occupying Syria under the French Mandate: Insurgency, Space, and State Formation*. Cambridge: Cambridge University Press, 2012.

Neier, Aryeh. *The International Human Rights Movement: A History*. Princeton: Princeton University Press, 2012.

Nelson, Benjamin. "Civilizational Complexes and Inter-Civilizational Relations." *Sociological Analysis* 34, no. 2 (1973): 79–105.

Neumann, Iver. "Returning Practice to the Linguistic Turn: The Case of Diplomacy." *Millennium* 31, no. 3 (2002): 627–51.

Newland, Kathleen. "Ethnic Conflict and Refugees." In *Ethnic Conflict and International Security*, edited by Michael Brown, 143–65. Princeton: Princeton University Press, 1993.

Niebuhr, Reinhold. *Moral Man and Immoral Society*. London: Charles Scribner, 1932.

Niemann, Holger, and Henrik Schillinger. "Contestation 'All the Way Down'? The Grammar of Contestation in Norm Research." *Review of International Studies* 43, no. 1 (2017): 29–49.

Nojum, Neamatollah. *The Rise of the Taliban in Afghanistan: Civil War, Mass Mobilization, and the Future of the Region*. New York: Palgrave Macmillan, 2002.

Nussbaum, Martha, and Jonathan Glover. *Women, Culture, and Development: A Study of Human Capabilities*. Cambridge: Clarendon Press, 1995.

O'Mahoney, Joseph. "Why Did They Do That?: The Methodology of Reasons for Action." *International Theory* 7, no. 2 (2015): 231–62.

Orwell, George. "Arthur Koestler." In *Fifty Orwell Essays*, 234–236. Oxford: Oxford City Press, 2010.

Orwell, George. "Reflections on Gandhi." In *Fifty Orwell Essays*, 5–12. Oxford: Oxford City Press, 2010.

Orwell, George. "Shooting an Elephant," in *A Collection of Essays*, 148–155. New York: Harvest, 1946.

Owen, John. "The Foreign Imposition of Domestic Institutions." *International Organization* 56, no. 2 (2002): 375–409.

Owen, John. *Liberal Peace, Liberal War: American Politics and International Security*. Ithaca: Cornell University Press, 1997.

Packer, George. *The Assassins' Gate: America in Iraq*. New York: Farrar, Strauss, and Giroux, 2005.

Paris, Roland. *At War's End: Building Peace after Civil Conflict*. Cambridge: Cambridge University Press, 2004.

Peterson, Howard. "The Quest for Moral Order: Emile Durkheim on Education." *Journal of Moral Education* 4, no. 1 (1974): 39–46.

Pinker, Stephen. *The Better Angels of Our Nature: Why Violence Has Declined*. New York: Viking Press, 2011.

Pollack, Oliver. "A Mid-Victorian Coverup: The Case of the 'Combustible Commodore' and the Second Anglo-Burmese War, 1851–1852." *Albion* 10, no. 2 (1978): 171–83.

Pollack, Oliver. "The Origins of the Second Anglo-Burmese War." *Modern Asian Studies* 12, no. 3 (1978): 483–502.

Prager, Carol. "Intervention and Empire: John Stuart Mill and International Relations." *Political Studies* 53, no. 3 (2005): 621–40.
Price, Richard, and Nina Tannenwald. "Norms and Deterrence: The Nuclear and Chemical Weapons Taboos." In *The Culture of National Security*, edited by Peter Katzenstein, 114–52. New York: Columbia University Press, 1996.
Provence, Michel. *The Great Syrian Revolt and the Rise of Syrian Nationalism*. Austin: University of Texas Press, 2005.
Putnam, Robert. "Bowling Alone: America's Declining Social Capital." *Journal of Democracy* 6, no. 1 (1995): 65–78.
Rabe, Stephen. *Eisenhower and Latin America: The Foreign Policy of Anti-Communism*. Chapel Hill: UNC Press, 1988.
Rawls, John. *Justice as Fairness: A Restatement*. Cambridge: Belknap Press, 2001.
Reus-Smit, Christian. "The Concept of Intervention." *Review of International Studies* 39, no. 5 (2013): 1057–76.
Reus-Smit, Christian. *The Moral Purpose of the State: Culture, Social Identity, and Institutional Rationality in International Relations*. Princeton: Princeton University Press, 1999.
Richardson, James. "Contending Liberalisms: Past and Present." *European Journal of International Relations* 3, no. 1 (1997): 5–33.
Ricoeur, Paul. *Freud and Philosophy: An Essay on Interpretation*. Translated by Denis Savage. Hartford: Yale University Press, 1977.
Riley, Alexander. *The Social Thought of Emile Durkheim*. Thousand Oaks, CA: SAGE, 2015.
Risse, Thomas. "Let's Argue!: Communicative Action in World Politics." *International Organization* 54, no. 1 (2000): 1–39.
Rist, Gilbert. *The History of Development: From Western Origins to Global Faith*. New York: Zed Books, 2002.
Roche, George Charles. *Frédéric Bastiat: A Man Alone*. New Rochelle, NY: Arlington House, 1971.
Rostow, WW. *The Stages of Economic Growth: A Non-Communist Manifesto*. Cambridge: Cambridge University Press, 1960.
Rousseau, Jean-Jacques. *The Social Contract and Other Later Political Writings*. Cambridge: Cambridge University Press, 1997.
Ruggie, John. "Continuity and Transformation in the World Polity: Toward a Neorealist Synthesis." In *Neorealism and Its Critics*, edited by Robert Keohane, 131–57. New York: Columbia University Press, 1986.
Russett, Bruce, and John Oneal. *Triangulating Peace: Democracy, Interdependence, and International Organizations*. New York: W. W. Norton, 2001.
Sager, Paul. "A Nation of Functionaries, a Colony of Functionaries: The Antibureaucratic Consensus in France and Indochina, 1848–1912." *French Historical Studies* 39, no. 1 (2016): 145–82.
Said, Edward. *Culture and Imperialism*. New York: Vintage, 1994.

Said, Edward. *Orientalism*. New York: Vintage, 1978.
Sandel, Michael. *Liberalism and the Limits of Justice*. Cambridge: Cambridge University Press, 1982.
Sandholtz, Wayne. "Dynamics of International Norm Change: Rules Against Wartime Plunder." *European Journal of International Relations* 14, no. 1 (2008): 101–31.
Sarraut, Albert. *Grandeur et servitude coloniales*. Paris: L'Harmattan, 2012.
Saunders, Elizabeth. *Leaders at War: How Presidents Shape Military Interventions*. Ithaca: Cornell University Press, 2011.
Saunders, Elizabeth. "Transformative Choices: Leaders and the Origins of Intervention Strategy." *International Security* 34, no. 2 (2009): 119–61.
Scheuer, Michael. *Osama Bin Laden*. Oxford: Oxford University Press, 2012.
Schimmelfennig, Frank. "The Community Trap: Liberal Norms, Rhetorical Action, and the Eastern Enlargement of the European Union." *International Organization* 55, no. 1 (2001): 47–80.
Schlag, Gabi, and Axel Heck. "Securitizing Images: The Female Body and the War in Afghanistan." *European Journal of International Relations* 19, no. 4 (2013): 891–913.
Schmidt, Vivien. "Discursive Institutionalism: The Explanatory Power of Ideas and Discourse." *Annual Review of Political Science* 11 (2008): 303–25.
Schmitt, Carl. *The Concept of the Political: Expanded Edition*. Translated by George Schwab. Chicago: University of Chicago Press, 2007.
Searle, John. *Speech Acts*. Cambridge: Cambridge University Press, 1969.
Sen, Amartya. *Development as Freedom*. Cambridge: Oxford University Press, 1999.
Shklar, Judith. "The Liberalism of Fear." In *Liberalism and the Moral Life,* edited by Nancy Rosenblum. Cambridge: Harvard University Press, 1989.
Shusterman, Richard. "Pragmatism and Liberalism between Dewey and Rorty." *Political Theory* 22, no. 3 (1994): 391–13.
Simms, Brenda, and DJB Trimm, eds. *Humanitarian Intervention: A History*. Cambridge: Cambridge University Press, 2011.
Simpson, Gerry. "Two Liberalisms." *European Journal of International Law* 12, no. 3 (2001): 537–72.
Simpson, MCM, ed. *Correspondence and Conversations of Alexis de Tocqueville with William Nassau Senior from 1834–1859*. 2 vols. London: Henry S. King, 1872.
Slater, Jerome. *Intervention and Negotiation: The United States and the Dominican Revolution*. New York: Harper and Row, 1970.
Smith, Martin. *Burma: Insurgency and the Politics of Ethnicity*. London: Zed Books, 1991.
Smuts, Jan. *The League of Nations: A Practical Suggestion*. London: Hodder and Stoughton, 1918.
Snodgrass, John James. *Narrative of the Burmese War Detailing the Operations of Major-General Sir Archibald Campbell's Army from the Landing at Rangoon in May 1824 to the Conclusion of a Treaty of Peace at Yandaboo in February 1862*. London: John Murray, Albemarle-Street, 1827.

Sørensen, Georg. *Liberal World Order in Crisis: Choosing between Imposition and Restraint.* Ithaca: Cornell University Press, 2011.

Spencer, Herbert. *Essays: Scientific, Political, and Speculative.* Vol. 3. London: Williams and Norgate, 1891.

Stewart, David. "The Hermeneutics of Suspicion." Journal of Literature and Theology 3 (1989): 296–307.

Stoler, Ann. *Carnal Knowledge and Imperial Power: Race and the Intimate in Colonial Rule.* Berkeley: University of California Press, 2010.

Stoler, Ann. *Race and the Education of Desire: Foucault's History of Sexuality and the Colonial Order of Things.* Durham: Duke University Press, 2012.

Strauss, Leo. *The City and Man.* Chicago: University of Chicago Press, 1964.

Stuckey, Mary, and Joshua Ritter. "George Bush, 'Human Rights,' and American Democracy." *Presidential Studies Quarterly* 37, no. 4 (2007): 646–66.

Swedberg, Richard. "A Note on Civilizations and Economies." *European Journal of Social Theory* 13, no. 1 (2010): 15–30.

Swidler, Ann. "Culture in Action: Symbols and Strategies." *American Sociological Review* 51, no. 2 (1986): 273–86.

Taffet, Jeffrey. *Foreign Aid as Foreign Policy: The Alliance of Progress in Latin America.* New York: Routledge, 2007.

Talmon, Jacob. *The Origins of Totalitarian Democracy.* London: Secker and Warburg, 1952.

Talmon, Jacob. *Romanticism and Revolt: Europe, 1815–1848.* New York: Harcourt, Brace, and World, 1968.

Tannenwald, Nina. "The Nuclear Taboo: The United States and the Normative Basis of Nuclear Non-Use." *International Organization* 53, no. 3 (1999): 433–68.

Tatum, Dillon Stone. "Discourse, Genealogy, and Methods of Text Selection in International Relations." *Cambridge Review of International Affairs* 31, nos. 3/4 (2018): 344–64.

Tatum, Dillon Stone. "Liberal Pessimism: An Intellectual History of Suspicion in the Cold War." In *Pessimism in International Relations: Provocations, Possibilities, Politics*, edited by Tim Stevens and Nicholas Michelsen, 67–81. Basingstoke, UK: Palgrave MacMillan, 2020.

Tatum, Dillon Stone. "A Pessimistic Liberalism: Jacob Talmon's Suspicion and the Birth of Contemporary Political Thought." *British Journal of Politics and International Relations* 21, no. 4 (2009): 650–66.

Taylor, Dianna. *Michel Foucault: Key Concepts.* London: Routledge, 2010.

Tesón, Fernando. "The Liberal Case for Humanitarian Intervention." In *Humanitarian Intervention: Ethical, Legal, and Political Dilemmas*, edited by J. L. Holzgrefe and Robert O. Keohane, 93–129. Cambridge: Cambridge University Press, 2003.

Thacker, Andrew. "Foucault and the Writing of History." In *The Impact of Michel Foucault on the Social Sciences and Humanities,* edited by Moya Lloyd and Andrew Thacker, 29–53. Basingstoke, UK: Palgrave MacMillan.

Thakur, Vineet, Alexander Davis, and Peter Vale. "Imperial Mission, 'Scientific Method': An Alternative Account of the Origins of IR." *Millennium* 46, no. 1 (2017): 3–23.

Thelen, Katherine. "Historical Institutionalism in Comparative Politics." *Annual Review of Political Science* 2 (1999): 369–404.

Thérien, Jean-Philippe, and Philippe Joly. "'All Human Rights for All': The United Nations and Human Rights in the Post-Cold War Era." *Human Rights Quarterly* 36 (2014): 373–96.

Thomas, Claire. "Why Don't We Talk about 'Violence' in International Relations?" *Review of International Studies* 37, no. 4 (2011): 815–36.

Thompson, James. "Democracy." In *The Oxford Handbook of Modern British Political History, 1800–2000*, edited by David Brown, Robert Crowcroft, and Gordon Pentland, 471–89. Oxford: Oxford University Press, 2018.

Tilly, Charles. "Reflections on the History of European State-Making." In *The Formation of National States in Western Europe*, edited by Charles Tilley, 3–83. Princeton: Princeton University Press, 1975.

Towns, Ann. *Women and States: Norms and Hierarchies in International Society*. Cambridge: Cambridge University Press, 2010.

Tripp, Charles. *A History of Iraq*. 3rd ed. Cambridge: Cambridge University Press, 2007.

Turku, Helga. *Isolationist States in an Interdependent World*. London: Routledge, 2009.

Turshen, Meredith. *Gender and the Political Economy of Conflict in Africa*. New York: Routledge, 2016.

Tyrell, Ian, and Jay Sexton, eds. *Empire's Twin: US Anti-Imperialism from the Founding Era to the War on Terrorism*. Ithaca: Cornell University Press, 2015.

Varouxakis, Georgios. *Mill on Nationality*. London: Routledge, 2002.

Vidal, Gore. "Theodore Roosevelt: An American Sissy." In *The Selected Essays of Gore Vidal*, 357–72. New York: Vintage, 2008.

Vucetic, Srdjan. "Genealogy as a Research Tool in International Relations." *Review of International Studies* 37, no. 3 (2011): 1295–1312.

Vuori, Juha. "Illocutionary Logic and Strands of Securitization: Applying the Theory of Securitization to the Study of Non-Democratic Political Orders." *European Journal of International Relations* 14, no. 1 (2008): 65–99.

Walker, RBJ. "Culture, Discourse, Insecurity." *Alternatives* 11, no. 4 (1986): 485–504.

Webster, Anthony. "Business and Empire: A Reassessment of the British Conquest of Burma in 1885." *The Historical Journal* 43, no. 4 (2000): 1003–25.

Webster, Anthony. *The Debate on the Rise of the British Empire*. Manchester: Manchester University Press, 2006.

Webster, Anthony. *Gentlemen Capitalists: British Imperialism in Southeast Asia, 1770–1890*. New York: IB Tauris, 1998.

Wedeen, Lisa. "State Fragility, Piety, and the Problems with Intervention." *Noref Report*, March 3, 2010. https://ciaotest.cc.columbia.edu/wps/noref/0018450/f_0018450_15803.pdf.

Weiner, Antje. "Contested Compliance: Interventions on the Normative Structure of World Politics." *European Journal of International Relations* 10, no. 2 (2004): 189–234.

Weiner, Antje. "The Dual Quality of Norms and Governance beyond the State: Sociological and Normative Approaches to 'Interaction.'" *Critical Review of International Social and Political Philosophy* 10, no. 1 (2007): 47–69.

Welch, Richard. *Response to Imperialism: The United States and the Philippine-American War, 1899–1902.* Chapel Hill: University of North Carolina Press, 1979.

Wendt, Alexander. "Driving with the Rearview Mirror: On the Rational Science of Institutional Design." *International Organization* 55, no. 4 (2001): 1019–49.

Wendt, Alexander. "On Constitution and Causation in International Relations." *Review of International Studies* 24 (1998): 101–17.

Wendt, Alexander. *Social Theory of International Politics.* Cambridge: Cambridge University Press, 1999.

Wendt, Alexander. "The State as Person in International Theory." *Review of International Studies* 30 (2004): 289–316.

Wendt, Alexander. "Why a World State is Inevitable." *European Journal of International Relations* 9, no. 4 (2003): 491–542.

Whatmore, Richard. "War, Trade, and Empire: The Dilemmas of French Liberal Political Economy." In *French Liberalism from Montesquieu to Present Day*, edited by Raf Geneens and Helena Rosenblatt, 169–91. Cambridge: Cambridge University Press, 2012.

Wheeler, Nicholas. *Saving Strangers: Humanitarian Intervention in International Society.* Oxford: Oxford University Press, 2003.

Whelan, Frederick. *Edmund Burke and India: Political Morality and Empire.* Pittsburg: University of Pittsburg Press, 1997.

Wight, Colin. *Agents, Structures, and International Relations: Politics as Ontology.* Cambridge: Cambridge University Press, 2006.

Williams, David. "Development, Intervention, and International Order." *Review of International Studies* 39, no. 5 (2013): 1213–31.

Williams, Michael. "Securitization and the Liberalism of Fear." *Security Dialogue* 42 (2011): 452–63.

Williams, Michael. "Words, Images, Enemies: Securitization and International Politics." *International Studies Quarterly* 47, no. 4 (2003): 511–31.

Wolin, Sheldon. *Politics and Vision: Continuity and Innovation in Western Political Thought.* Expanded ed. Princeton: Princeton University Press, 2004.

Woodward, Bob. *Obama's Wars.* New York: Simon and Schuster, 2010.

Wright, Harrison, ed. *The "New Imperialism": Analysis of Late Nineteenth Century Expansion.* 2nd ed. Lexington, MA: DC Heath, 1976.

Yack, Bernard, ed. *Liberalism without Illusions: Essays on Liberal Theory and the Political Vision of Judith N. Shklar.* Chicago: University of Chicago Press, 1996.

Zastoupil, Lynn, *John Stuart Mill and India*. Palo Alto: Stanford University Press, 1994.

Zimmern, Alfred. *The League of Nations and the Rule of Law: 1918–1935*. New York: MacMillan, 1936.

Žižek, Slavoj. *Did Somebody Say Totalitarianism? Five Interventions in the (Mis)Use of a Notion*. London: Verso, 2011.

INDEX

24 (television series), 125-126
Addams, Jane 32, 36, 64, 68-71, 74
Afghanistan, 27, 111, 126-136, 139
    Coalition war in, 27, 111, 126-136, 139
Africa, 2, 75, 91, 96-97, 113-114, 116-117
Albright, Madeleine, 116
Alliance for Progress, 98-99
Al-Qa'ida, 126
American Anti-Imperialist League, 55
Annan, Kofi, 130
Arendt, Hannah, 26, 86, 92, 95, 108
Arida, Anthony II Peter, 81
Aristotle, 145
Aron, Raymond, 88
Ashdown, Paddy, 112
Aubert, Louis, 79
Australia, 75, 127
Austro-Hungarian Empire, 72
Azerbaijan, 124

Bastiat, Frédéric, 46-48, 55, 70
Economic Harmonies, 46-47
Beauvoir, Simone de, 94-95
Bell, Gertrude, 83-84
Benedict, Wes, 132
"Benevolent assimilation," 54
Bengal, 57
Berlin, Isaiah, 10, 88, 90, 92-93
    "Two Concepts of Liberty," 90
Bin Laden, Osama, 126, 128-129
Blair, Tony, 128-129
Boer Wars, 69-70
Bosch, Juan, 102, 104
Bosnia and Herzegovina, 117, 134
Brailsford, Henry Noel, 75-76

Brissot, Jacques-Pierre, 1, 152
Brown, George, 91
Burke, Edmund, 44
Burma, 33, 56-62, 83
    and British intervention, 33, 35, 41, 56-62, 83
Bush, George W., 2-3, 27, 114-115, 123, 127-130
Bush, Laura, 127

Cabral, Donald Reid, 102
Cambodia, 124
Canada, 126
Capitalism, 2, 75, 99-100
Carbillet, Gabriel, 77-78
Caribbean, 2, 24-25, 29, 32, 101, 103
Carlyle, Thomas, 43
Carr, E.H., 139
Case selection, 37-38
Castro, Fidel, 103, 108
Catholicism, 89
Cato Institute, 132
Central Intelligence Agency (US), 126
Charlemagne, 51
Chateaubriand, François-René de, 47
Cheney, Richard, 123
"Child races," 21, 27, 30, 31, 65, 67-71, 73, 81, 91
Chile, 99
China, 45, 53, 75, 95
Chomsky, Noam, 21
Churkin, Vitaly, 134-135
"Civilization," 2, 8, 12-14, 22, 29, 33, 40-43, 45-78, 80, 82, 84-85, 88-91, 109, 120-123, 139-140, 147

199

Clausewitz, Carl von, 12
Clemenceau, Georges, 76
Clinton, Bill, 112, 124
Clinton, Hillary, 133
Cold War, 1, 11, 13-14, 21-22, 25, 29-30, 32, 34-35, 86-113, 118, 120-121, 123-124, 127, 133, 135, 140
Committee on US-Latin American Relations (CUSLAR), 107
Common sense, 26-28, 31-32, 52-53
Communism, 29, 32, 86-87, 89-91, 95-99, 101-103, 105-107, 113, 116
Concert of Europe, 146
Constitutionalism, 80, 82-83, 107, 122, 125-126
Constructivism (International Relations theory), 138, 146-147
Content analysis, 37
Cornell University, 107
Cosmopolitanism, 5, 8, 89
Cox, Percy, 82
Crimean War, 45
Critique, 10
Cuba, 29, 54, 103

Dalhousie, Lord James BR, 56
Decolonization, 35
Democracy, 8, 10, 16, 33, 64-65, 68, 71, 81-82, 84, 86-87, 92-94, 100-101, 103, 108, 112, 117, 119, 122, 124, 131, 135, 137-152
   radical 13, 142-143
Democratic Republic of Congo, 148
Derrida, Jacques, 13, 21
Development, 7, 16, 22, 25, 28-29, 40-43, 46-51, 55-56, 58-69, 72, 82, 84-88, 96-102, 105-108, 110, 113-115, 117, 119, 121-126, 130-132, 135, 138-140, 147
Dewey, John, 142, 144
Discourse, 3
   definition of, 10-13, 18-19
   genealogical analysis of, 10, 20
   and culture, 3, 10-11, 26-28
   and identity (*see also* identity) 20-23
   and institutions (*see also* institutions) 23-26
Dodd, Thomas, 103
Dominican Republic, 16, 32, 35, 87-88, 101-108, 147
   and Dominican Crisis (1965) 16, 32, 35, 87-88, 101-108, 147
Durkheim, Emile, 65, 73-74

Eastern Europe, 2, 112-114, 117
Egypt, 76
Eisenhower, Dwight, 102, 105
El Salvador, 96
Ethology, 50
Equality, 5, 21, 40
European Union, 134
Existentialism, 94

Failed states, 22, 26-27, 32, 35, 110-120, 124-125, 127-132, 134-136, 141
Faisal I, 76-77
Fascism, 94-96, 112
Feminism, 94-95
Feudalism, 5
First Opium War, 62
Fonctionnairisme, 46
Foreign Affairs, 79
Foreign Policy, 116
Fortas, Abe, 104-105
Foucault, Michel, 10, 12, 16-17, 19-20, 25-26, 28, 33, 36
France, 1, 17, 22, 40-42, 45-48, 54-56, 60, 64-65, 68, 71-82, 88, 92-94, 124
Fraser, Nancy, 145
French Revolution, 1-2, 92-94
Freud, Sigmund, 93
Fukuyama, Francis, 1-2, 17, 113
Fulbright, William, 16, 103-104
Fund for Peace, 115-116
Furnivall, John, 59

Gamelin, Maurice, 80
Genealogy, 36-37, 87, 92-93, 116, 118, 138-140

Germany, 67, 70, 72, 75, 79, 82, 96
Gladstone, William, 62
Gouraud, Henri, 77, 81
Gramsci, Antonio, 27
Green, T.H., 93
Grenada, 24-25
Guam, 54
The Guardian, 124-125
Guyot, Yves, 36, 65, 72, 74
   Les causes et les consequences de la guerre, 72

Habermas, Jürgen, 142
Haiti, 124
Hall, Harold Fielding, 59-60
Hawaii, 54
Hegel, Georg Wilhelm Friedrich, 1, 17, 33, 89
Heraclitus, 47
Herder, Johann, 92
Hinduism, 75
Hitler, Adolf, 104
Hobbes, Thomas, 116, 118, 124-125
Hobhouse, Emily, 68-71, 74
Hobson, J.A., 45
Holocaust, 92
Holy Roman Empire, 22
Hong Kong, 53
Honneth, Axel, 142-143
Hull House, 69
Human Development Index, 119
Humanitarian intervention, 2. 7, 9
Human Terrain Systems, 131-132
Huntington, Samuel, 113, 121-124, 126

Identity, 9, 19-23, 43-45, 47-48, 51, 53, 57, 59
   as subject position, 11-12, 20, 23
Imperialism, 2, 6, 12, 23, 34, 36, 40-52, 54-85, 88, 90-91, 95, 107-108, 120-121, 133, 139-140, 147
Independent, 124
India, 45, 48, 56-59, 75, 121
Institutions, 19, 23-26, 35, 48-51, 53, 59, 66, 139

International law, 8, 66
Iran, 76, 119
Iraq, 2-3, 25, 27, 29, 31-32, 35, 64-65, 71, 76, 82-84, 111, 123, 132-133, 147, 149
   war in (2003), 2-3, 25, 27, 31, 34, 111, 123, 132-133, 149
   British mandate in, 25, 29, 31-32, 35, 64-65, 71, 76, 82-84, 147
Ireland, 43
Islam, 121-123

Jackson, Andrew, 2
Japan, 75, 96
Jefferson, Thomas, 122-123
Johnson, Lyndon, 87, 98-99, 101-106, 109
Judaism, 75
Justification, 28-31, 46, 48, 50, 57-59, 77-78

Kant, Immanuel, 8, 93
Karen (ethnic group), 61
Kennedy, John F., 97-99, 108
Koestler, Arthur, 89
Korea, 97

Lambert, Commodore George, 56
Laski, Harold, 89
Latin America, 29, 98-99, 102-104, 107-108
Lavrov, Sergey, 134
League of Nations, 6, 24-25, 32, 64-71, 74-85, 139
   and Mandates, 16, 24-25, 32, 64-71, 74-85, 139
Lebanon, 76, 78
Le Temps, 79
Lewis, Bernard, 122-124, 126
Liberal Peace Theory, 7-8
Liberalism
   general definition of, 5-6
   emancipatory (definition), 3, 9
   minimalist, 3-4, 13-14, 137-152
   internationalism, 4, 6, 10, 24, 36, 139
   neo-, 7, 99-100, 140

Liberia, 124
Libertarianism, 132
Locke, John, 116, 118-119
London School of Economics, 75
Lughard, Frederick, 75
Luther, Martin

Machiavelli, Niccolò, 90
Manifest Destiny, 55
Mann, Thomas, 99
Mansfield, Mike, 103
Martel, Comte de, 81
Marx, Karl, 86, 93, 108
Marxism, 87, 90, 108
McKinley, William, 54
Mead, George Herbert, 142
Mill, John Stuart, 2, 37, 43-44, 46-53, 55, 58, 88, 148
   Principles of Political Economy, 43, 48-51
   On Liberty, 51-52, 148
   "A Few Words on Non-Intervention," 52
Millerand, Alexandre, 16, 77, 81
Modernization Theory, 22, 27, 98, 105-107, 121
Molinari, Gustav de, 72
Montesquieu, Charles de, 73
Murray, Gilbert, 6
Mussolini, Benito, 96

Nationalism, 66, 69, 76, 79, 81
Nation building, 31, 80, 106, 130-136
Native Americans, 2
Netherlands, 60
The New Republic, 75-76
New York Review of Books, 96
New York Times, 99, 103, 112, 115, 124, 128
"New Wars," 7
Nicaragua, 96, 101
Nice (France), 1
Niebuhr, Reinhold, 139

Nietzsche, Friedrich, 93
Nixon, Richard, 95
Norms, 9-10, 12, 22, 30, 138-139, 146-147
North Atlantic Treaty Association (NATO), 113, 127, 129, 130-131, 134
   and Provincial Reconstruction Teams (PRTs), 131
North Korea, 119
Nuclear Weapons, 138

Obama, Barack, 128, 132
Organization of American States, 35, 103, 109
Organization of Eastern Caribbean States (OECS), 24-25
Orientalism, 26, 45, 53, 59, 111, 120-126, 132
Orwell, George, 62, 89-90
Ottoman Empire, 67, 76

Pakistan, 126
Palmer, Bruce, 106
Paraguay, 43, 50, 58
Paternalism, 3, 9, 13, 21, 42, 60-61, 67-68, 74, 80, 90-91, 113, 118, 120, 142-149
Peacebuilding, 31, 33, 127, 131-132, 140, 148
Peace Corps, 106
Perle, Richard, 115
"Philippine Organic Act," 54
Philippines, 54-55, 62
   US annexation of, 54-55, 62-63
Playboy Magazine, 96
Pluralism, 7, 13-14, 90, 101, 108, 144, 147
Popper, Karl 88
Positive liberty, 10, 50, 90, 134, 144
Pragmatism, 13, 137, 141-148
Puerto Rico, 54
Putin, Vladimir, 134-135

Reagan, Ronald, 96, 101, 108
Realism (International Relations theory), 17, 24, 89, 139-140

Index

Religion, 46-47, 92
Resistance, 17, 32, 61, 76, 81-82, 107, 132-133
Revolutionary Association of the Women of Afghanistan (RAWA), 133
Ricoeur, Paul, 92-93
Rights, 5, 8-9, 16, 27, 42, 110-133, 135-136
    Human rights, 2, 8-9, 27, 110-133, 135-136
Rockefeller, Nelson, 103
Rogers, Bill, 107
Roosevelt, Theodore, 55, 96
Rorty, Richard, 144-145
Rostow, Walt W., 98, 105-106, 121
Rousseau, Jean-Jacques, 1, 73, 93-94, 116
Rusk, Dean, 91
Russia, 45, 76, 133-135
Rwanda, 124

Said, Edward, 26
Sandinistas, 101
San Remo Conference (1920), 76
Santo Domingo, 102
Sarrail, Maurice, 81
Sarraut, Albert, 68
Saudi Arabia, 126
Savoy (France), 1
Scheldt River, 1
Schmitt, Carl, 1
Second Anglo-Burmese War (1852-1853), 56, 59, 61
Securitization, 110, 140
Self-determination, 32-34, 42, 48, 64-71, 73-74, 76, 78, 80-85
Sen, Amartya, 119
Senior, William Nassau, 45
Sepoy Rebellion, 45
September 11 Attacks, 113-116, 124-128, 130
"Shared governance," 33, 118-120
Shaw, George Bernard, 89
Slavery, 49

Smith, Bromley, 104-105
Smuts, Jan, 16, 64, 67, 70
Snodgrass, JJ, 57-58, 61
Social Contract Theory, 116
Socialism, 45, 89-90
South Africa, 64, 67, 69-71
South Sudan, 115
Soviet Union, 2, 88, 90-91, 94-99, 101, 108-109, 111-114, 116, 123
Spain, 54
Spanish-American War, 54
Sparta, 22
Speakes, Larry, 101
Spearman, Horace, 61
Speech act theory, 17, 26, 28-30
Spencer, Herbert, 44, 48, 55, 72
State building, 31, 127
Stevenson, Adlai, 99
Strauss, Leo, 86
Sudan, 126
Suffragist movement, 32, 68-71
Sykes-Picot Agreement (1916), 76
Syria, 16, 64-65, 71-72, 76-82
    and French intervention, 71-72, 76-82
    and the Druze, 76-77, 80
    and Maronite Christians, 78, 81

Taliban, 126-128, 133
Talmon, Jacob L, 36, 88, 92-96
    Origins of Totalitarian Democracy, 92, 94
Terrorism, 2-3, 7, 22, 26-27, 110-111, 120-129, 133, 136
Textual analysis, 36-37
The Times, of London, 53, 59
Third Anglo-Burmese War (1885), 57, 61
Tilly, Charles, 116-117
Tirard, Pierre, 72
Tocqueville, Alexis de, 45, 48, 53, 55, 60
Totalitarianism, 11, 16, 21-22, 32, 86-90; 92-101-108; 110-113, 138, 140, 147
Treaty of Paris (1898), 54

Treaty of Yandabo, 56
Troupes Speciales de Levant, 80
Trujilo, Rafael, 101-102
Truman, Harry, 97

Ukraine, 133-135
  Russian intervention in (2014), 133-135
United Kingdom, 2, 6-7, 25, 29-33, 35,
    40-41, 43-45, 48-65, 67-72, 75-76, 82-84,
    88, 91, 112, 121, 124, 126, 128-129, 147
  and British empire, 2, 6-7, 25, 29-33,
    35, 40, 41, 43-45, 48-65, 67-72, 76,
    82-84, 91, 121, 147
United Nations, 23-25, 35, 48, 91,
    99, 112-113, 115, 118-119, 124, 127,
    129-131, 134-135
  Security Council, 25, 91, 113, 127,
    129-130
  Development Program (UNDP), 119
  Mission in Haiti (UNMIH), 124
  International Security Assistance
    Force (ISAD), 127
  UN Assistance Mission in Afghanistan (UNAMA), 131
United States, 2-4, 13, 16, 21, 24-25, 34-35,
    40, 54-56, 62-66, 68, 75; 87-88, 90-91,
    95-110, 112-115, 123-133-135, 139, 147-149
  anti-imperialist movement in, 54-55, 63
  and US Civil War (1861-1865), 55
  and indigenous peoples, 56, 63

Vanity Fair, 115
Vidal, Gore, 21, 96
Vienna Declaration (1993), 112

Vietnam, 91, 95-96, 103, 105
  war in, 91, 95-96, 103, 105
Violence, 8-9, 140
  definitions of, 8-9
Voltaire, 1

Wallas, Graham, 75
Wall Street Journal, 123, 134
Washington, DC, 23, 105, 107
Washington Post, 97, 99, 124
Weber, Max, 116
Wheeler, Earle, 106
Wilson, A.T., 83
Wilson, Harold, 91, 104
Wilson, Woodrow, 64-66, 79, 84, 101
Wizard of Oz, 16, 137
Women's International League for Peace
  and Freedom (WILPF), 68
Women's Peace Conference (1915), 69
Women's Peace Party (United States), 68
World Bank, 23, 100
World War I, 16, 24, 64-70, 72, 74, 76,
  79, 82, 101
World War II, 82, 86, 89-91, 95, 97,
  108, 112, 124

Yanukovych, Viktor, 134
Yemen, 124
Yugoslavia, 117

Zaire, 124
Zimbabwe (Rhodesia), 91
Zimmern, Alfred, 6, 67
Žižek, Slavoj, 125